Design Anthropology

Object Cultures in Transition

Edited by Alison J. Clarke

BLOOMSBURY ACADEMIC
AN IMPRINT OF BLOOMSBURY PUBLISHING PLC

BLOOMSBURY
LONDON · OXFORD · NEW YORK · NEW DELHI · SYDNEY

Bloomsbury Academic

An imprint of Bloomsbury Publishing Plc

50 Bedford Square	1385 Broadway
London	New York
WC1B 3DP	NY 10018
UK	USA

www.bloomsbury.com

BLOOMSBURY and the Diana logo are trademarks of Bloomsbury Publishing Plc

This edition first published 2018
A previous version of this book was published by Springer, 2011, with the title
Design Anthropology: Object Culture in the 21st Century

British Library Cataloguing-in-Publication Data
A catalogue record for this book is available from the British Library.

ISBN: HB: 978-1-4742-5904-0
           PB: 978-1-4742-5903-3
           ePDF: 978-1-4742-5905-7
           eBook: 978-1-4742-5906-4

Library of Congress Cataloging-in-Publication Data
A catalog record for this book is available from the Library of Congress.

Cover design: David A Gee

Typeset by Lachina
Printed and bound in China

To find out more about our authors and books visit www.bloomsbury.com.
Here you will find extracts, author interviews, details of forthcoming events and the option
to sign up for our newsletters.

Table of Contents

For Constance and Solomon

Illustrations

2.1 New York City subway turnstiles. © Noah McClain

2.2 Toilet Fountain, San Francisco Exploratorium. © Harvey Molotch

2.3 Frustrated mover, New York City subway turnstiles. © Noah McClain

3.1 A set of wooden Japanese combs collected by Papanek as exemplars of indigenous design tied to cultural ritual and evolved ergonomics (in this case the elegant aesthetic of Geisha hairstyling). Victor J. Papanek Foundation, University of Applied Arts Vienna

3.2 A collection of fishing hooks from Papua New Guinea, used by Papanek to show design development within indigenous cultures. Victor J. Papanek Foundation, University of Applied Arts Vienna

3.3 Victor Papanek and his wife Harlanne in their Copenhagen apartment 1973, with a backdrop of indigenous artifacts. Victor J. Papanek Foundation, University of Applied Arts Vienna

3.4 Tin Can Radio: radio receiver designed for use in the developing world at 9 cents a piece. By Victor Papanek and George Seeger at North Carolina State College. Originally published in Victor J. Papanek, *Design for the Real World* (New York: Pantheon Books, 1971), 163. Victor J. Papanek Foundation, University of Applied Arts Vienna

3.5 Tin Can Radio receiver decorated with colored felt cutouts and seashells by a user in Indonesia according to their own taste. Originally published in Victor J. Papanek, *Design for the Real World* (New York: Pantheon Books, 1971), 163. Victor J. Papanek Foundation, University of Applied Arts Vienna

3.6 Front cover, *Global Tools* bulletin no. 1, design by Remo Buti, Edizioni L'uomo e l'arte, Milan, 1974.

5.1 Billboard without an advertisement. This caught Gen Suzuki's eye as he passed it in a Tokyo subway station. He understood later that what intrigued him was the boundary between the object and its environment. © Gen Suzuki

5.2 The coffee Gen Suzuki was served on a summit in the Alps; the whipped cream on top was the shape of the mountain he had just climbed. © Gen Suzuki

5.3 Gen Suzuki's design for a pen stand was inspired by his observation of rolls of tape stacked on a friend's desk. © Gen Suzuki

8.5 Fine, traditional Koniaków lace tablecloth worked in silk (detail), 2009. Designer: Beata Legierska. © Nicolette Makovicky

8.6 A young man inspects the designs of his mother, Ana Gemera. They sell lace and refreshments from a small stall outside their home near the summit of the Ochodzita Mountain. © Nicolette Makovicky

9.1 Vladimir Antipov`s shovel, Moscow, Russia, 1998. © Vladimir Arkhipov

9.2 Vasilii Arkhipov's television antenna, Kolomna, Russia, about 1993. © Vladimir Arkhipov

9.3 Albina Leonidovna Falko`s children's steering wheel, Perm, 1978. © Vladimir Arkhipov

9.4 Alexei Tikhonow`s 'close-stool,' the Ryazan region, Russia, 1990. © Vladimir Arkhipov

9.5 Sven Hünemörder`s balalayka, Russia, Altai region, 2003. © Vladimir Arkhipov

9.6 Vladimir Arkhipov`s case, Bordeaux, France, 2009. © Vladimir Arkhipov

10.1 Car on a homeland. © Diana Young

10.2 Blue and white car, Ernabella. © Diana Young

10.3 Blue Toyota 4WD on a homeland. © Diana Young

10.4 Red and white car. © Diana Young

13.1 A Digicel mobile money outlet in downtown Port-au-Prince. © Erin B. Taylor

13.2 T-Cash's logo, Se lajan kontan! aims to convince customers that mobile money is just as good as cash. © Erin B. Taylor

13.3 Branding in a Digicel office in Port-au-Prince, with advertisements in both French and Haitian Creole. © Erin B. Taylor

13.4 A vendor wearing a Digicel t-shirt in the Marche en Fer, Port-au-Prince. © Erin B. Taylor

13.5 A mobile money transfer using Digicel's TchoTcho Mobile uses French. © Erin B. Taylor

13.6 Mercy Corps developed leaflets in Haitian Creole to explain how mobile money works to recipients of conditional cash grants in Saint Marc, Haiti. © Erin B. Taylor

13.7 A T-Cash instructional leaflet and a TchoTcho Mobile cartoon. © Erin B. Taylor

Contributors

Vladimir Arkhipov

Vladimir Arkhipov, born 1961 in the USSR, collects and curates 'self-made' objects and runs the database www.folkforms.ru as a resource for objects with 'biographies.' His collection of re-made and self-made objects is internationally renowned and has been exhibited in art galleries across Europe. He is the author of *Home-Made: Contemporary Russian Folk Artifacts* (2006; 2012), *Design del popolo: 220 inventori della Russia post-sovietica* (2007), and *Home-Made Europe: Contemporary Folk Artifacts* (2012).

Maria Bezaitis

Maria Bezaitis is a principal engineer with the Intel Experience Group in CCG where she leads the UX Pathfinding and Platform team. Maria's own research has focused on the changing nature of the smart technology landscape and the rise of technologies that augment human skill. She finished her PhD at Duke University in French Literature. Maria started her post-academic career as managing partner at E-Lab, a firm that pioneered the use of ethnography and design planning for product development. She serves on the advisory board of TTI Vanguard, a global technology thought leadership organization and is the president of the Ethnographic Praxis in Industry Conference.

Alison J. Clarke

Alison J. Clarke is professor of Design History and Theory and director of the Victor Papanek Foundation at the University of Applied Arts Vienna. An extensively published design historian (MA, RCA/V&A) and social anthropologist (PhD, UCL), Alison is co-founding editor of *Home Cultures: The Journal of Design, Architecture and Domestic Space*, editor of *Design Anthropology: Object Culture in the 21st Century*, and author of the award-winning *Tupperware: The Promise of Plastic in 1950s America*. A regular contributor to media, including *The Genius of Design* (BBC), Alison is presently completing a monograph for MIT Press exploring the activist politics of 1960s and 1970s design.

Lane DeNicola

Lane DeNicola is a researcher, analyst, and critical designer working at the intersection of information, education, and culture. Currently the director of Institutional Research for the College of Arts and Sciences at Emory University, he has been a lecturer in digital anthropology at University College London, a programmer at the Center for Space Research at MIT, and an analyst at the MIT Lincoln Laboratory and the Johns Hopkins University Applied Physics Laboratory.

Arturo Escobar

Arturo Escobar is Kenan Distinguished Teaching Professor of Anthropology at the University of North Carolina at Chapel Hill. His work concerns social movements, women and place, the World Social Forum, globalization and the decolonial option as well as, most recently, pluriversal studies and design. His main academic publications include *Encountering Development: The Making and Unmaking of the Third World* (2011 [1995]), *Territories of Difference: Place, Movements, Life, Redes* (2008), and two collections of essays in Spanish, *El final del salvaje. Naturaleza, cultura y política en la antropología contemporánea* (1999) and *Más allá del Tercer Mundo. Globalización y diferencia* (2005).

Jane Fulton Suri

Jane Fulton Suri is partner and chief creative officer at IDEO. Educated as a social scientist, she has pioneered a human-centered approach to design through work with clients representing diverse organizations, from governments and nonprofits to Fortune 500 companies. A practitioner of careful observation to stimulate empathic creativity, she authored *Thoughtless Acts: Observations on Intuitive Design* (Chronicle Books 2005). In 2015, Fulton Suri taught IDEO U's online design thinking course Insights for Innovation.

Pauline Garvey

Pauline Garvey is lecturer in anthropology in Maynooth University, National University of Ireland, as well as co-editor of *Home Cultures: The Journal of Architecture, Design and Domesticity Space*. Her research interests include material culture, Nordic domesticity, and design anthropology. Recent publications include a special issue of the *Journal of Design History* ("Design Dispersed: Design History, Design Practice and Anthropology," 2016 with Adam Drazin). Her ethnography of Swedish Design and Ikea was published in the 2017 monograph *Unpacking Ikea: Swedish Design for the Purchasing Masses* (Routledge).

Heather A. Horst

Heather A. Horst is a principal research fellow (professor) and a vice-chancellor's senior research fellow in the School of Media and Communication at RMIT University, Melbourne. Her books include *The Cell Phone: An Anthropology of Communication* (with Daniel Miller, Berg 2006), *Hanging Out, Messing Around, and Geeking Out* (with Mizuko Ito et al., MIT Press 2010), *Digital Anthropology* (with Daniel Miller, Berg 2012), and *Digital Ethnography* (with Sarah Pink et al., Sage, forthcoming 2015).

Jamer Hunt

Jamer Hunt is the director of the MFA Transdisciplinary Design program at Parsons The New School for Design, New York. His academic teaching and professional practice, Big + Tall Design, focus on conceptual, collaborative, and communication design as a means for exploring the politics and poetics of the everyday. Hunt served on the board of directors of the American Center for Design and the editorial board of *Design and Culture*. For seven years, he was director of the Masters Program in Industrial Design at the University of the Arts in Philadelphia and is co-founder of DesignPhiladelphia.

Susanne Küchler

Susanne Küchler is professor of anthropology at University College London. Her research focuses on the material in art and design, the nature of innovation, and the cognitive work of Images. Küchler is currently working on a new manuscript, *The Material Mind*, which develops the theoretical implications of her past ethnographic research into the making of sculpture and social memory. It takes insights into the nature of innovation in Oceania to the laboratory context of material science and offers a critical review of existing theorization of material aesthetics and the formalized nature of thought symptomatic of knowledge economies.

Nicolette Makovicky

Nicolette Makovicky is lecturer in Russian and East European studies at the University of Oxford. She has published extensively on the relationship between craft, modernity and ideology as well as craft and the post-socialist informal economy. Makovicky is the editor of *Neoliberalism, Personhood, and Postsocialism: Enterprising Selves in Changing Economies* (Ashgate 2014) and co-editor of *Economies of Favour After Socialism* (University of Oxford Press 2016).

Daniel Miller

Daniel Miller is professor of material culture at the Department of Anthropology at University College London. He is currently running the *Why We Post* project (www.ucl.ac.uk/why-we-post). Recent books include *Social Media in an English Village* (UCL Press 2016), *Webcam* (with J. Sinanan, Polity Press 2014), *Digital Anthropology* (with H. Horst, Bloomsbury 2012), *Stuff* (Polity 2009) and *The Comfort of Things* (Polity 2008).

Harvey Molotch

Harvey Molotch, professor of sociology at New York University, conducts research on product design as well as urban development and security. His books include *Against Security: How We Go Wrong at Airports, Subways, and Other Sites of Ambiguous Danger* (Princeton 2012); *Urban Fortunes* (California 2007); *Where Stuff Comes From: How Toasters, Toilets, Cars, Computers and Many Other Things Come to Be As They Are* (Routledge 2003); and *Toilet: Public Restrooms and the Politics of Sharing* (NYU 2010).

Rick E. Robinson

Rick E. Robinson is professor of practice in the Department of Information Science at the University of Colorado Boulder. He holds a PhD in human development from the University of Chicago. As a co-founder of E-Lab and iota partners, he has been a pioneer in using observational research for new product development. Robinson's current work focuses on understanding the interactions people have with increasingly pervasive data about themselves, others, and the world.

Erin Taylor

Erin Taylor is an economic anthropologist and since 2011 has held the position of research fellow at the University of Lisbon. She is the author of *Materializing Poverty: How the Poor Transform Their Lives* (2013 AltaMira) and editor of *Fieldwork Identities in the Caribbean* (2010, Caribbean Studies Press). Additionally, she is the managing editor of *PopAnth: Hot Buttered Humanity* and sits on the editorial board of the *Journal of Cultural Economy*.

Diana Young

Diana Young is a social anthropologist. Her research is focused on visual and material culture including color, art and photography, space, ecology and architecture, anthropology of museums and consumption, with a regional focus on Indigenous Australia and the Pacific. Forthcoming publications include "Colour as Palettes" for the *Routledge Handbook of Beauty* and an edited volume *Rematerializing Colour*. Recent exhibition curation includes *written on the body (2014)* and *In the red (2012)*.

Acknowledgments

This book is the outcome of a lengthy and stimulating journey into the various objects, disciplines, and debates that form the bridges between contemporary design and anthropology. Many of the contributors are colleagues from academia, industry, and design with whom I have shared discussions, or to whom I simply listened intently, at conferences, workshops, and events over the last two decades. *Design Anthropology* is a testament to the generosity of the contributing authors, whose articles arose from a genuine collective interest in disseminating knowledge beyond the tight parameters of their disciplines to specifically address the phenomenon of design anthropology and its future potential as an emerging field.

I would like to thank enormously Martina Grünewald whose academic insight, inspiring observations, and adroit editing skills underpinned this edition from start to finish, and Kathrina Dankl with whom this project was first initiated. My thanks also to Rebecca Barden, Daniel Miller, Harvey Molotch, Jane Fulton Suri, Bill Moggridge, and the designers and students with whom I have explored the intersections of design and anthropology.

Introduction

Alison J. Clarke

Design Anthropology: Object Cultures in Transition brings together leading practitioners and academics from the fields of anthropology and design as a means of opening up a dialog around their joint potentialities and shared commonalities. Set against the backdrop of an exponential rise, over the last decade, of transdisciplinary design areas (design studies, critical design, design sciences, co-design, post-design, transition design, design ethnography, speculative design, et al.), this volume explores the ways in which the methodologies and theoretical emphases of anthropology serve design as a socially engaged activity. Since an earlier edition of the book was published under the title *Design Anthropology: Object Culture in the Twenty-First Century* in 2011, there has been a proliferation of networks, companies, projects, publications, and initiatives made within an area loosely defined as 'design anthropology.' Despite the ongoing expansion of the field, both as curricular component and area of study within itself, this volume does not make claims for design anthropology as a discrete discipline, area of research, or methodology (Gunn, Otto and Smith 2013).

While the volume broadly concurs with wider claims of design anthropology's capacity to build "closer relations between using and producing, designing and using, people and things" and acknowledges that a "move is required away from a problem-orientated approach towards designing" (Gunn and Donovan 2012: 1), it considers the respective methods and historiographies of anthropology and design as having a discrete worth within and of themselves. As anthropologist Susanne Küchler puts it in the opening chapter of this volume "[D]esign distinguishes itself from mere things . . . by the 'inherence' of intellectual expectations in the work itself, and anthropology's contribution has been in unraveling the intersubjective nature of the kind of thought that is made concrete in design." (Küchler, this volume: 1)

Early Genres of Design Anthropology

In the early 1960s, Victor Papanek, the staunch critic of market-driven Western industrial design, devised a low-tech radio receiver for 'underdeveloped' countries based on the ethnographic observation of Indonesian indigenous cultures. The design comprised a recycled juice can, transistor, earplug, wire, paraffin wax and wick, and could be topped up using local cow dung as a sustainable power source. The stark industrial utility of the tin can lent itself to customization through the application of surface decoration (shells, traditional embroidery, etc.) easing the artifact's appropriation into traditional rituals and rites. This vernacularized form, a synchronous artifact framed by the contemporary media theories of Marshall McLuhan and 'sensitivity' toward local cultures, aimed at promoting mass communication among dispersed tribal groups and isolated communities in non-literate areas. Manufactured for less than nine cents a unit, the design received UNESCO sanction as a user-based project fostering participatory and appropriate technology approaches. In the broadest sense, the object foretold of a potential future in which design and anthropology co-joined in addressing cross-cultural issues of social inequality, rather than a burgeoning consumer culture, bolstering informal and alternative economies of product design.

Further into the twenty-first century, the "tin can radio" has come to stand for the broader ambitions of a late-postwar design counter culture geared towards social inclusion and pitted against corporatized power (Blauvelt 2015). This genre of the 'humanitarian object' perfectly summarizes the main thesis of Papanek's best-selling polemic *Design for the Real World: Human Ecology and Social Change* (1971), which promulgated the concept of design as a natural extension of anthropological analysis and practice (see Clarke, this volume). Yet, early on, these materialized forms of design anthropology caused disquiet among the established design fraternity. In 1973, Gui Bonsiepe, a former faculty member of the high modernist Hochschule für Gestaltung in Ulm (HfG), condemned objects like Papanek's tin can radio as "paternalistic design covered with a humanitarian coating," a crude post-colonial mechanism "doused in the ideology of the noble savage." (Bonsiepe 1973: 13–16) Both design and designer were condemned as being complicit in furthering American military dominance and capitalist expansionism. Anthropology was fraught with the legacy of its colonial past and the ethical dilemmas of fieldwork, while design had to strive to establish itself as a serious mode of social and critical intervention operating beyond a Western model of rational modernism.

Indeed, the idea of 'design anthropology' as a recent phenomenon emanating from 1970s post-industrial society and manifest in the rise of human-computer interaction design, systems thinking, social innovation strategy as well as user-centered research, crucially overlooks how the early political histories of design and anthropology were intertwined within the project of Cold War development politics (Clarke 2016). As post-development anthropologist Arturo Escobar argues in this volume, a branch of ontological design built on the legacy of 1960s design activism still harbors the potential for transforming post-development and ecological discourse:

> [T]ransitions towards entirely new ways of being-in-the-world are possible however unthinkable they might seem in particular current situations. These transitions are possible based on an ostensibly simple observation: that in designing tools (objects, structures, policies, expert systems, discourses (even narratives) we are creating ways of being. Change, from this ontological perspective, can be understood as residing firmly within the scope of design [...]. (Escobar, this volume: 202)

Escobar views the contemporary rise in 'critical design studies' as a direct successor to the early, if failed, attempts to unite the shared social imperative of design and anthropology.

From the embrace of phenomenological theory within 1960s and 1970s architectural discourse to the central role of anthropology and interpretative archaeology in highlighting the significance of material culture as a non-literary historical source through which to understand the agency of design as an expression and maker of power relations (Rudofsky 1964; Glassie 1975; Shanks and Tilley 1987), design and designers have been an integral part of social science discourse (Miller 1987). Indeed, from the early 1960s onwards, even within the upper echelons of professionalized design—namely, the International Council of Societies of Industrial Design (ICSID)—anthropology and the broader social sciences were brought to bear on international policy as affiliations with the United Nations Industrial Development Organization (UNIDO). This union, which saw anthropological methods and considerations applied to industrial design as a tool for 'development,' ultimately resulted in industrial design's key role in 1970s entente Cold War politics and the signing of the Ahmedabad Declaration of 1979, a pivotal event, which saw design dispersed within broader post-colonial social science.[1]

The 'Agentive Turn' and the New Design Politics

The mutuality of people and things, the confluence of the material and the social is, as sociologist Harvey Molotch (this volume) contends, an ongoing process. Since the 1990s, the separation of object and subject has been made all but redundant in theorizing around our contemporary material world. In bio- and nanotechnology, design innovation and engineering, the sheer proliferation of materialities, which cut across definitions of nature and culture, has brought the artifactual theories of the academe, from Bruno Latour to Alfred Gell, into the realm of mainstream design discourse (Gell 1992, 1999; Latour 1993, 1996). And, while anthropology was arguably the first discipline to take the consumption of things and the agency of artifacts seriously, it is now the area of materiality that promises to be the shared disciplinary concern of design and anthropology (Drazin and Küchler 2015).

A large-scale transdisciplinary "material turn" has expanded interest in design as a broader facet of the politics of ontology, the politics of making and the agency and social life of materials (Swenarton, Troiani, and Webster 2007; Bennett and Joyce 2010; Coole and Frost 2010). The once peripheral question of 'where stuff comes from,' in the broadest theoretical sense, is now central to the social sciences (Molotch 2003). As Molotch contends in his overview of this 'material turn,' if sociologists (as opposed to anthropologists) write about mass-produced goods at all, they "treat them as distractions from other putatively more worthwhile aspects of existence.

---

1. Adopted in 1979 at a meeting convened by UNIDO, ICSID and the Indian National Institute of Design, the "Ahmedabad Declaration on Industrial Design for Development" called for developing countries to strategically embrace industrial design in political policy-making across a broad spectrum from design education, promotion and cooperation to actions in industry and ecology. (Clarke, this volume; Clarke 2016)

[Sociologists] inherit as a Freud-Marx blend, a vision of consumer goods as fetish. Stuff provides noxious evidence of corrupted sensibilities, hegemonic oppression, or false needs." (Molotch, this volume: 19)

The non-hierarchical and holistic approaches of material culture as embraced within anthropology have opened up the definitions of design beyond formalistic and aesthetic analysis. The 'found,' vernacular and homemade artifact, borne of adhocism and the improvisation of everyday life, is a trope through which design and anthropology come together in re-assessing the socially embedded, informal and anti-commodity form (Jencks and Silver 1972). Contemporary movements such as 'post-craft,' in which the boundaries of making in analog and digital realms merge, and 'slow design,' in which the designer's focus shifts from object- to process-oriented approaches, bring new economies of design to the fore. Yet, anthropologists have long acknowledged the mutability and diasporic nature of vernacular forms and their ability to transgress, unsettle, and agitate cultures, as much as bind them. Designed goods, genres of making and materials are increasingly understood as embedded in, and constitutive of, the broader politics of neo-liberalism and personhood, as anthropologist Nicolette Makovicky highlights in her ethnographic case study of the merging of vernacular craft traditions with erotic underwear in Poland, as demanded by marketization and shifting nature of informal economies (this volume; Makovicky 2014).

Similarly, the work of sculptural artist Vladimir Arkhipov (this volume) centers on the curation of found and retrieved self-made utilitarian design, plucked from derelict post-socialist homesteads and the roadside of his native Ryazan, Russia. Disassembling the logic and hegemony of commodified product culture, objects such as a Soviet-era TV antenna modeled from discarded cutlery are re-cast as 'commodity folklore' invoking a methodological approach, as much as an aesthetic statement, that exposes design as integrally bound to internalized notions of State, technology, and personhood. Adapted, salvaged, and reinvented, these commodity folk forms, which once littered the post-Socialist landscape, embody the anthropology of everyday life as it is actually lived, rather than envisaged in the large-scale design studios of vast corporations.

The social life of objects has been a preoccupation of anthropology since the rise of consumption and material culture studies of the late 1980s (Appadurai 1986; Miller 1987). As scrutiny has shifted even further from the lives of goods beyond initial production cycles into the post-consumption phase, anthropology's emphasis upon geo-political understandings of informal economies and modes of appropriation has inverted design's concern with sustainability as a production-phase phenomenon. Disposal, waste and recycling are now understood as cultural, as well as logistical concerns, which design anthropology is ideally poised to navigate. With degradation, decay and the movement into alternative realms of value beyond the market inherent in the complexity of designed stuff (material and immaterial), new areas of design-anthropological discourse (e.g., transition design and post-development discourse) emerge and a new politics of design is forged (Norris 2012; Tonkinwise 2014; Gregson and Crang 2015).

The notion of what actually constitutes a 'designed product' has taken on expanded transnational and cross-cultural meaning, crucially disassociating design from a linear process of mediation toward a holistic model. As well as acknowledging 'designed things' as having agency beyond that conferred by a singular designer, Diana Young's ethnographic study of customized, discarded motor vehicles, among the Anangu desert peoples of Western Australia shows how apparently discarded and functionally dilapidated technological artifacts 'live,' through color and landscape, beyond the auspices of their corporate makers. Their chromatic significance extends beyond the dictums of a global forecasting industry; instead, these vehicles add to a world of "colorful goods," providing a "means of materializing and developing ideas and connections about the presence of the Creation Ancestor, which hitherto had been confined to evanescent effects across the landscape or painstakingly produced during ritual." (Young, this volume: 151) Young's vivid account of the aboriginal currency of cars as modes of color inseparable from an indigenous cosmological scheme, challenges a type of design studies that has sought to mark distinctions between social, technical, and aesthetic functions (Crilly 2010).

Design Anthropology, the Brand, and the Corporation

Design, of course, is not restricted to the materiality of things; but rather operates as a dispersed phenomenon. The global design entity IKEA is a case in point. The single largest globalized purveyor of mass branded furnishings goods should not be understood simply as a corporation, neither as a brand or typology of objects, argues anthropologist Pauline Garvey in this volume. Far from embodying the superficiality and transience of contemporary consumer culture, the extraordinary extent of IKEA's transnational reach relies rather upon its relevance as a practice. It is not the agency of the designers or the behind-the-scenes manipulation (by anthropologists and marketing experts), which manifest the corporate behemoth that is IKEA. Theories around brand sociality and value co-creation imply IKEA is "putting shoppers to work not only in obliging them to assemble flat-pack furniture but also in absorbing and territorializing their expertise, skills and creativity." (Garvey, this volume: 103) Yet, Garvey counters this idea through extensive comparative ethnography of the brand, spaces, and social relations, arguing instead that IKEA operates as 'collectivized inspiration' in which designers are merely creative brokers, rather than guiding innovators.

The corporate role of anthropologists and their 'complicity' in branding, advertising, and consumer persuasion stretches back at least as far as the 1950s (Packard 1957). In more recent decades, urban myths and legends have abounded regarding the rise of the corporate design anthropologist. As early as 1991, the *New York Times* featured an article titled "Coping with Cultural Polyglots" (Deutsch 1991) exploring the role of anthropologists within commercial and technological corporations. *Business Week*, later that year, reported that anthropologists were "Studying Natives on the Shop Floor (Garza 1991)." A wealth of similar stories about the intervention of anthropologists into the corporate workplace, with titles such as "Anthropologists Go Native in the Corporate Village" (Kane 2007) and "Into the Wild Unknown of the Workplace Culture" (Koerner 1998), sketch out a kind of parody of 'authentic' anthropologists whose attentions have turned from ancient Papuan New Guinea gift cultures to the banality of Western corporate and consumer culture. This popular fascination with the reversed role of the anthropologist as an observer of 'ourselves' persists under newspaper bylines hailing corporate anthropologists as fortune-tellers of our design and technological futures. Figures such as prominent Intel anthropologist Genevieve Bell take on guru-like roles (similar to figureheads of the future forecasting industries) seen to mediate between technological innovation and social worlds (Phelan 2013).

Anthropologist Lucy Suchman's oft-retold involvement with Xerox PARC, as part of a research and development strategy in the late 1980s, was feted in the business media as a best practice example of how design, transfigured by anthropology, might enhance a product's success. Legend had it that Suchman's ethnographic study of Xerox users led to the development of the 'break-through' design of the big, green photocopier button. According to the hero of the tale herself, this myth of corporate anthropology's 'magical' power is in fact an entire fiction that undermines the intent of deep research and its findings. Far from being an advocate of the 'simple' green button, Suchman's user-research challenged its very existence. As she puts it herself, "the green button actually masked the labor that was needed to become familiar with the machine and incorporate it effectively into use." (2007: 3) The branding of corporate anthropology in this reductionist way, she suggests, arose with the need to understand the worker and consumer beyond the economic paradigm; anthropology had a role both as a brand (offering human interest and public relations *caché* to corporate employers via the media) and as social science promising new and appropriable insights into worker and customer culture and experience.

Technology-based corporations like Intel (see Bezaitis and Robinson, this volume) engaged anthropologists during this period to expand their understanding of ever-fragmenting global markets. Design models like the ubiquitous 'smart home' offer a homogenizing vision of technological innovation. But an anthropological approach, which promotes cross-cultural and non-secular understandings of everyday life (from Hindu to Buddhist culture), takes into account 'soft' factors such as notions of pollution, sacredness, humility, and modesty otherwise overlooked in Western discourse around the appropriation of technologies (Bell 2006). Similarly, design companies such as IDEO encourage designers themselves, not just adjunct anthropologists, to use their observational skills and intuition in thinking beyond functional problem solving and into the social realm of things (Fulton Suri, this volume).

The shift towards cultural sensitivity through ethnography, while underpinned by a market-driven agenda, could optimistically be construed as a move towards socially responsive design. But early on, some critics pointed to the inherently reactionary nature of using consumers themselves to generate 'bottom-up' innovation, much as politicians have moved in the last decades towards focus groups as a means of trading complicity for 'real' social innovation. To quote one such critic from the neo-Marxist online journal *spiked*:

As an example of a relatively new form of immersive research, the discipline of ethnography emerged out of social anthropology: that is, white men studying black natives in the jungle, in an attempt to understand and control them. Today, we are the natives, caricatured in the interests of research. (Perks 2003: 1)

The commodification of ethnography and the incorporation of anthropology within corporate and political settings, as well as the ethical dimensions of design ethnography have more recently been opened up to much more rigorous academic scrutiny (Moeran 2012; Baba 2014). As examples of ethnographic research into aging, social exclusion, and the value of peripheral economic cultures reveal, anthropological methods have the capacity to generate effective social innovation. But where are the crucial points at which design and anthropology diverge? Jamer Hunt's essay critically unravels the ways in which the relative practices deal with issues of temporality (anthropology is of the now, design is of the imagined future) and points to the largely unproblematized incorporation of 'quick and dirty' ethnography within business. Advocating the role of critical and experimental design in helping to address global-scale problems, Hunt concludes that "we can no longer be content with anthropology's hands-off sensibility and design's 'more is more' mentality" (Hunt, this volume: 87, 88) and likewise "it is no longer sufficient for only a few in the academy to encounter the incisive work of anthropologists and for the vicissitudes of commercial interests to drive the work of designers," argues Hunt. As the realm of speculative and critical design has increasingly dealt with (often dystopic) design futures reaching beyond Modernist rationalism and progressivism (Dunne 2006; Dunne and Raby 2013), the idea of anthropology as a discipline 'applied' to design (as method or cultural contextualizing) has given way to a co-joined practice; asking what it is to be human now and how humanity might be further imagined.

Design in the Pre-Digital and Post-Digital

What of the post-digital shift to 'non-thing' design, the digital spaces between people and things in an immaterialized context? Early user-based and ethnographic research was carried out under the auspices of human-computer interaction (HCI) in the 1960s and 1970s, joined later in the 1980s by the field of 'interaction design.' Digital anthropology and interaction design have moved theory and practice around twenty-first-century object culture far beyond the remit of those early corporate design anthropologists and myths of big, green photocopier buttons. Yet, while the shift from analog to digital life and its ensuing social relations has long been the concern of those involved in designing interactions (Moggridge 2007), the emergence of digital anthropology has thwarted any residual conceptual divide between the 'para-world' of the digital and the 'real world' of the analog (Horst and Miller 2012). Whereas the less mediated world of the pre-digital was formally lent greater authenticity, the focus on digital design anthropology has led to a radical overturning of this basic supposition. Design anthropology, in its most diluted form, is reduced to little more than a social add-on for co-design projects needing 'tick-box' solutions for user-engagement. Yet, it has much greater potential to analytically engage with emerging areas such as critical algorithm studies, which urgently need methodologies and expanded insights into micro and macro implications of non-transparent forms of design and engineering (Baker and Potts 2013; Pasquale 2015; Demos 2016).

In this respect, Lane De Nicola (this volume) brings into question the core rhetoric of the 'Internet of Things' designers and corporations routinely build upon. Challenging the inherently optimistic vision of 'techno-science' and the social egalitarianism embodied in Latour's commonly appropriated notion of "The Parliament of Things" (with its quasi-objects and networked human-object relations), De Nicola provocatively proposes an alternative model under the title the "The Pub of Things." A "wilder, woolier terrain" of inquiry for the anthropologist, "The Pub" filled with "opportunists and miscreants," he argues, works as a more succinct model for researching the objects that populate everyday human lives in the post-digital context. As corporate research ostensibly considers the ways in which users talk and practice the digital in bounded ways, theorists focus on the agencies of objects. De Nicola postulates that just as a traditional anthropologist asks "What of the people on the ground in this discourse?" so too must the critical design anthropologist by considering the less obvious and 'checkered terrain' of actors and agents in the Internet of Things, "[t]he voyeur spying on his neighbors" or the exploitation of increasingly personalized data gleaned by poaching advertisers.

Daniel Miller, in his chapter dealing with the practice of interior design as "a foundational attribute of merely being human" further challenges the artificial divide between offline and online, and the imperative of critical anthropological inquiry to look beyond definitions of 'professional' design spheres. Building on a long-term global ethnography of social media (Miller et al. 2016), online, argues Miller, is as much a place of habitation as any physically embodied space which involves perpetual acts of interior design. Critical anthropology that ceases to differentiate between offline worlds and online worlds can open up crucial questions regarding the contemporary nature of ordinary human lives—issues of migration, social relations, and co-living beyond a 'bricks and mortar' approach. Ultimately, argues Miller, "the shift of our skills as interior decorators from offline to online does not make us less human or post-human," rather design anthropology must look precisely to "de-exoticize" the online world, understanding this type of crafting as a type of design "that makes us all ordinarily human" (Miller, this volume: 176).

Just as design processes form an integral part of what it is to be human in an everyday sense, the anthropology of design is, of course, inseparable from the larger frameworks of cultural, economic and social life. The poignant significance and power relations of design are made evident in the nuanced ethnography of mobile money services, which over the past decade have grown primarily across Africa, Asia, and Latin America, explored in Erin Taylor and Heather Horst's chapter "Designing Financial Literacy in Haiti" (this volume). As the use and availability of mobile handsets has increased, their role in broadening the constituency of financial inclusion for the poor through access to mobile money services has been embraced by governments, industry, and development sectors alike. Yet, through the application of a design anthropological approach, Taylor and Horst complicate this seemingly simple equation of 'access' and 'availability,' arguing instead that a design perspective encompasses a broadened understanding of literacy as an index of aesthetics, branding, and historically located value around specific forms of technology and material culture. This branching out into anthropology offers design a timely intervention into alternative and new economies, beyond the mass scale of industrial object-based production; whereby social innovation might lie at the core, rather than the periphery, of its practice.

This collection of essays outlines a seismic shift in the way experts and users conceptualize, envisage, and engage in object cultures. As the output of contemporary design becomes evermore diverse, the term design itself is increasingly redundant in its capacity to capture the sheer heterogeneity of the processes, practices, and materialities involved in the making of stuff. Designers are now as likely to engage in social research as they are in the making of form: Once an intuitive process, gauging cultural relevance has become part of a burgeoning area—design anthropology. Observational techniques, human focus and emphasis on the machinations of the everyday are essential in interpreting the complex implications of consumer culture, technological interaction, and media. As the values of expanding new markets challenge homogenous, globalized understandings of product worlds and users, the desire for indigenous, grassroots, and nuanced insights has never been more acute. Similarly, a social imperative, the challenge to the monopoly of market models with the creation of alternative economies of design, has reignited critical design discourse. It is precisely this pressing recognition of a need for change with which the agencies and lives of products and technologies, as much as their designers and users, are now explored and probed beyond disciplinary boundaries; consequently propelling social understanding to the forefront of the design agenda and moving contemporary object cultures firmly into the center of academic inquiry.

References

Appadurai, A. ed. (1986), *The Social Life of Things: Commodities in Cultural Perspective*, Cambridge: Cambridge University Press.

Baba, M. L. (2014), "De-Anthropologizing Ethnography: A Historical Perspective on the Commodification of Ethnography as a Business Service," in R. Denny and P. Sunderland (eds.), *Handbook of Anthropology in Business*, 43–68, Walnut Creek: Left Coast Press Inc.

Baker, P. and A. Potts (2013), "'Why Do White People Have Thin Lips?' Google and the Perpetuation of Stereotypes Via Auto-Complete Search Forms," *Critical Discourse Studies,* 10 (2): 187–204.

Bell, G. (2006), "The Age of the Thumb: A Cultural Reading of Mobile Technologies from Asia. Knowledge," *Technology and Policy,* 19 (2): 41–57.

Bennett, T. and P. Joyce (2010), *Material Powers: Cultural Studies, History and the Material Turn*, London and New York: Routledge.

Blauvelt, A. (2015), *Hippie Modernism: The Struggle for Utopia*, Minneapolis: Walker Art Center.

Bonsiepe, G. (1973), "Bombast aus Pappe," *form* 61 (1): 13–16.

Clarke, A. J. (2016), "Design for Development, ICSID and UNIDO: The Anthropological Turn in 1970s Design," *Journal of Design History*, 29 (1): 43–57.

Coole, D. and S. Frost (2010), *New Materialism: Ontology, Agency, and Politics*, Durham: Duke University Press.

Miller, D., E. Costa, N. Haynes, T. McDonald, R. Nicolescu, J. Sinanan, J. Spyer, S. Venkatraman, and X. Wang (2016), *How the World Changed Social Media*, London: UCL Press.

Crilly, N. (2010). "The Roles that Artefacts Play: Technical, Social and Aesthetic Functions," *Design Studies*, 31 (4): 311–44.

Demos (2016), "The Use of Misogynistic Terms on Twitter," research summary report. Available online: http://www.demos.co.uk/wp-content/uploads/2016/05/Misogyny-online.pdf (accessed June 15, 2016).

Deutsch, C. H. (1991), "Managing; Coping with Cultural Polyglots," *New York Times*, February 24.

Drazin, A. and S. Küchler (2015), *The Social Life of Materials: Studies in Materials and Society*, London: Bloomsbury.

Dunne, A. (2006), *Hertzian Tales: Electronic Products, Aesthetic Experience and Critical Design*, Cambridge: The MIT Press.

Dunne, A. and F. Raby (2013), *Speculative Everything*, Cambridge: The MIT Press.

Garza, C. E. (1991), "Studying Natives on the Shop Floor," *Business Week*, September 30.

Gell, A. (1992), "The Technology of Enchantment and the Enchantment of Technology," in J. Coote and A. Shelton (eds.), *Anthropology Art and Aesthetics*, 40–66, Oxford: Oxford University Press.

Gell, A. (1999), "Vogel's Net: Traps as Artworks and Artworks as Traps," in E. Hirsh (ed.), *Alfred Gell, The Art of Anthropology: Essays and Diagrams*, London: Bloomsbury Academic.

Glassie, H. (1975), *Folk Housing in Middle Virginia: A Structural Analysis of Historic Artifacts*, Knoxville: University of Tennessee Press.

Gregson, N. and M. Crang (2015), "From Waste to Resource: The Trade in Wastes and Global Recycling Economies," *Annual Review of Environment and Resources* 40: 151–76.

Gunn, W., J. Donovan and R. C. Smith (eds.) (2012), *Design and Anthropology*, Farnham: Ashgate.

Gunn, W. and T. Otto (eds.) (2013), *Design Anthropology: Theory and Practice*. London: Bloomsbury.

Horst, H. and D. Miller (2012), *Digital Anthropology*, Oxford: Berg Publishers.

Jencks, C. and N. Silver (1972), *Adhocism: The Case for Improvisation*, Cambridge: The MIT Press.

Kane, K. A. (2007), "Anthropologists Go Native in the Corporate Village," *Fastcompany.com* (December 18). Available online: http://www.fastcompany.com/magazine/05/anthro.html (accessed June 15, 2016).

Koerner, B. I. (1998), "Into the Wild Unknown of the Workplace Culture," *US News and World Report*, August 10: 56.

Latour, B. (1993), *We Have Never Been Modern*, Cambridge: Harvard University Press.

Latour, B. (1996), *Aramis or the Love of Technology*, Cambridge: Harvard University Press.

Makovicky, N. (2014), *Neoliberalism, Personhood, and Postsocialism: Enterprising Selves in Changing Economies*, Farnham: Ashgate.

Miller, D. (1987), *Material Culture and Mass Consumption*, Oxford: Blackwell.

Moggridge, B. (2007), *Designing Interactions*, Cambridge: The MIT Press.

Molotch, H. (2003), *Where Stuff Comes From: How Toasters, Toilets, Cars, Computers, and Many Other Things Come to Be As They Are*, New York: Routledge.

Moeran, B. (2012), "Opinion: What Business Anthropology Is, What It Might Become . . . and What, Perhaps, It Should Not Be," *Journal of Business Anthropology*, 1 (2): 240–97.

Norris, L. (2012), "Economies of Moral Fibre: Materializing the Ambiguities of Recycling Charity Clothing into Aid Blankets," *Journal of Material Culture*, 17 (4): 389–404.

Packard, V. (1957), *The Hidden Persuaders*, New York: D. McKay Co.

Papanek, V. (1971), *Design for the Real World: Human Ecology and Social Change*, New York: Pantheon Books.

Pasquale, F. (2015), *The Black Box Society: The Secret Algorithms That Control Money and Information*, Cambridge: Harvard University Press.

Perks, M. (2003), "Ethnography Exposed," *spiked*, December 30. Available online: www.spiked-online.com/articles/00000006E039.htm (accessed June 15, 2016).

Phelan, D. (2013), "Technology's Foremost Fortune Teller: Why Intel Has an Anthropologist on Its Payroll," *Independent*, September 25. Available online: http://www.independent.co.uk/life-style/gadgets-and-tech/features/technologys-foremost-fortune-teller-why-intel-has-an-anthropologist-on-its-payroll-8839723.html?version=meter+at+null&module=meter-Links&pgtype=article&contentId=&mediaId=&referrer=https%3A%2F%2Fwww.google.at%2F&priority=true&action=click&contentCollection=meter-links-click (accessed June 15, 2016).

Rudofsky, B. (1964), *Architecture Without Architects: An Introduction to Non-Pedigreed Architecture*, New York: Museum of Modern Art.

Shanks, M. and C. Tilley (1987), *Re-Constructing Archaeology: Theory and Practice*, Cambridge: Cambridge University Press.

Suchman, L. (2007), "Anthropology as 'Brand': Reflections on Corporate Anthropology," paper presented at the *Colloquium on Interdisciplinarity and Society*, February 24, Oxford University.

Swenarton, M., I. Troiani and H. Webster, eds., (2007), *The Politics of Making*, Abington and New York: Routledge.

Tonkinwise, C. (2014), "Design Studies—What Is It Good For?," *Design and Culture* 6 (1): 5-43.

1 Materials and Design
Susanne Küchler

Materials, once thought of as determined by form and function, are now the function-
ing thing itself. Crunchable, foldable and portable, reactive and proactive, materials
designed in laboratories range from the practical to the unsettling. What they have in
common is to draw our attention to a material world that is composed, akin to music,
as 'poiesis,' the numerical and temporally sequenced logic that is capable of enchanting
without knowing, and of inspiring relational actions without similitude.

Design has been a longstanding concern in anthropology with a formative tradition of thought reaching back to the eighteenth-century historian and philosopher Johann Gottfried Herder ([1778] 2002). Herder's theory of sculpture pointed to the poetic nature of communication, shared by both language and repetitive actions of the body, and the relation between this poetic element of communication and the emotional pull of the resulting product. These ideas were famously developed by Franz Boas (1955 [1927]) into a concept of 'virtuosity'—understood as the pleasures of practice that are given substance in basket making, pottery making, or Northwest Coast wood carving—as well as by Marcel Mauss (1934), who drew attention to highly developed body actions that embody aspects of a given culture. More recently, this notion of the algorithmic and relational nature of technical action was taken forward by Gregory Bateson (1973) in his theory of "style, grace, and information," by Fred Myers (1999) in his analysis of the prototyp-icality of Aboriginal painting, and by Alfred Gell (1998) in his theory of the indexical logic of manufactured artifacts. Design distinguishes itself from mere things, in the words of David Freed-berg (1991), by the 'inherence' of intellectual expectations in the work itself, and anthropology's contribution has been in unraveling the intersubjective nature of the kind of thought that is made concrete in design.

Despite these formative ideas that open up the world of design to anthropological introspection, there has been one notable lapse of attention. As Margaret Conkey (2006) has shown in her discussion of style, design, and function in the *Handbook of Material Culture*, anthropology took with ease to the conceptual nature of the classical notion of 'disegno,' in which an act of drawing was thought to be prefigured by a concept, embedding wherever possible the representation of mental schema into the context of social practice. It has coped very badly, however, with materials and their functional, sensorial, and technical capacities, which must enter into conference with the algorithmic and poetic qualities of making in order for a shared concept of form and function of designed objects to arise (Reckwitz 2002; Miller 2005). In failing to include materials in their reckoning of design, anthropologists have missed a chance to question what is social about design, assuming it to reside in the process of production known as 'co-creation' in which designers, standing in for the 'ideal' consumer, inform the inventive discovery and deployment of commodities (Barry 2005; Barry and Thrift 2007). Other disciplines, notably the history of science and the history of art, have delivered studies of historical and institutional contexts of design with an increasing emphasis on materials and the manifold ideas that inspire their trade and their use in design (Wagner 2001; Schiebinger and Swan 2005; Klein and Lefèvre 2007; Rubel and Hackenschmidt 2008; Lange-Berndt 2015). The publication of studies on the agency of matter and the re-emergence of materials as paradigm for the social sciences that coincided with the end of the first decade in the twenty-first century summarized what materials science had long recognized, namely, that the question of what is social about design and design's relation to material and immaterial frames of reference required to be fundamentally reconsidered (Bensaude-Vincent 2004; Bennett 2010; Coole and Frost 2010; Buchli 2015). To understand the theoretical and also methodological implications for disciplines concerned with the study of design, we need to look closely at design's changing relation to materials.

Materials by Design

"We live," as Mike Ashby and Kara Johnson (2002) have pointed out, "in a world of materials"; we make things out of materials, and we see potential in materials before giving form to it. Yet, the materials we use for our design are no longer just found or grown, but are themselves subject to design in being "made to measure" (Ball 1997). Bernadette Bensaude-Vincent and William R. Newman (2007) have pointed to the growing polarity between the natural and the artificial in a world in which the majority of materials that surrounds us is engineered to assume functions that we used to associate with technical devices hidden in objects. What is distinctive about these materials is their composite nature and membrane-like quality, which allows them to stretch over any shape, merging formal and functional qualities in the very fabric of the material. Materials, once thought of as covers, such as the surface of a wireless keyboard, are the functioning thing itself—the keyboard is crunchable, foldable, and eminently portable, and feels to the touch like denim. Known as 'smart materials,' materials by design range from the practical to the hilarious and unsettling, but in common they draw our attention to a material world that does not just represent who we are, but also is capable of standing in for us, substituting some of our own capacities. The goal of research into smart materials and structures is the animation of the inanimate world, by endowing it with more and more of the attributes of living things, and by creating networks of integrated artifacts that work relationally, forming huge complex systems of sensate things that (eventually) really learn (Küchler 2008). Alongside such chemically engineered materials, the rediscovery of 'old' materials today plays a prominent role in the fabrication of environmentally friendly materials for the future through new engineering techniques. Materials such as flax, bamboo, and hemp, typically found in archaeological and ethnographic collections, evoke ideas of heritage, identity, and place, but also open up debates about cultural rights and property.

The rediscovery of known materials shows that all materials are potentially new. What distinguished the material we associate with the rise of modern imagination, however, involved making the technical function part of the material itself. This material was rubber, first processed by Charles Goodyear in 1839. It was soon followed by the innovation of synthetically produced, stretchable, and moldable materials with the invention of Bakelite, the first synthetic resin chemically formulated in 1909, and later, around 1938, of polystyrene for plastic materials and perlon fiber as well as coatings such as Teflon. Arguably, it was the capacity of natural rubber and its synthetic variants to cover any surface, irrespective of form, that created the capacity for new artifacts with new functions, such as the diver's suit, the rubber hose, and the raincoat (Mossmann and Smith 2008). New ways of life in domains reaching from leisure to work were made possible by a 'stretchable' material that came to compare fittingly to the many new actions that took life beyond its known limits (Meikle 1995).

Social science's interest in the legacy of the chemical revolution and in the design and the take-up of new materials has classically been low in the English-speaking world. Anthropology, ironically, has arguably borne witness to the chemical revolution's social effects perhaps more than other disciplines, as the rise of chemical engineering provoked shifts in political economy, which led to the local touchdown of the ethnographic method. An example of the distant effect of the chemical revolution that anthropology came to chart is New Guinea, where European incursion followed the chemical development of soap in 1823 by Chevreul, who first separated natural dyes from the complex mixtures of oils, resins, and gums. This was made possible, in turn, by an earlier discovery by Nicholas Leblanc, who in 1801 extracted alkali from common salt and thereby created the basis for the development of the first chemical industry in Europe. From the 1830s onward, soap and candles were made with chemically manufactured vegetable oils instead of animal tallow, and by 1840 coconut oil extracted from copra was imported from the Pacific Islands into Europe. Local histories of the global reach of an economy that began to function increasingly on the back of trade in raw materials for chemical engineering are, however, as yet largely unwritten, albeit from a purely historical, Eurocentric perspective (Smith and Findlen 2002; Schiebinger and Swan 2005).

Much without us noticing, in a move that was as swift as it was seemingly unremarkable, a rapidly advancing material technology has invaded into every aspect of daily life in the modern world, subtly altering the infrastructure of life in a manner far more effective than paradigm shifts in scientific knowledge (Latour 1992; Hansen 2000). Nanotechnology, materials, and information technology are now combining with biology and the life sciences to enable further integrations with pervasive effects from design (biomimetics) to end product (bionics). A world of materials, readily equipped with technical function, now cuts across all known classifications of nature and culture in quantities that now reach into the tens of thousands (Silberglitt 2001). Bruno Latour has captured the vanishing of the relevance of existing systems of classification in which 'things' were radically other to 'persons,' inventing for us a vocabulary that makes manifest the agency of nonhumans and the recalcitrant materiality of humans (Latour and Woolgar 1979; Latour 1996). Latour (2001) speaks of a "parliament of things" to draw attention to the ways in which material technologies form assemblages that interrupt, revise, or restructure political life.

As anthropology has come to appreciate artifactual agency (Gell 1998), following the history and philosophy of science where materials made by 'design' have become the new epistemic object par excellence (Daston 2004; Bensaude-Vincent and Newmann 2007), it is dawning on us that distinctions—between the social and the material, the natural and the artificial—upon which our most trusted methods have rested for the past century have indeed become obsolete. As connections of molecules made tangible in materials take on a presence in our lives without us even being fully aware that they do so, materials by design have become far more than the mere technical substrata of a world lived in analog to a digitized presence. Ready-made with a use and a user in mind, virtually un-reconstructable yet affecting the very infrastructure of life, new materials challenge anthropology to respond with a theory of design that enables us to understand how materials work and what they do from a social science perspective.

Libraries of materials are wrestling with an avalanche of designed materials, estimated at between 40,000 and 70,000, that no longer fit existing classificatory paradigms. Such libraries have sprung up since the mid-1990s, a commercial example of which is *material connexion*, with its outlets in New York, Milan, and Beijing. As the need for material consultants is increasing in all sectors of industry, design, and architecture, such libraries are rapidly becoming the main knowledge resource about what materials can do. As new materials are not just composites, which cannot be easily disentangled either conceptually or physically, impeding such actions as copying and recycling, but are also at least potentially aggregates in their systemic capacity for propagation and replication, those that need to select materials are facing a real problem. Knowing materials to the extent that one can select from a range of several thousand materials that more or less fulfill the same function has become a specialist domain for the material consultant. To assist designers in steering through this minefield, there is now burgeoning literature on the huge range of engineered materials from which designers and manufacturers can choose in the fabrication of any artifact (Benyus 1997; Hongu and Philips 1997; Askeland and Pradeep 2002; Ashby and Johnson 2002; Gay, Suong, and Tsai 2002; Mori 2002; Addington, Miller and Schodek 2004; Wessel 2004). Publications on new materials also comprise handbooks directed at a specialist audience in design and industry (Satas and Tracton 2000; Stattmann 2003; Beylerian, Dent, and Moryadas 2005).

Handbooks furnish the designer with an image of a material, its functional characteristics such as luminosity or tensile strength, but leave out any discussion of experience of use. Ashby and Johnson (2002) have recently begun to fill this gap in writing a phenomenologically oriented guide to designed materials, modeling the range of effects of materials so that designers can take these effects into consideration. Using grid systems, they map out acoustic, olfactory, tactile, and motion-sensitive factors inherent in materials and arrange these on a spectrum at the center of which is the egocentric and relative sensorial space of a person. Most new materials take the form of screens or fibrous membranes, a fact that cannot quite be explained by the perceptual paradigm implicit in this phenomenological account of new materials. Simulating cloth, such membranes, much like skin, form both a boundary and a point of contact between the human and the material world, binding people in social and economic relationships while simultaneously defining their difference. Individuation, which we used to associate with the consumption stage of commodity production, is now taking place at the moment of materials design and selection in a manner that is raising important issues about the difference such materials will make to our notion of and intellectual expectations directed to diversity.

The thriving economy in new materials revolves around highly mobile and complex materials, moving from institution to institution as they are adopted, transformed, and manufactured into products to suit a number of distinct functions. The inseparable link between materials and knowledge is now recognized to present a huge potential for growth but also to be highly vulnerable to factors affecting transmission and take-up. The materials industry in the United Kingdom—in which new materials are presenting a steady increase—has today an annual turnover of around £200 billion, contributing 15 percent of GDP to the economy, and employing 1.5 million people directly and supporting a further 4 million jobs. In 2006, a report by the Department of Trade and Industry (DTI) identified a number of challenges to the UK materials sector's place as a world leader in materials science. Recognizing the volatility of an economy run on the back of materials that need to be known in order to be taken up, the report emphasized that central to any future success would be the transfer of knowledge of materials across a network of stakeholders: an interconnected web of customers, universities, research and technology organizations, designers, and other intermediaries. As a result, the UK government created the Materials Knowledge Transfer Network in 2006 in order to improve the capacity of the United Kingdom's innovation performance by increasing the breadth and depth of knowledge transfer.

Designers and industry are facing the new relation between materials and knowledge with anxiety, as untold numbers of designed materials fail to reach a market. Over and above the question of how to design with materials in mind, what material knowledge actually is when the distinction between nature and culture is meaningless, how this knowledge is transmitted, and what 'new' materials do when they come to replace existing materials in artifacts that are pivotal to identity are concerns that have not yet even begun to be addressed (McDonough and Braungart 2009). It is here that anthropology can contribute with a theoretical understanding of the nature of materials selection drawn from ethnographies, which testify to the absence of the distinction of the natural and the artificial in societies we tend to have disregarded in studies of design (Strathern 1999).

New Materials: A Story of Uncertainty and Risk[1]

Global policy makers have embraced cutting-edge scientific research that takes the potential societal benefit of newly invented materials as axiomatic. Governments in the United States, Germany, China, Japan, and South Korea posit the development of advanced materials as crucial to global competitiveness and national security, and essential for addressing the broader challenges of clean energy, food security, and human health and well-being. As a result, the early twenty-first century is being defined by a flourishing new materials economy driven by a flood of engineered technological materials whose capacities offer far-reaching promises—but just how sustainable are they and what may the difference be that they make to society and culture?

In science, innovation for its own sake is privileged, with a trajectory that goes from invention to successful initial application on a case-by-case basis; failures are not highlighted or even acknowledged. From this perspective, new technology looks entirely positive, and tends to be adopted by policy makers without a broad evidence base as to its potential consequences. In social science, which focuses on the societal use of new materials *after* initial application, over a prolonged period of time, the view is very different. From this perspective, production quickly segues into overproduction, and use often into misuse.

Recent ethnographic research shows that a staggering percentage of materials invented and manufactured at great cost fail to establish a secure market within the first five months, often for social rather than scientific reasons. One example of failed materials is Azlon, a class of regenerated protein fibers developed as a wool substitute during the 1930s and 40s. Fibers made from milk (Aralac) and peanuts (Ardil) were commercially produced in the United States and United Kingdom during World War II shortages and marketed as patriotic fibers; however, they were

---

1. This section was written jointly with Lucy Norris and Kaori O'Connor and was presented at the III Open Systems Conference in October 2014.

structurally weak and had to be blended. The range of unfamiliar trade names resulted in 'forgetta-ble' fibers that were both physically and cognitively difficult to identify and failed to create a strong niche market. After 1945 they came to be culturally associated with wartime deprivation and sub-stitution, and only recently have they re-emerged as luxury sustainable fibers with health-giving properties. 'Qmilch' is one such contemporary milk fiber being developed in Germany and mar-keted as highly desirable and beneficial to the skin.

New materials may not be effectively mobilized, designers may remain ignorant of their potential, or consumers may fail to become attached to them. For every lasting 'success,' therefore, many materials come into circulation and then fail, exacerbating the very problems new materials are supposedly developed to solve. At the same time, the privileging of innovation drives the devel-opment of yet more new materials, instead of fully exploring the potential and qualities of recent inventions, leading to waste, overproduction, increased risk and uncertainty, and an increasing lack of knowledge about the materials that surround us. Indeed, there is a general resistance to thinking about materials at all.

The new materials market has produced two distinct phenomena, each taken individually presenting huge problems for society and the environment—together they present perhaps one of the greatest challenges. The first is overproduction—materials innovated in the laboratory do not offer resistance to tools and skills and thus can, with the right machinery, be produced in any quantity and quality for as long as there is a demand in the market. The second is disposal—new synthetic materials do not degrade or degrade in time spans that are unknown to human civilizations. The precedent for this was set in the 1950s with the commercialization of the first mass-market new material: plastic (Mossmann and Smith 2008).

The consequences unleashed by the unbridled development of plastics comprise some of the greatest environmental challenges of our times, and yet people are still hypnotized by what Meikle (1995) called the 'exuberant proliferation' of design and new materials. And in our obsession with novelty, we overlook the fact that materials are not inert; they leak, transform, and interact with what is around them in ways that are invisible and unsuspected. Asbestos and plastics are two examples that immediately come to mind (Norris 2010).

We are all familiar with the overwhelming representations of the Great Pacific Garbage Patch; there are vast areas of miniscule particles of plastic marine debris suspended in columns in each of the five major gyres in the world's oceans. Its impact on marine life has been catastrophic. Various artists have attempted to convey the enormity of our falling out of love with these plastics and our wastefulness, potently brought to mind by Chris Jordan's images of dead baby albatrosses whose stomachs are full of plastic, or sea turtles bound with netting. The effects of these marine rubbish dumps are inconceivable, and research has only just begun on the impact of molecular changes as plastic breaks down. Indeed, the term 'plastisphere' refers to ecosystems that have evolved to live in human-made plastic environments, such as the image by Andrea Westmoreland. But this disguises the hidden dangers of the Garbage Patch, the 'shadow' it casts over the marine life below it, turning vast areas of the ocean floor and the deep sea into marine deserts we cannot see, but the consequences of which are already affecting us, in the loss of edible marine resources.

There are at present two competing approaches to how best to mitigate the uncertainty and risk that surround the discovery, deployment, and disposal of materials: one calling for increased governance, the other emerging from open access models for developing shared knowledge resources. But both approaches are hampered by existing economic and management systems set up for commodity production that either unnecessarily restrict movements of materials or are totally unaware of the possibilities and consequences.

The governance model directs almost exclusive attention to identifying and securing materials resources, driven by narratives of risks, volatility, scarcity, frontiers, resilience, and governance, and calling for a holistic approach that includes (a) strategic, diplomatic efforts in the international arena to boost supply through trade agreements and knowledge exchange; (b) increasing the efficiency of resource use; and (c) improving the husbandry of resources through reuse, remanufacture, and recycling in secondary markets. The governance model argues that it is *de facto* resource politics, not environmental preservation or sound economics, that is set to dominate the global agenda, played out through trade disputes, climate negotiations, market manipulation strategies, aggressive industrial policies, and the scramble to control frontier areas.

The open access model on the other hand is all about finding innovative advanced alternatives through increased connectivity, with narratives of opportunity, experimentation, and collaboration. Examples of its implementation are the United States's 'Materials Genome Initiative,' launched in 2011, which aims to double the speed of new materials innovation and deployment through computational research, and develop a national public–private infrastructure to integrate emerging data into generic open-access materials databases within an evolving intellectual property (IP) framework. The computational research uses algorithms to generate millions of potential new materials and model their physical properties without their ever having been manufactured, and models spatially and temporally the new materials' behaviors and properties during product design.

Supercomputing clusters at Berkeley have been harnessed for the Materials Project, which aims to compute the properties of all known materials and make them available to researchers, thus improving software's predictive capacities for new material combinations and allowing for targeted screening of the potentially most useful materials before they have been synthesized in a lab. It is claimed that such advanced combinatorial techniques accelerate tenfold the transition from new materials discoveries to practical applications. In contrast, Harvard's open-access 'Clean Energy Project' is seeking a clearly defined advanced-material solution to a practical problem. Aiming to develop high-performance organic photovoltaic candidates for solar cell materials, it is currently the world's largest computational chemistry experiment. Using IBM's World Community Grid, the global public can participate by donating idle computer time for computational research. This has so far generated 2.3 million candidate materials, whose properties have been made available in online databases, allowing other materials scientists and engineers to design experimental new products.

The screening and selection of suitable virtual candidates results in what Andrew Barry (2005) has termed 'informed materials,' whose properties are simulated by computers and whose proposed use is built into their very existence, yet whose real social use once manufactured cannot be predicted or imagined. The story of these millions of computed new materials can be seen to offer a counterpoint to the by now familiar narrative of lack-of-sustainability determined by resource depletion. But is simply speeding up advances in technology really going to solve the global challenges that confront us today?

This new materials economy also throws up uncertainties, risks, and anxieties attached to the potential social life of these materials. What kinds of meanings will be embedded in them, what relationships will we build with them? How much will be wasted? The pursuit of novelty and innovation for their own sake, and the reluctance to develop the full potential in new materials before moving on to develop further new ones, many of which will be discarded, is not new, and a famous industry story may serve as a cautionary example. Dupont developed the elastane fiber Lycra over twenty years before launching it in 1959 (O'Connor 2011). Lycra was specifically invented for use in women's girdles, and since all women wore girdles in the 1950s, a huge mass market was ensured. Then came Women's Liberation. Women abandoned the girdle and the market for Lycra collapsed. No one wanted it. Bales of Lycra fabric lay unused in warehouses until the aerobics movement erupted, and Lycra was rediscovered for use in the workout outfits Jane Fonda made famous. Suddenly, everyone wanted clothes that stretched—not just for gymnastics, but for everyday use; now Lycra is ubiquitous, mixed with many other fibers. In this case, working together, science and society created a new market for the fiber that had been on the edge of being abandoned, fully developing its potential.

The problem is fundamentally anthropological—how do people from very different and overlapping cultures interact with, use, and understand highly mobile materials in their changing environments? An understanding of the use and usefulness of materials is a vital factor in the success of any solution to a sustainable materials economy, as high-velocity materials alone will not enable us to overcome our current strategic reliance on simply improving remanufacture and recycling. For this to happen, materials, and the understanding and actions we direct toward them, have to be taken seriously as objects of research by both materials and social science. With theoretical traditions that balance cultural relativism with universalist principles and a disciplinary foundation in fine-grained ethnography as a methodology, anthropological studies of the cultural perceptions of materials in use have never been more urgently needed.

The story of materials use, the inter-subjective, often surprising, and yet deeply empathetic understanding that communities bring to materials is a story that is sensitive to the needs, hopes, and aspirations of society and that sees success not in the scale of consumption, but in the duration and quality of use. Ironically, in a world in which potentially millions of materials compete to be turned into objects with rather more limited forms and functions than they are technically capable of, we are now generally ignorant of the properties, levels of sustainability, and future impact of the material objects that surround us. And this precisely at a moment when materials are beginning to take over the technical functions we once associated exclusively with object forms.

The step-change in both the quantity and inherent qualities of materials is swift and largely unrecognized outside the laboratory environment, arriving in the marketplace as a *fait accompli*, apparently undifferentiated from previous materials. This leaves existing structures of training, monitoring, and planning for their long-term impact hopelessly behind and unable to respond intelligibly. Without a deep understanding of the role of the social in materials development and use, how can we define the criteria of success and understand how and why some materials fail? How are we to evaluate the 'usefulness' of materials and, by the same token, avoid wasting their potential and simply creating more waste? Understanding the value of new materials through a nuanced study of social and cultural values is a core contribution that social science ought to be making.

In the rush to create future forms of living and burdened by our industrial past we have forgotten the very simple fact that, like humans, materials need two to tango: scientists who study how to think with materials and social scientists who study how materials are used and experienced. The task ahead is not just about finding the right way to innovate materials and bring them to market but how to break down the silos of training that have been with us since the mid-nineteenth century by partnering up materials and social science in ways fit for the demands of the twenty-first century, from the bottom up.

The making of futures has always been shrouded in uncertainty and risk; in our material world, the challenges can only be overcome if science and social science work together. Social science, and anthropology in particular, is called upon to assist brokering conversations across disciplines in ensuring that the question of the difference made by materials designed in laboratories includes questions of society and culture. For what enables materials to be taken up and resonate—spurring on new imaginaries and new actions much beyond the potential originally informing the design of a material—has been revealed by recent ethnographies sensitive to the question of what materials are, what happens when they are taken up, and what they do unwittingly to cultural imaginaries and actions (Drazin and Küchler 2015). The following section is a brief excursion into one such ethnographic study, which shows that a material such as fiber, let alone the woven and dyed fabric that is made from it, is taken up with intentions that are rather surprising and with effects that are reaching far beyond the society within which the material has come to resonate.

Material, Substance, and Effect

This section discusses a case study of the take-up and transformation of cloth in a Pacific society. The Pacific Islands are famous for the diversity and visual complexity of their art traditions, which are an inseparable part of trade and exchange, and flamboyant rituals. The rich and complex intellectual expectations that resonate with the world of the concrete have been the subject of numerous ethnographies that have provoked the theorizing of the analogical relation between concepts of the social and the material. The ethnography with the most lasting theoretical impact has been Marilyn Strathern's (1986) work *The Gender of the Gift*, which explored the relational nature of actions and their intellectual understanding, which is thought to effect the making of persons and things alike. Social and biographical relations in Melanesia are internally defined and are likened to the aggregates of the gendered identities of bodily substances that need to be disaggregated (decomposed) for discrete persons to emerge, capable of physical and ideological reproduction. Such actions of taking apart invisible, composite substances involves the selection of material substances that are likened in terms of their transformative capacities, rather than merely their physical properties, to the relational capacity ascribed to bodily substances. When specific materials with concrete properties are chosen, such as, for example, softness and malleability as found in types of wood, associations with skin and bounded surface make the matriline materially manifest in ways that paradoxically effect the momentary accentuation of the fiction of patrilineal descent. Gendered substance and material effect are complementary entities in a ritualized opposition scenario that makes visible and conceptually present what is at once the same and different (Bateson 1958).

Distinctions such as natural and artificial, person and thing, bodily substance and material, do not apply here, where effects are derived from fusions of the alchemy of materials with the properties of persons. The unlikely 'likeness' of Pacific ethnography with the condition of contemporary design is underscored by the way materials are handled and transferred as knowledge, access to which is hotly contested (Barth 1990). For those interested in the articulations of a knowledge-based economy run on the back of materials, it is to Pacific ethnography that they should turn.

No better example has been given of how to excavate the inherent socialness of material knowledge, relating to the calculated selection of concrete materials, than Frederick Damon's (2004) analysis of the materials used for the construction of the Kula Canoe, famous in anthropological literature as the material expression of an image of the social body and of the cultural imaginary surrounding mobility in an island world. Damon shows how the many different types of wood chosen in the construction of the seafaring canoe are at once significant for the technical function of the canoe, as they are for the cultural imaginary supporting social identity, as they are taken from trees that are grown in places associated with the biographical relations that make up a matriline and also with the temporal cycles unique to the practice of the shifting cultivation of land. When making a canoe as a gift to secure an affinal relation, the knowledge that is required to create a socially acceptable and seaworthy canoe demands an understanding of the complex relation between material, substance, and effect.

The transformative effect that is unleashed when translating artifact production from one material to another, subtly altering daily life and relations of labor and loyalty, has been examined by ethnographers in relation to the introduction of cloth in the Pacific (Colchester 2003). Readily colored and often patterned, yet otherwise recalling the known and much desired material properties of partibility and portability, alongside the ability to be folded and to be wrapped around bodies and three dimensional forms, cotton cloth was readily seized in many areas of the Pacific when it became available through traders. As Nicholas Thomas (1999) has argued convincingly for Eastern Polynesia, it was Polynesians, rather than missionaries, who carried a wave of Christianization across the Pacific on the back of the new material, which was harnessed and transformed in ways redolent of established notions of status and deportment associated with prosperity and fortune.

Arguably, the impact of cotton cloth was marginal across areas in the Pacific where a cloth aesthetic prevailed already, maintained by and existing alongside indigenous fiber technologies utilizing the bark of the paper mulberry tree and the leaves of the pandanus plant. Others, like Lissant Bolton (2001) and Hauser-Schaublin (1996), have argued that in areas of the Pacific where non-cloth aesthetics prevail, articulated in the emphasis not on the planar surface of the wrap but on the line, the string, and the frond, cotton cloth was met with a very different response. Jarring with a fundamentally different conception of status, based not on temporal but on spatial modalities of differentiation, imported cotton cloth was resisted and/or acted upon in a manner that led to the transformation of the material in ways that made it compliant with an established material aesthetic. Sweaters are still today unraveled, dresses shredded before being reworked into open-work forms. Where the donning of cotton clothing was enforced, relations of labor and loyalty changed dramatically, as women no longer could maintain their work in gardens unhindered by the new strictures of cleanliness and modes of bodily deportment.

The complex relation between the work demanded by the new material and the relations that became associated with the worked upon product is best illustrated with the case of the Polynesian quilt in the Cook Islands, a chain of tiny islands in the eastern part of Polynesia where cotton cloth was greeted enthusiastically (Küchler and Eimke 2009). Cook Islanders had for long been preoccupied with the coloration of its bark-cloth and the patterning of its pandanus sleeping mats, both difficult to achieve and requiring a lengthy process of soaking, burying, and drying. Ready colored cotton relieved of this time-consuming work so convincingly that already 25 years after Chinese traders had arrived in the footsteps of missionaries, the main island of Rarotonga had its own cotton plantation.

Yet, cotton cloth was not merely used for the purpose destined by missionaries who encouraged the sewing of clothing and the domestication of the household, which followed in the wake of the new material with its demand for cleanliness and care. Women began to sew large and complex planar sheets from shredded pieces of cloth, known later as *tivaivai* or patchwork quilts. Competitive, potlatch-like presentations of quilts and the sewing of quilts for important life-cycle events in which they figured as major items of exchange sustained the development of sewing bees, which began to run the political economy of the islands. Elevated with the support of the church, which regarded them as eager followers of its mission, women had—already by the mid-nineteenth century—taken over the positions of *ariki*, the partially divine and partially human-ordained office of the chief, taking these positions from men who, since the condemnation of their ritual artifacts as idols and the acceptance of Christianity, could no longer pool divine power through the mechanism of sacrificial exchange. In a move that was as swift as it was seemingly unremarkable, women, who had previously moved in marriage in the opposite direction to divine power, access to which was granted to wife-giving groups among islands that became enchained in such exchanges, had assumed control over the relational nature of such actions.

Patchwork, in the Cook Islands, thus provoked a radical shifting of the axis of power relations, from a vertical topology of a chiefly polity centered in particular locations to the horizontal topology of a decentered polity that began to grow its radius by means of reconnecting the lost and the forgotten touchdowns of power through the circulation of products of women's labor (Siikala 1991). Relations of labor that came to be associated with the actions upon shredding and re-stitching patches of cloth were able to effect the transformation of Cook Island society from nucleated island groupings to an expanding transnational community by means of what is known as skeuomorphism, or a translation of properties of form expressed in one material into another. In the same way as cotton cloth was not really new, but merely enabled the exploration of new properties in a material medium already central to actions at the heart of the configuration of the social body, patchwork was not new, as the missionaries had thought, but a material translation of the topology of a sculpture onto the planar surface of cloth. It was this move that enabled patchwork to partake in the concepts surrounding the actions that had been central to the strategic calculation of biographical relations right up to European incursion.

The formal relation between sculpture and patchwork is plain to the eye in an overtness that is not dissimilar to the quite unnecessary vertical seam at the back of the Wellington boot that allows us to recall its affinity with its counterpart made from leather. In the quilt, it is its scale that stands out, connecting the miniaturized with the magnified through a process of the multiplication of proportionally self-similar motifs in ways that are reminiscent of the sculpted wood of god staffs. Rendered invisible in the sculpture, which was tightly bound with tapa cloth, sennit cordage, and feathers, was the relational nature of acts of sacrificial exchange that accompanied the refashioning of the polity over time. The relational nature of acts of exchange through which women reconstitute their connectedness across the expanded diaspora is also invisible in the patchwork. Hardly ever coming together in one place, Cook Island patchwork is made by three distinct modalities of technical acts, which can be described as partitioning, grouping, and mirroring. The resulting quilts have different names and are associated with distinct types of social relations. There is the patchwork proper (*taorei*) whose reduplicated motifs are made of tiny patches of cloth, which is gifted in an asymmetric, transitive, and relational manner between grandmother and granddaughter. Then there are the symmetrically appliquéd motifs of a quilt (*tat aura*) that are gifted between affines, and the mirrored motif of the snowflake or cut out quilt (*manu*), which is gifted between friends and casual acquaintances. What we are looking at is, in fact, an instantiation of a modular time-map hidden in the sculpture beneath its wrap and hidden in the quilt in the seeming divide of its distinct material techniques.

The work that Pacific Islanders put into the quasi-alchemic combination of materials would defy understanding were it not for the intuitive manner by which one can grasp the analog relations that are foundational to the social fabric. Methodologically speaking, inter-artifactual relations and the reconstruction of the temporal and sequential nature of a logic of which they partake become important in the analysis in ways that remind of Bruno Latour's analysis of the complex web of relations between human and nonhuman actants in the laboratory setting, where seemingly very different materials are designed in a not too dissimilar manner.

Enchantment by Inherence: Material Properties and Design Responsibilities

The anthropology of design has to be cognizant of the complexity of contexts that are not so much referenced by the objects as they are inherent within them and that objects activate as logic capable of inspiring new actions and new thoughts, rather than merely reflecting in a representational manner contexts of production and consumption. This chapter has argued that it is not, as conventionally thought, the form and function, but the material properties of objects that carry the propensity for enchantment for reasons that are by definition complex and difficult to predict and reconstruct. It is for this reason that the designing of materials in the laboratory is not to be taken lightly, and it is also for this reason that designers need to be both materials and anthropologically savvy.

References

Addington, D., D. Miller and L. Schodek (2004), *Smart Materials and Technologies in Architecture*, Burlington: Architectural Press.

Ashby, M. and K. Johnson (2002), *Materials and Design: The Art and Science of Material Selection in Product Design*, Oxford: Butterworth-Heinemann.

Askeland, D. and P. Pradeep (2002), *The Science and Engineering of Materials*, Salt Lake City: Thomson Engineering.

Ball, P. (1997), *Made to Measure: New Materials for the 21st Century*, New Jersey: Princeton University Press.

Barry, A. (2005), "Pharmaceutical Matters: The Invention of Informed Materials," *Theory, Culture and Society*, 22 (1): 51–69.

Barry, A. and N. Thrift (2007), "Gabriel Tarde: Imitation, Invention, and Economy," *Economy and Society*, 36 (4): 509–25.

Barth, F. (1990), *Cosmologies in the Making: A Generative Approach to Cultural Variation in Inner New Guinea*, Cambridge: Cambridge University Press.

Bateson, G. (1958), *Naven: A Survey of the Problems Suggested by a Composite Picture of the Culture of New Guinea Tribe Drawn from Three Points of View*, Stanford: Stanford University Press.

Bateson, G. (1973), "Style, Grace, Information in Primitive Society," in A. Forge (ed.), *Art in Primitive Society*, 78–90, Oxford: Oxford University Press.

Bennett, J. (2010), *Vibrant Matter: A Political Ecology of Things,* Durham: Duke University Press.

Bensaude-Vincent, B. (2004), *Le libérer de la matière? Fantasmes autour de la nouvelles technologies*, Versailles: Inra.

Bensaude-Vincent, B. and W. R. Newmann (eds.) (2007), *The Artificial and the Natural: An Evolving Polarity*, Cambridge: MIT Press.

Benyus, J. (1997), *Biomimicry*, New York: Perennial.

Beylerian, G., A. Dent and A. Moryadas, eds. (2005), *Material Connexion: The Global Resource of New and Innovative Materials for Architects, Artists and Designers*, New York: Wiley & Sons.

Boas, F. (1955 [1927]), *Primitive Art*, New York: Dover Publications.

Bolton, L. (2001), "Classifying the Material: Food, Textiles, and Status in North Vanuatu," *Journal of Material Culture*, 6 (3): 251–68.

Buchli, V. (2015), *Immateriality*, London: Routledge.

Colchester, C., ed. (2003), *Clothing the Pacific*, Oxford: Berg.

Conkey, M. (2006), "Style, Design and Function," in C. Tilley et al. (eds.), *Handbook of Material Culture*, 355–73, London: Sage.

Coole, D. and S. Frost (2010), *New Materialism: Ontology, Agency and Politics*, Durham: Duke University Press.

Damon, F. H. (2004), "On the Ideas of a Boat: From Forest Patches to Cybernetic Structures in the Outrigger Sailing Craft of the Eastern 'Kula' Ring, Papua New Guinea," in C. Sather and T. Kaartinen (eds.), *Beyond the Horizon: Essays on Myth, History, Travel and Society*, 123–44, Helsinki: Finnish Literature Society.

Daston, L., ed. (2004), *Things That Talk: Object Lessons from Art and Science*, New York: Zone Books.

Department of Trade and Industry (DTI), Materials Innovation and Growth Team (2006), "A Strategy for Materials." Available online: http://www.matuk.co.uk/docs/DTI_mat_bro.pdf (accessed May 8, 2017).

Drazin, A. and S. Küchler (2015), *The Social Life of Materials*, London: Bloomsbury Press.

Freedberg, D. (1991), *The Power of Images: The Study of the Nature of Response*, Chicago: University of Chicago Press.

Gay, D. V., H. Suong and S. Tsai (2002), *Composite Materials: Design and Application*, Boca Raton: CRC Press.

Gell, A. (1998), *Art and Agency*, Oxford: Oxford University Press.

Hansen, M. (2000), *Embodying Technesis: Technology Beyond Writing*, Ann Arbor: University of Michigan Press.

Hauser-Schaublin, E. (1996), "The Thrill of the Line, the String and the Frond, or Why the Abelam Are a Non-Cloth Culture," *Oceania*, 67 (2): 81–106.

Herder, J. G. ([1778] 2002), *Sculpture: Some Observations on Shape and Form from Pygmalion's Creative Dream*, trans. and ed. J. Gaiger, Chicago: University of Chicago Press.

Hongu, T. and G. O. Philips (1997), *New Fibers*, Cambridge: Technomic Publishing Company.

Klein, U. and W. Lefèvre (2007), *Materials in Eighteenth-Century Science: A Historical Ontology*, Cambridge, MA: MIT Press.

Küchler, S. (2008), "Technological Materiality: Beyond the Dualist Paradigm," *Theory, Culture and Society*, 25 (1): 101–20.

Küchler, S. and A. Eimke (2009), *Tivaivai: The Social Fabric of the Cook Islands*, London: British Museum Press.

Lange-Berndt, P., ed. (2015), *Materiality*, Cambridge and London: The MIT Press.

Latour, B. (1992), "Where Are the Missing Masses: The Sociology of a Few Mundane Artifacts," in W. Bijker and J. Law (eds.), *Shaping Technology/Building Society: Studies in Socio-Technical Change*, 225–58, Cambridge, MA: MIT Press.

Latour, B. (1996), *Aramis, or the Love of Technology*, Cambridge, MA: Harvard University Press.

Latour, B. (2001), *Das Parlament der Dinge*, Frankfurt am Main: Suhrkamp.

Latour, B. and S. Woolgar (1979), *Laboratory Life: The Construction of Social Facts*, London: Sage Publications.

Mauss, M. (1934), "Les Techniques du corps," *Journal de Psychologie*, 32 (3–4): 271–93. Reprinted in Mauss, M. (1936), *Sociologie et anthropologie*, Paris: PUF.

McDonough, W. and M. Braungart (2009), *Cradle to Cradle*, London: Vintage.

Meikle, J. L. (1995), *American Plastic: A Cultural History*, New Brunswick: Rutgers University Press.

Miller, D., ed. (2005), *Materiality*, Durham: Duke University Press.

Mori, T. (2002), *Immaterial/Ultramaterial: Architecture, Design and Materials*, New York: Braziller.

Mossmann, S. and R. Smith (2008), *Fantastic Plastic: Product Design and Consumer Culture*, London: Black Dog Publishing.

Myers, F. (1999), "Aesthetics and Practice: A Local Art History of Pintupi Painting," in H. Morphy and M. Smith Bowles (eds.), *Art from the Land*, 218–61, Charlottesville: University of Virginia.

Norris, L. (2010), *Recycling Indian Clothing: Global Contexts of Reuse and Value*, Bloomington: Indiana University Press.

O'Connor, K. (2011), *Lycra: How A Fiber Shaped America*, London and New York: Routledge.

Reckwitz, A. (2002), "The Status of the 'Material' in Theories of Culture: From 'Social Structure' to 'Artefacts,'" *Journal for the Theory of Social Behaviour*, 32 (2): 195–217.

Rubel, D. and S. Hackenschmidt (2008), *Formless Furniture*, Frankfurt: Hatje Cantz.

Satas, D. A. and A. Tracton (2000), *Coatings Technology Handbook*, New York: Marcel Dekker.

Schiebinger, L. and C. Swan (2005), *Colonial Botany, Science, Commerce and Politics in Early Modern Europe*, Philadelphia: University of Pennsylvania Press.

Siikala, J. (1991), *Akatokamava: Myth, History and Society in the Southern Cook Islands*, Auckland/Helsinki: The Polynesian Society in Association with the Finnish Anthropological Society.

Silberglitt, R., ed. (2001), *The Global Technological Revolution: Bio/Nano/Materials Trends and Their Synergies with Information Technology by 2015*, Santa Monica: Rand.

Smith, P. and P. Findlen, eds. (2002), *Merchants and Marvels: Commerce, Science and Art in Early Modern Europe*, London & New York: Routledge.

Strathern, M. (1986), *The Gender of the Gift: Problems with Women and Problems with Society in Melanesia*, Berkeley: University of California Press.

Stattmann, N. (2003), *Ultra Light—Super Strong: A New Generation of Design Materials*, Basel: Birkhäuser.

Strathern, M. (1999), *Property, Substance and Effect: Anthropological Essays on Persons and Things*, London: Athlone Press.

Thomas, N. (1999), "The Case of the Misplaced Ponchos—Speculations Concerning the History of Cloth in Polynesia," *Journal of Material Culture*, 4 (1): 5–21.

Wagner, M. (2001), *Das Material in der Kunst: Eine andere Geschichte der Moderne*, Munich: H. C. Beck.

Wessel, J. (2004), *The Handbook of Advanced Materials: Enabling New Design*, New York: Wiley-Interscience.

2 Objects in Sociology
Harvey Molotch

In the ongoing stream of mutuality between person and object, the objects forge the body and vice versa. Tools of many sorts and very broadly defined extend human physicality and mentality into the world. Objects are a kind of prosthesis of our own minds. But we are more than tool users: The human body is a 'tool-being.'

It has been a mystery to me why my fellow sociologists have paid so little attention to objects—to their creation, design, and the specifics of their consumption. If they write about mass-produced goods at all, sociologists tend to treat them as distractions from other putatively more worthwhile aspects of existence. We inherit as a Freud–Marx blend, a vision of consumer goods as fetish. Stuff provides noxious evidence of corrupted sensibilities, hegemonic oppression, or false needs. Thorstein Veblen, foreshadowing the French social theorist Pierre Bourdieu (1984), warned of conspicuous consumption and the role of elites in using the consumption apparatus to set up anxieties that reinforced elite dominance over everyday life. Depending on the telling, for the poor as well as the strivers somewhat higher up, materiality ensnares with its symbolic 'come-ons.'

Although the Left critique pervades most, anti-goods ideology takes many forms and emerges from all sorts of premises, including, for example, eighteenth-century British worries that importing French products would spread degrading sensualities into the English population (Lubbock 1995). Especially as revealed in post-war science fiction but also in the work of highly sophisticated sociologists (e.g., Bittner 1983), there was fear of the machine—especially the computer—taking over. The object, usually as 'independent variable,' impacts social life from outside, causing misery or threat of future misery. The object itself goes missing. Even in the work of the most astute of our observers of mundane existence, Erving Goffman, artifacts are primarily incidentals in the scene. Goffman noted, for example, the role of objects as "markers" through which a person could show they "owned" a restaurant table by leaving their coat on the chair (Goffman 1971: 41). But what kind of coat? What kind of chair?

At the same time that this negativity comes down on goods, a second theme ironically runs almost opposite. For those who worry about social inequality (and this overlaps with scholars who decry the goods), the problem is not that there is so much stuff at all, but that some people have too little of it. Although often framed as an inability of the poor to meet 'basic needs,' it is clear enough that *inequality* of access is the key issue. Reformers do not just want to provide basic nutrition, clothing, and a roof over the heads of the masses; they want them to have more of what others have—home appliances, commodious living spaces, and late-model cars. To imply that the poor of rich countries should make do without such amenities, positional goods though they may be, would surely be noxiously elitist as well as plain mean.

Earlier in the history of the sociological discipline, at least in the United States, empirical study of goods did factor in as part of documenting equality. Most prominently perhaps, F. Stuart Chapin (1928) developed a 48-item "scale for rating living room equipment" to determine social standing. This allowed him to show, for example, the "equipment" level of a household "on relief" compared to other subgroups. He could pinpoint which social groups had "vases, telephone, radio, statues, mirror, piano, sheet music" or other goods (1928: 386). The prominent sociologist William Sewell followed on with fifty-four material items on his scale, including iron, piano, "living room windows decorated," and "linoleum on kitchen floor" (Sewell 1940: 28). There were also extensive discussions, in other classics, of the importance adolescents give to having *au courant* clothing (Lynd and Lynd 1937: 163), and discussions of the automobile and radio as introducing changes in lifestyle differences among social classes and age groups (Warner 1949). Yet, the goods are still of primary use as class indicator rather than, with minor exception, embedded in concrete practices of life. There are not studies of how people actually use the goods. Instead, the banner was picked up, albeit sporadically and unevenly in other disciplines: material culture studies in anthropology; cultural studies; science-technology studies; and, among sociologists, the still only begrudgingly accepted field of actor-network theory. Otherwise, artifacts primarily arise as props in the course of describing something not material.[1]

The anthropologists Mary Douglas and Baron Isherwood pointed the better way with their 1982 book, *The World of Goods*, which had the subtitle *Towards an Anthropology of Consumption*. In dealing with, respecting, being stopped by, creating, judging, buying, discussing, envisioning, altering, placing, and disposing of goods, people are simultaneously manipulating and deploying the makeup of their own lives (see also Csikszentmihalyi and Rochberg-Halton 1981). Going a bit further, it is possible, indeed, to see inanimate objects as "actants"—a word used, apparently independently, by the British anthropologist Alfred Gell and the French polymath (theology,

---

1. For an important exception to the practice of avoiding mundane materiality, see Csikszentmihalyi and Rochberg-Halton, 1981, for what could have been a sociologically inspired program of material culture studies.

philosophy, anthropology, sociology) Bruno Latour to acknowledge the inanimate as part of a persistent mutuality of the material and the social (Latour 1996). Latour (and probably Gell, who died midcourse in his work) argues for symmetry of methodological approach between humans and objects. They do not have some idealized vision of ontological equality (see Preda 1999); they are promoting a strategy for understanding material–social confluence. This means you can pick up the trail of sociality by focusing on the goods as much as the reverse. The objects are, to again invoke Latour, the "missing masses" from sociological investigation (1992). The goal becomes to follow up the material–social nexus as it unfolds historically and as people experience it as ongoing process.

In the remainder of this chapter, I try to show how objects help in sociological projects that, although not explicitly objects-centered, use them in productive ways. I want to display their utility across the sociological spectrum. I include some of my own work. Taking up objects one way or the other, I aim to demonstrate through commonplace conceptual and methodological problems, ways that sociology and objects can work together.

What to Do about the Body?

In the ongoing stream of mutuality between person and object, the objects forge the body and vice versa. Tools of many sorts and very broadly defined extend human physicality and mentality into the world. Objects are a kind of prosthesis of our own minds. But we are more than tool users, the usual social scientific categorization. As the geographer Nigel Thrift remarks, "the evidence suggests that organs like the hand, the gut, and the various other muscle and nerve complexes" and the brain itself have evolved in synch with tool use. Through this interpretation, "the human body is a tool-being" (Thrift 2007: 10).

A striking display of mutuality, albeit less genetically ambitious, comes from the case of the chair (Cranz 1999; see also Rudofsky 1980). Chairs historically arose from a need to display status (e.g., the throne) and offer respect ("have a seat"). As the chair became ubiquitous, human musculature adapted, with the result that people then came to need it. The chair along with the pew and the toilet snatches the body, creating what Latour calls a "hybrid" (a chair-human) and philosopher/biologist Donna Haraway (1991) calls a "cyborg." But the hybrid/cyborg consists of more than artifact and musculature. It also consists of the stuff of ordinary sociology: the deviance of people who do not use chairs (some for medical reasons) and children who "can't sit still." For peoples who specialize in chair sitting (not Japanese, for example), it fosters the idea that those who crouch, eat on rugs, or squat when they defecate must indeed be primitive.[2]

---

2. In defending treatment of immigrant workers in his country, an official of the Dubai government explained that some come from backgrounds so impoverished "they don't know how to use the toilet; they will sit and do it on the ground" (DeParle 2007).

Even in the poorest groupings, vast resources—relative to the wealth base—go into body goods: jewelry, headdresses, costumes, and cosmetics. These expenditures extend beyond the practical, erasing any clear boundary between decoration and appliance. Wearing clothes at all in some locales and almost all places at some time (Manhattan in summer, for example) cannot be understood in terms of utility. But nudity in general as well as nudity precisely (exactly what to expose and how) display cultural belonging and subcultural distinction.

Attention to some artifacts, linked to body modification, yield up solutions of clinical import. In investigating prevalence of US AIDS infections, Philippe Bourgois and his colleague Daniel Ciccarone focus on the interaction of heroin type and the mechanics of the syringe used to inject it (Ciccarone and Bourgois 2003). In some parts of the United States—like San Francisco where the researchers were based—heroin users inject "Mexican black tar," which is a tacky, heavy type of substance that gums up a syringe. For this reason, users rinse their syringes frequently to keep them from clogging, so much so that Bourgois was worried that he might be infected by the splash from the users nearby. But all the rinsing happens to have the positive consequence of removing blood traces from prior injections (and injectors), an act that decreases the risk of AIDS. This contributes to lower rates of AIDS infection among users of this type of heroin compared to the main alternative, which is powder form. Bourgois and Ciccarone needed to explain geographic variation in AIDS infection among drug users and noticed a correlation between US region and type of heroin used. Through close attention to the syringe in action (something that could be done by the ethnographer Bourgois), the researchers were able to explain an outcome that might have otherwise remained elusive. The focus on an appliance *in situ*, along with an ecological correlation, contributes to a causal explanation.

As a general rule of thumb, the body–artifact connection reveals the nature of 'affordance.' As used by industrial designers, the term indicates the capacity of an object to help people do something by virtue of its 'interface' features—how it invites and facilitates some particular action. One of the pleasures and satisfactions of everyday life is meeting up with an affordance—experiencing the right 'give' of a door or the 'feel' of a lever whose downward motion signifies one's competence and capacity to move the world. Some types of affordance are probably universal, like the 'peel-ability' of a banana skin, but others—like working a kayak oar or cell phone feature—are specific to a historic and social niche. Getting intellectual access to affordances—what turns on whom and when with what—enables identification of similarities and differences of peoples across time and place. Such understandings also, of course, work the other way around: Knowing the cultural features of affordance makes the designer more likely to come up with a viable artifact.

What about Beauty?

The question is a sociological baffler. People have an aesthetic dimension, operative—some say—in all they do, including the way they invent new technologies, political systems, and economic structures (Smith 1980). Sociologists of art plot the distribution of taste but in a realm they mark off as 'art'—something quite segregated from the give and take of daily life. In his book *Inside Culture*, the sociologist David Halle (1996) gets one step closer to life-as-lived by investigating 'art' in the sphere of ordinary domestic spaces. He went into people's houses and apartments, noticing (and asking about) what they had on their walls and atop their TV sets. He learned they have lots of landscape paintings, family photos, and religious artifacts—with systematic differences across social class (abstract art, for example, happens among those higher up).

A more radical move than Halle's is to see ordinary goods as, in a sense, art—or at least having an artistic dimension. They give off aesthetic impressions and persist because their evocations are inspiring, pleasant, or provide intrigue that draws people toward them. This is an intrinsic part of how any practical device works; its appearance, shape, and textures invite action toward it and in a particular way. The lever of my toaster calls forth one or two of my fingers, not my fist or open palm. Its curvilinear shape has been made friendly and not fearsome, in part by my exposure to the abstract artists who also influenced the designer of the product. If the toaster were frightening, it would not be practical. Hence, form and function, beauty and practicality are not opposed to one another but can only work when in synch. Studying the history of art and the history of goods as an interacting system—not the usual approach—would help clarify the coevolution of sentiment, expressivity, and economic development. Products are the people's art.

People of all races, classes, and genders, including the very young, buzz with sensual evaluations; you can hear it in their everyday talk. You can also get preference data from stores, trade journals, and the financial press. You can do participant observation behind the counter or watch folks compliment, appreciate, or razz one another for what they got or didn't get (see Zukin 2005). Why restrict the aesthetic to the pre-category of 'art'? If you ask people about 'art,' it makes them uptight. It hinders gaining access to the relation between aesthetics and other aspects of existence. Products are the missing masses in the sociology of art.

One of the virtues of studying products as art is that it informs how change happens. People want something new. Taken to larger problems of social organization, the art of stuff allows us to see that some change happens for its own sake. The fashion system reveals a more general feature of social systems. For sociologists, a constant hypothesis needs to be that part of any given shift in belief or practice comes from the human appeal of novelty. Fashion, in this large sense, needs to be part of any explanatory model, at least a null hypothesis that nothing is going on except the drive for something new. Stanley Lieberson (2000), in his study of first name use in the United States (e.g., the rise of Jennifer and decline of Stanley), shows how such 'matters of taste' operate; people think they are making choices out of personal (and largely ahistorical) preferences, when in fact they are part of a collective connoisseurship specific to time and social context. Again, from the design perspective, there is always a drive toward the new, albeit constrained by the history of what has come before and the practicalities of the present.

Enforced Consumption

Some products are acquired by third parties rather than the end user. These products include public goods like transit infrastructure (see Figure 2.1). Compared to the acquisition of most ordinary products, the users' mode of consumption is enforced by instrumentation selected by others. In research on the New York City subway system, Noah McClain and I focus on the instruments, physical layouts of the stations, and workers' equipment (Molotch and McClain 2008). One of our prime artifacts is the turnstile, a mechanism to prevent people from riding for free. The Metropolitan Transit Authority (MTA) has created increasingly restrictive designs aimed at frustrating fare beaters, for example, by slanting slide panels that otherwise could be used to boost oneself over the turnstile bar. There is also a horizontal bar just above head level as further discouragement. Where once even old people and the rather unfit could climb over or crawl under, now only the extremely agile can cheat. Hence, the equipment shapes the demography of deviance (McClain 2011). This most recent twist in the machinery follows from a Tom-and-Jerry succession of designers' efforts to stay a step ahead of users' work-arounds. A focus on the artifacts enabled us to elaborate some of the organizational and individual struggles of urban life.

2.1 New York City subway turnstiles. © *Noah McClain*

Public monuments are an enforced kind of symbolic consumption, and hence there are quarrels and political upheavals of just what will be shown and how (Hayden 1995), with struggles in places like Jerusalem representing a dramatic apogee of the stakes. Taking advantage of materiality to become so socially loaded, some contemporary artists insert their works as deliberate 'provocation.' They intervene into ongoing social pathways, including modes of organizational functioning. For example, the artist Hans Haacke created a 1971 show for New York's Guggenheim Museum depicting, on museum-lobby type plaques, the corporate identity of the museum's founders (see Becker and Walton 1976). Successive plaques in the same series listed others in the Guggenheim corporate retinue, including those running the family's copper mining operations in Chile (Kennecott Copper). The brief statements of affiliations (and accompanying company revenues) ended with the fact of Salvador Allende's death and the restitution of corporate assets that followed—all inscribed in the same typeface and manner. The museum canceled the show and fired its curator. The Haacke installation thus displayed, through press commentary and actions taken, the power of capital over art.

This all suggests a method: doing something with things (or at least raising the prospect of intervention) as a way to elicit cultural information. The researcher might propose only a modest change; say a sign on a building, a different color for the school, or a new icon for the church recreation hall. Or perhaps create an artifact that forms a breach into everyday life, like the toilet water fountain at the San Francisco Exploratorium that crowds of people hesitate to drink from (see Figure 2.2). However, in defiance of the 'fly on the wall' idealization for the field researcher or strictures from the University Human Subjects Committee, those who propose (or enact) changes in the local material world can generate useful information—about culture, about anxiety, about politics.

Understanding History

The shape and design of relatively simple objects drive history. The historical sociologist Michael Mann (1986) shows how the pike (yes, the thing men on horses use to charge the enemy) helped transform pre-modern Europe. Fighters who had it won out over those who did not. Mann shows how this weapon gained its efficacy through organizational and ideological structures themselves of a changing sort that, as all sociologists know[3] work with material artifact to shape outcomes. The light bulb, whatever the motivations of its creators, has bent work and pleasure toward 24/7 schedules. Like all inventions, its capacity depended on complexly intersecting organizational structures. Scholars like Hughes (1989), Bazerman (1999), and Bijker (1995) use a sociological prism (although of the three only Bijker is a card-carrying sociologist). Not only did the light bulb emerge out of specific (and not inevitable) organizational contexts, it refracted on the attitudes and

---

3. In contrast, for example, to the perspective of the non-sociologist Jared Diamond in his influential book on the history of most of the world (Diamond, 1999).

2.2 Toilet Fountain, San Francisco Exploratorium. © *Harvey Molotch*

organizations that brought it into being. And as increasing numbers of adjustments were made, including in how factories got built (less need for windows), family schedules arranged (night shifts), and entertainments devised (thrills at Times Square), the artifact became "interactively stabilized" (Pickering 1995).

The artifact can also facilitate macro-comparative work akin to collective ethnography. Hence, the anthropologists Miller and Woodward (2010) use denim as the basis for international comparison. Issuing a "Manifesto for the Study of Denim," they invite participation from scholars across the world to add in their own cases of just how people form and use this ubiquitous fabric in each setting. In this way, diverse scholars can participate without the need for close monitoring, expensive coordination, or rigid protocols. Concentrating on the particular and the specific, including its ethnographic present, can help clarify what is local, what is global, and the relation between the two.

A focus on luxury goods accesses the consumption patterns of elites, who have their own special impact on history. The wealthy have extraordinary power to gain what they want and turn things topsy-turvy to get it. In the histories of, say, Renaissance rulers, obtaining jewelry, tableware, textiles, palaces, and frescoes was a historical force. Indeed, that is why much of the stuff came to exist. As with Polynesian chiefs who decorated their boats and houses to signal might (Gell 1998), such displays were a tool of power, including the capacity to attract imperial allies. The zeal for gold and spice launched the colonial enterprise and all the mayhem that came to pass. Keeping up with the Habsburgs influenced marriage, resource use, and political alliance. What was important to Louis XIV about the gardens of Versailles was that visitors would see "French wealth, taste, and power" (Mukerji 1997: 317). The chateau artifacts and the garments of residents—both in their general splendor as well as specific shaping—were exhibitions of his court's significance on the world stage as well as in constituting, metaphorically and otherwise, the territory of France. Whatever role the glorious stuff played in intimidating the peasants (few of whom likely had any idea what was going on), it forged relations among elites, near and far.

Regimes have not lost their dependence on goods. In explaining the outcome of the Cold War, the low quality of Soviet artifacts ordinarily gains barely a mention. Sociologist David Riesman (1964: 65–77) was something of an exception, advising, albeit facetiously, that the United States bomb the Soviet people with vacuum cleaners, nylon hose, and other consumption goods. That would make them rebel against their masters, who gave them so little that was durable and attractive. But it may be at the elite level where shoddiness had its historic consequence. The Gorbachevs, it was reported, experienced "profound shock" (McCauley 1998: 30) that villagers in a poor country defeated in the war—specifically Italy—lived in some ways better than the Soviet elite (Matthews 1978: 177). Commentators noted that the Gorbachevs dressed and ate "well"; the *New York Times* referred to Raisa Gorbachev as "chic" in its obituary of her life (Bohlen 1999). People with increasingly world-class sensibilities (Zemtsov 1985: 98) sat astride a system unable to produce for such a niche—to understate the case. Richard Nixon seemed to agree with Riesman when he informed Khrushchev, in front of a US kitchen exhibit (the famous "kitchen debate"), that home products would be the site of Soviet defeat. In this light, Soviet demise was not so much a failure of the economy in some general sense as deficiencies in the specific goods. Starting with particular artifacts might have helped social scientists better keep up with Nixon in anticipating this great transformation.

A focus on materiality helps explain the way cities become different from one another, even under common conditions of industrialization (or capitalism or globalism). City leaders' decisions implant a fateful physical apparatus. So, for example, a study of the siting of the same freeway as it moved through different California coastal localities revealed to a research group in which I participated (Molotch, Freudenburg, and Paulsen 2000) how prior decisions that permitted spot industrialization at the waterfront in Ventura, California, lowered the amenity value of the coast, thus making it cheaper, financially and politically, to acquire ocean front land for road building than it otherwise would have been. The freeway, in turn, undermined 'higher uses' in the future, in particular, hindering successive efforts to build ocean-related tourist facilities or an amenity-based so-called creative economy. These realities then reverberated throughout the cultural, political, and economic life of the locality, reinforcing place direction and sharpening its distinction from other coastal places. So it is not the physical or the social that determines outcomes, but the way they conjointly operate to form something like a character of the place, made durable over time.

It is possible, indeed, to use objects not just to shed light on a particular place, historic event, or epoch, but on the nature of history itself. The economist Paul David (again, where was the sociologist?) fixed on the QWERTY keyboard as instructive of how history works (David 1985, 1997). Once in existence—and there is some debate of how it took original form—the QWERTY comes to be a semiautonomous force. As some individuals master its usage, they become stakeholders in its perpetuation. The more users, the greater the stability for the keyboard as the cost rises for producing a different kind or learning how to type with an alternative configuration. The keyboard case—thanks to David and as popularized by Malcolm Gladwell (2002)—displays how path dependency works. We can use material things to discover the practices that make up any path dependency, a methodologically opportunistic point to presume a 'stop' in the infinite flows over time, space, and relationships (Strathern 1996: 525). Scholars in the actor-network theory tradition now move in this direction.

Interview and Entre Tool

Objects are storehouses of the tacit "documents of life" (Plummer 2001) and are thus useful as tools for qualitative research. Talking to people in the presence of their stuff and watching them interact with artifacts (recall Bourgois on needle injection) provides a route into the understandings and ordering mechanisms of life, including its satisfactions and dangers.

With exquisite precision, Douglas Harper details life in a one-person machine shop/auto garage in rural New York—an ethnography of repair. He asks his main subject and the occasional visitor-clients about the old cars, tractors, and other miscellaneous artifacts and parts thereof. He zeroes in on the specifics of cams, pistons, and housings just as these machine parts, in real time, intersect with hands and tools. He uses his own finely wrought photographs of hands, tools, and machines to prompt and collaboratively evaluate, with his subjects, just how repair work is done, including the social relations on which it rests. "Roles are reversed," Harper says (1992: 12), "as the subject becomes the teacher" and slowly communicates to him what Harper calls "kinesthetic correctness" (p. 117). Sociologist Elizabeth Shove et al. (2008), in their studies of Do-It-Yourself projects, start with homeowners' tools and/or completed works, like a new bathroom or bookcase. They then work outward from those objects and projects to other goods with which they interconnect, but also to a family's aspirations and tensions within it. In our interviews with subway workers, McClain and I gain much by pointing to tools and widgets in the worker's purview and asking them: "What's that for?" and "When do you use that?" From this, we have learned how workers physically protect themselves, keep trains running on time, and discipline recalcitrant passengers (e.g., those who hold open the doors).

In still another approach, sociologist Stephen Riggins (1994) uses the artifacts in his own parents' living room to perform what he calls an "autoethnography." Assiduously adhering to strictures that all items be systematically included along with their relation to one another, their "artifactual ecology" (p. 110), Riggins leaves no knickknack unturned. Because this is the house he grew up in, he can use its contents to contrast the meaning and uses things have for him versus what they do in his parents' lives. Developing his own sensibilities over his years of growing up (and beyond), he came to disapprove of many of the items. But his parents apparently appreciated them enough not only to retain them, but also to keep many in the same positions over the long *durée*. This high degree of stability provides evidence for Riggins that, contrary to the idea of contemporary society as "the rapid flow of signs and images which saturate the fabric of everyday life in contemporary society" (quoted by Riggins from Featherstone 1992: 270), domestic artifacts give stability to lives, "like a score that the self can follow to endlessly retell the stories through which its social identity is selectively constructed." Details of the goods reveal balance of stasis and change.

Exposition

Descriptions of products bring mnemonic capacities into sociological texts. Objects, finely observed and maybe also photographed or drawn, can make sociological texts more memorable, otherwise a great problem for the discipline. In *Slim's Table*, sociologist Mitchell Duneier's (1994) prize-winning ethnography of life among a group of working class men who meet regularly in the same restaurant for lunch, the author provides an inventory of objects, including brand names, used by "Slim"—the central figure of the study. He characterizes him, in the view of his colleagues, as "one of the most respected mechanics on the South Side" (p. 10). Part of the evidence, memorable evidence, I think, comes from what is in Slim's pockets:

> Slim keeps a chain with many keys (a symbol of responsibility in the ghetto) and a plastic wallet compliments of the Internal Auto Parts Co. Inside are family pictures, an Aamco bond card, a driver's license, and an automobile I.D. He also carries a pack of Camel cigarettes, business cards from some of the firms he relies on as a mechanic, and loose papers with information related to the various jobs he is engaged in down at the garage. (Duneier 1994: 9–10)

Duneier here trades on the shared familiarity his readers, including sophisticated social scientists, have of these artifacts from their own everyday lives and shows their contextual deployment.

Objects also arise, with at least some effect, in a number of works taken by sociologists as among the classics. Jane Jacobs (1961) famously tells us about the house keys (keys again) that residents leave with the street corner merchant, showing how people organize their urban lives through trust and proximity. And she beautifully illustrates the importance of physical configurations of street life, with exposition sufficient to have had vast impacts on urban planning and architecture worldwide. But even she has little space for the modest scale of artifacts; they do not appear in her work. I did hear her once in a small informal talk explain how her love of Greenwich Village took form after she saw beautiful handmade jewelry in a shop window. She knew she could not afford to buy such a thing, but wanted, she said, to live in a place where such things could be seen. I wish she had had the opportunity to describe, and make memorable in her writings, her neighborhood at this level of detail.

Sampling Frame

Making an object the basis of a case study can create a vehicle for selecting other details and connections to investigate. In *Slim's Table*, Duneier uses the table as a device to select the individuals who will matter in his analysis; they are the people who regularly congregate together at lunch. This brings him to activity that takes place at the table, in preparation for coming to the table, or results from having been at the table. This is a different kind of use than he made of the keys: The keys were important analytic tools in themselves, not a basis for discovering the people and elements to be investigated.

Nina Wakeford (2003) uses a long London bus route to locate Internet cafés that she makes the basis of her research. The bus zigzag takes her through diverse neighborhoods—by class, race, and consumption practices. She learns things about some of the social patterns in those neighborhoods by watching passengers board and exit. But she then focuses on the Internet cafés that dot the route. Again, these cafés have no necessary relation one to the other, nor do their customers. But the bus route gains for her a series of interactions (on the bus) and settings (the cafés) that come her way through a mechanism other than specific selections. She learns how people use buses and use Internet cafés.

Using a physical artifact puts aside sampling bias that might derive from a researcher making choices out of preconceptions or from too limited a list of differentiations. Wakeford might have started with the idea that, for example, black versus white neighborhoods differ in how cafés are used. The bus route method gave her a richer variety of settings to study. In Latour's phrasing (2007), she allows London transport to help "assemble the social." This provides for an empirical openness instead of a prestructuring of the sample via variables already presumed to be relevant (see Nippert-Eng 1996). This is not the only way to do it, but it is a way to do it—one with certain advantages.

Power to Which People?

Goods are notoriously the stuff of inequality. But focusing on them in detail provides new ways to understand the process. In his example of the common spring-loaded door closure, Latour (1992) points out that however much this everyday instrumentation increases convenience for many, it yields disadvantages for some. Automatic door closures can trap individuals with crutches or those carrying unwieldy packages (delivery people, for example). Certain New York subway turnstiles (see Figure 2.3) greatly magnify such effects. Latour's approach opens empirical investigation, through close-in focus, to the differential costs and benefits of any object.

Some examples have long been well-known. Poor people end up with products that have lead paint. Given women's physiological and cultural needs, public restrooms create special problems for them—long waits and cramped stalls. The design of walls and gates in Israel yield hindrance for Palestinians. When harmed or frustrated by the impediments, victims may blame some dominant group (or even engage in violence against its members) or merely mutter to themselves, perhaps in self-blaming for their "clumsiness" or some other inadequacy. How people respond politically to artifacts is still another venue for design research.

Some of the great battles occur intra-class, including at the elite level. Product development and distribution is inherently political and not just in terms of working class resistance. In the great contest to determine whose patent for the incandescent bulb would win out, the primary players were Joseph Swan of the United Kingdom and Thomas Edison of the United States—and their respective backers. Although best known, these were only two of the competing parties in an international contest that had great consequence in terms of fame, fortune, and the distribution of resources to various points of the globe.

Those who won the battle over the incandescent bulb then fought to keep it as the standard means of light. Drawing on documents and testimony produced at anti-trust hearings of the US Congress in 1940, Wiebe Bijker (1995) argues that important stakeholders conspired, with aid from the power companies, to block usage of fluorescents. As we all now acknowledge, fluorescents are more efficient with greatly lower consumer costs, which is why the utilities, Bijker says, did not want them around. Fluorescents did have certain disadvantages, like the harsh quality of light and the tendency to flicker. But a conspiracy apparently undermined the capacity of consumers to consider the trade-offs and select accordingly. Again, massive wealth shifts (and ecological consequence) followed.

The arena of standard-setting makes some of the great infrastructural conflicts visible. Within nineteenth-century Britain, opposing railroad companies fought over railroad gauge; whoever lost would see their tracks become useless. Sony Beta-max, arguably superior to

2.3 Frustrated mover, New York City subway turnstiles. © *Noah McClain*

US-based VHS, lost out as US consumption tipped away from the Sony product (Arthur 1988). In the effort to establish a world standard for HDTV, the giant Japanese conglomerate NHK, which first developed the new technology in the mid-1980s, could not prevail (Braithwaite and Drahos 2000). Contests over radio frequencies, aircraft equipment, and many other product types similarly yield information about intra and international oppositions, all with huge implications for dispersing profit and wealth among individuals, groups, and nations.

Objects tend to anchor arrangements in ways that can thus be concretely investigated. Their special fixity sets up ongoing inducements and impediments. Further, objects do not just exist as one-offs, but as part of "suites," as Shove calls them (Shove et al. 2008). One thing leads to and connects to the next and, as evidenced in how computer peripherals multiply in large ensembles, sometimes sequentially but also with simultaneity. As the complementarity builds, each element gains more solidity until it may become a taken-for-granted part of the world, like electrical outlets in a house.

Now add in the social relations that are themselves complimentary with each artifactual element—creating a mutually reinforcing system of inertia, as Howard Becker (1995) terms it. The automobile is itself a system of intersecting mechanical parts, each with its own history of agreements and conflicts. But it is also sustained through a vast array of interacting elements like petroleum suppliers, drive-in banks, dating behavior, and Beach Boys songs. However true it may be that corporate power advanced the agenda of the automobile industry, the end-up involves far more than corporate domination. For those who want to generate ecological and lifestyle reforms, a capitalist plot would be better news. Never mind people's attitudes (brain washings, false needs, or whatever), the reorganization of economic and social life to undo the car remains a vast challenge.

And this brings up the natural environment more generally. Sociologists need to address the great infrastructures that shape nature and distribute life chances, through the social-material bits and pieces that create and rely on them. Only by bringing the material into the sociological sphere—the technologies, the gizmos, and nature—will there be any hope of analytic capacity (or reform).

We all know that goods are thick with meaning and consumers are thick with aspiration. One of the consequences of these two thicknesses is how little it takes for people to think a difference exists between one object and another. People will go through "too much" to have the latest style of tennis shoe and spend their money "foolishly" by upgrading to a different shade of lipstick. This great capacity for subtlety, so much the bane of critics, is the basis for hope. That people can make so much of so little means that status systems can really exist with much less social and ecological mayhem. Indeed, only a small amount of inequality is sufficient to trigger great striving. Think about the distribution of benefits among academic colleagues—intense quarrels over crumbs. Strong regulation of production systems as well as wealth redistribution would have no radical consequence on the use of goods for identity and difference. People would still revel in their stuff and use it for distinction and belonging. So now we come to a new way to address the moral dimension that has so drenched sociological thinking about products. By following up on the goods, how they are made and function in people's lives, we can facilitate social and ecological reform. What we now have is not just dangerous waste of nature, but useless social overkill.

References

Arthur, W. B. (1988), "Self-Reinforcing Mechanisms in Economics," in P. W. Anderson, K. J. Arrow and D. Pines (eds.), *The Economy as an Evolving Complex System*, 9–32, Redwood City, CA: Addison-Wesley.

Bazerman, C. (1999), *The Language of Edison's Light*, Cambridge, MA: MIT Press.

Becker, H. (1995), "The Power of Inertia," *Qualitative Sociology*, 18: 301–09.

Becker, H. and J. Walton (1976), "Social Science and the Work of Hans Haacke," in J. Burnham and H. Haacke (eds.), *Framing and Being Framed*, 145–52, New York: New York University Press.

Bijker, W. E. (1995), *Of Bicycles, Bakelites, and Bulbs: Toward a Theory of Sociotechnical Change*, Cambridge, MA: MIT Press.

Bittner, E. (1983), "Technique and the Conduct of Life," *Social Problems*, 30 (3): 249–61.

Bohlen, C. (1999), "Raisa Gorbachev, the Chic Soviet First Lady of the Glasnost Era, Is Dead at 67," *New York Times*, 21 September.

Bourdieu, P. (1984), *Distinction*, London & New York: Routledge.

Braithwaite, J. and P. Drahos (2000), *Global Business Regulation*, Cambridge: Cambridge University Press.

Chapin, F. S. (1928), "A Quantitative Scale for Rating the Home and Social Environment of Middle Class Families in an Urban Community," *Journal of Educational Psychology* 19 (2): 99–111.

Ciccarone, D. and P. Bourgois (2003), "Explaining the Geographic Variation of HIV Among Injection Drug Users in the United States," *Substance Use & Misuse* 38 (14): 2049–63.

Cranz, G. (1999), *The Chair*, New York: Norton.

Csikszentmihalyi, M. and E. Rochberg-Halton (1981), *The Meaning of Things: Domestic Symbols and the Self*, Cambridge: Cambridge University Press.

David, P. (1985), "Clio and the Economics of QWERTY," *The American Economic Review*, 75 (2): 332–37.

David, P. (1997), "Path Dependence and the Case for Historical Economics: One More Chorus of the Ballad of QWERTY," University of Oxford Discussion Paper in *Economic and Social History*, 20: 3–47.

DeParle, J. (2007), "Restive Foreign Workers Have Fearful Dubai Eyeing Reform," *New York Times*, 6 August: A8.

Diamond, J. (1991), *Guns, Germs, and Steel: The Fates of Human Societies*, New York: Norton.

Douglas, M. and B. Isherwood (1982), *The World of Goods: Towards an Anthropology of Consumption*, New York: W. W. Norton.

Duneier, M. (1994), *Slim's Table*, Chicago: University of Chicago Press.

Featherstone, M. (1992), "Postmodernism and the Aestheticization of Everyday Life," in S. Lash and J. Friedman (eds.), *Modernity and Identity*, 265–91, Oxford: Wiley-Blackwell.

Gell, A. (1998), *Art and Agency*, Oxford: Oxford University Press.

Gladwell, M. (2002), *The Tipping Point: How Little Things Can Make a Big Difference*, Santa Ana, CA: Back Bay Books.

Goffman, E. (1971), *Relations in Public*, New York: Harper Colophon.

Halle, D. (1996), *Inside Culture*, Berkeley: University of Chicago Press.

Haraway, D. J. (1991), *Simians, Cyborgs and Women: The Reinvention of Nature*, New York and Abingdon: Routledge.

Harper, D. (1992), *Working Knowledge: Skill and Community in a Small Shop*, Berkeley: University of California Press.

Hayden, D. (1995), *Power of Place*, Cambridge, MA: MIT Press.

Hughes, T. (1989), *American Genesis*, New York: Viking.

Jacobs, J. (1961), *Death and Life of Great American Cities*, New York: Random House.

Latour, B. (1992), "Where Are the Missing Masses," in W. E. Bijker and J. Law (eds.), *Shaping Technology/Building Society*, 225–58, Cambridge, MA: MIT Press.

Latour, B. (1996), *Aramis, or the Love of Technology*, Cambridge, MA: Harvard University Press.

Latour, B. (2007), *Reassembling the Social*, New York: Oxford University Press.

Lieberson, S. (2000), *A Matter of Taste: How Names, Fashions, and Culture Change*, New Haven: Yale University Press.

Lubbock, J. (1995), *The Tyranny of Taste*, New Haven: Yale University Press.

Lynd, R. and H. Lynd (1937), *Middletown in Transition*, New York: Harcourt, Brace.

Mann, M. (1986), *The Sources of Social Power*, Cambridge, UK: Cambridge University Press.

Matthews, M. (1978), *Privilege in the Soviet Union*, London: Allen & Unwin.

McCauley, M. (1998), *Gorbachev: Profiles in Power*, London: Longman.

McClain, N. (2011), "The Institutions of Urban Anxiety: Work, Organizational Process and Security Practice in the New York Subway," PhD diss., Department of Sociology, New York University.

Miller, D. and S. Woodward (2010), *Global Denim*, Oxford: Berg.

Molotch H. and N. McClain (2008), "Things at Work: Informal Social-Material Mechanisms for Getting the Job Done," *Journal of Consumer Culture*, 8 (1): 35–67.

Molotch, H., W. Freudenburg and K. Paulsen (2000), "History Repeats Itself, but How?: City Character, Urban Tradition, and the Accomplishment of Place," *American Sociological Review*, 65: 791–823.

Mukerji, C. (1997), *Territorial Ambitions and the Gardens of Versailles*, Cambridge, UK: Cambridge University Press.

Nippert-Eng, C. (1996), *Home and Work*, Chicago: University of Chicago Press.

Pickering, A. (1995), *The Mangle of Practice*, Chicago: University of Chicago Press.

Plummer, K. (2001 [1983]), *Documents of Life: An Introduction to the Problems and Literature of a Humanistic Method*, London: Sage.

Preda, A. (1999), "The Turn to Things: Arguments for a Sociological Theory of Things," *Sociological Quarterly*, 40 (2): 347–66.

Riesman, D. (1964), *Abundance for What?*, New York: Garden City.

Riggins, S. (2004), "Fieldwork in the Living Room: An Autoethnographic Essay," in S. H. Riggins (ed.), *The Socialness of Things*, 101–47, New York: Mouton de Gruyter.

Rudofsky, B. (1980), *Now I Lay Me Down to Eat*, Garden City, NY: Anchor Books.

Sewell, W. (1940), A memorandum on research in income and levels of living in the South: Revision of a memorandum prepared for consideration at the Sixth Annual Southern Social Science Research Conference, Chattanooga, TN, 7–9 March, in Stillwater, Oklahoma: Agricultural and Mechanical College.

Shove, E., M. Watson, J. Ingram and M. Hand (2008), *The Design of Everyday Life*, London: Berg.

Smith, C. S. (1980), *From Art to Science*, Cambridge: MIT Press.

Strathern, M. (1996), "Cutting the Network," *Journal of the Royal Anthropological Institute*, 2 (3): 517–35.

Thrift, N. (2007), *Non-Representational Theory: Space, Politics, Affect*, London & New York: Routledge.

Wakeford, N. (2003), "A Research Note: Working with New Media's Cultural Intermediaries," *Information, Communication and Society*, 6 (2): 229–45.

Warner, W. L. (1949), *Social Class in America*, New York: Harper Torchbooks.

Zemtsov, I. (1985), *The Private Life of the Soviet Elite*, New York: Crane Russak.

Zukin, S. (2005), *Point of Purchase*, London & New York: Routledge.

3 The Anthropological Object in Design: From Victor Papanek to Superstudio

Alison J. Clarke

Objects and tools represent a particular field of investigation; they lend themselves much better to being used as keys in the interpretation of complex relationships. Objects are the direct witnesses of the creative drive.[1]

—Alessandro Poli, Superstudio 1973

This chapter explores the historical relation of design to anthropology, its objects and methodologies, focusing on the 1970s as a crucial point at which the design profession questioned its social and ecological role in the making of commodities. This period saw the emergence of a critical design culture, which sought to strip away the layers of 'false' meaning around commercial products, casting the indigenous and anthropological object as an alternative model of design in the rubric of 'non-capitalistic' creativity. This relationship stretched so far as to result, in the latter part of the decade, in the discipline of anthropology and the practice of design uniting formally through the policy making of the International Council of Societies of Industrial Design (ICSID) and the United Nations Industrial Development Organization (UNIDO). In the 1970s, design and anthropology coalesced with the emergence of radical, activist, and socially responsible design movements and conversely within the late Cold War development policies of major industrial nations.

---

1. Cited in Lang and Menking 2003: 226.

Critiquing the Commodity Form

In 1976, the Cooper Hewitt National Design Museum, New York, opened with a radical inaugural exhibition titled *MAN transFORMS*.[2] With its emphasis on process, rather than end product, the exhibition challenged the definition of design practice and its relationship to society. Austrian architect Hans Hollein was chosen to generate a provocative and interdisciplinary interpretation of design that avoided the paradigm of the 'genius maker' in favor of a broadly anthropological understanding of objects as the outcome of social processes. "The social concerns of the day," wrote the museum's director in describing the impetus behind the exhibit, "suggested the need to direct attention to issues far deeper than good taste" (Hollein 1989: 10).

Hollein's uncompromising concept had been set against those submitted by American design acolytes, such as Charles and Ray Eames and George Nelson, designers who would arguably have been a more obvious and predictable choice for the opening of the first US national design museum.[3] Coming from a critical European tradition, Hollein offered an unerringly theoretical approach focused on exploring the concept of design rather than the mere objects of design. The exhibit blurred the boundaries between product, urban design, and architectural design, and was refreshingly unhindered by the commercial and vocational pragmatism of American design culture. The installation, the designer insisted, was simply meant as "a statement about what Design is" (Hollein 1989: 13).

In place of the latest, branded must-have products or historical exemplars of the finest design, *MAN transFORMS* featured displays of anonymous objects. Cross-cultural specimens of bread loaves, from flat bread to pretzel, were featured on an extended monumental dining table (suggestive of Leonardo's "Last Supper") fully encased in a dramatically top-lit display case.

Adjoining *The Daily Breads of the World* exhibit, a wall installation titled *Variations of a Basic Item: Hammers* showed the evolution of the hammer with over a hundred types arranged according

---

2. The title of the exhibition, and the incorporation of anthropological schema, should also be understood in relation to feminist discourse of the period. In 1978, leading American feminist Mary Daly published *GYN/Ecology: The Metaethics of Radical Feminism*, part of which explored the consequences of patriarchal power relations of the destruction and control of 'nature.' Feminist discourse of this period also looked to non-capitalist economic models of production and consumption as a means of subverting patriarchal logic (that placed value on the mass-produced over the 'handmade' or indigenous). See, for example, Attfield 1989: 199–225.

3. The choice of a European curator may also have been prompted by the enormous success of the Museum of Modern Art's 1972 design exhibit *Italy: The New Domestic Landscape, Achievements and Problems of Italian Design* curated by Emilio Ambasz. According to architectural historian William Menking, this exhibit placed the young Florentines of Superstudio center stage in the New York design and architecture scene while "none of the other visionary architectural draftsmen of the period: Cedric Price, Archigram, or the Austrians: Coop Himmelbau, Haus-Rucker-Co, Hans Hollein, or Walter Pichler had a major museum exhibition at the time." See Lang and Menking 2003: 55.

to functional variation. From Paleolithic hammer stones to an upholsterer's tack hammer, the display self-consciously resembled that of a traditional ethnology museum.

The exhibit's objects were placed in a distinctly 'anthropological' setting and so, too, were the methods used in interpreting the material culture of the everyday. *Products: Daily Routine* featured candid photographs, captured during walking tours, focused on the observation of the minutiae of everyday rituals. By embracing a cross-cultural approach, spanning a timeframe from Ancient Egypt up to the advent of present day industrial society, the newly formed National Design Museum asserted a global remit that claimed the Indian sari as significant to design discourse as an avant-garde glass sculpture. Cross-cultural juxtapositions replaced the connoisseurial and chronological displays typical of decorative arts museums. Instead, a democratized vision of the designed world unreservedly conferred equal, if not greater, significance to non-Western material cultures from food to architectural structures.

Considering the overtly conservative nature of international design museums even today, which tend toward the hagiographical with their 'star' designers and objects, this 1976 intervention—highlighting both the critical and social role of design—appears jarringly radical to the modern eye. Its emphasis on the spiritual, emotional, and embedded meanings of space and 'things' preempts the move, in twenty-first-century design, toward meaning, value, and consumption as a framework for the making of design. Its approach is redolent of contemporary design ethnography and its claim to place 'the user' first.

But most of all, *MAN transFORMS* should be understood as a culmination of a broader 1970s move toward anthropology as a source of pre-modern promise. The vernacular and anthropological object was a remnant of a world as yet untouched by wanton commercialism, applied aesthetics, and alienating commodity culture. As a source, the objects of other cultures offered designers the opportunity to re-enchant society and free themselves from the stigma of being the "handmaidens" of capitalism, as the Neo-Marxist philosopher Wolfgang Haug had so brutally described them in his treatise *Kritik der Warenästhetik* (1971). Translated into English as *Critique of Commodity Aesthetics: Appearance, Sexuality, and Advertising in Capitalist Society* in 1986, Haug's work construed design as part of a broader "illusion-industry" of media and advertising; he likened the function of design under capitalism to that of the Red Cross in wartime, which boosted morale but was complicit in its cleaning up after the carnage (Haug 1986, quoted in Stairs 1997: 41). Furthermore, consumer culture, and its seductive guise, was cast as a feminized phenomenon with the debased products of modernity prostituting themselves to the whim of capitalism.[4]

In effect, *Critique of Commodity Aesthetics* summarized the intellectual Left's position regarding the role of designers in managing, generating, and promoting 'false consciousness' and insatiable desire in an advanced consumer society. But the critique of fangled consumer gadgets also emerged in the more populist form of a West Coast US counterculture publication, the *Whole*

---

4. See Teal 1995: 80–109 for a discussion on the gendered and sexualized discourse around "commodity aesthetics."

Earth Catalog, which, by 1971, had garnered an enormous following. Consumer catalogs, such as those distributed by the Sears and Roebuck department store, had long been understood as symbols of the American dream of abundance and social cohesion in the form of consumption. Uniting diverse social classes and ethnic groups, consumer catalogs had offered a bewildering array of goods and designs since the nineteenth century to rural and urban Americans alike.

The *Whole Earth Catalog*, as a semiparody of this consumer mechanism, entirely obviated the need for consumer goods, offering instead ecologically aware 'tools' for socially responsible living: from survivalist hardware to manuals on stargazing (Turner 2006). The catalog re-enchanted 'stuff' and made it relevant to the social and collective needs of its users; like the anthropological object, the meanings of its contents emanated from cultural significance rather than adulterated consumer desire. Distributed nationally, the *Whole Earth Catalog* offered readers a lexicon of tools for modern living—counterculture's own collectively devised blueprint for a new indigenous culture filled with objects of essential (rather than false) meaning.[5] The items featured ranged from Clarks' Wallabee walking shoes to diagrams for self-build pneumatic bubble shelters.

In his cultural history of lifestyle consumption in the 1970s, Binkley (2007) positions the phenomenon of the *Whole Earth Catalog* in the context of a more general 'loosening up' of ideas around selfhood and social relations, whereby the individual's lifestyle options became newly valorized. Choices within commodity culture and the discernment around 'things' brought with them new ethical concerns made visible in the rise of counterculture lifestyles. The catalog circulated among a range of similar best-selling publications, such as *How to Keep Your Volkswagen Alive*; *Grow Your Own: An Encounter With Organic Gardening*; *Living on Earth*; as well as *Other Homes and Garbage: Designs for Self-Sufficient Living*, which came to define a self-help culture aimed at co-opting the logic of commodity capitalism (Binkley 2007: 118). Books were seen as 'tools' in this endeavor, and the sensibility of the catalog, with its self-made style bazaar-like pages filled with 'found' images and alternative interpretation of goods, consciously steered away from the aesthetic conventions of commercial publishing houses. Considered by many commentators today as the precursor to open-access Internet sources, the *Whole Earth Catalog* drew on a genre of ecologically aware, countercultural index publications (access catalogs) formulated for those pursuing holistic, socially responsible lifestyles (Binkley 2007: 117).

The Designer's Indigenous Object

The *Whole Earth Catalog* was to counterculture what Victor J. Papanek's *Design for the Real World* (1971) was to design. Papanek's polemic was a clarion call to a generation of disillusioned designers who, even prior to Haug's theoretical condemnation, had been castigated as the masterminds of planned obsolescence in Vance Packard's best-selling book *The Waste Makers* (1960).

---

5. For an extensive discussion of the *Whole Earth Catalog* and the "Book as Tool" see Binkley 2007: 101–29.

Papanek's book chided the design profession for its wanton alliance with the wasteful and meaningless commodity culture of capitalism. First published in Swedish in 1970 under the title *Miljön och miljonerna: design som tjänst eller förtjänst?* (The Environment and the Millions: Design for Service or Profit?), it drew on anthropology as an antidote to this alienated condition (Clarke 2012; 2015). In a chapter titled "Snake Oil And Thalidomide: Mass Leisure and Phony Fads in the Abundant Society," Papanek summarized the twentieth-century designer's dilemma thus:

> *All right: the designer must be conscious of his social and moral responsibility. For Design is the most powerful tool yet given to man with which to shape his products, his environments, and, by extension, himself; with it, he must analyse the past as well as the foreseeable future consequences of his acts.*
>
> *The job is much harder to do when every part of the designer's life has been conditioned by a market-orientated, profit-directed system such as that in the United States. (Papanek 1977 [1971]: 87)*

As a leading design critic, Papanek interwove his interest in anthropology and the vernacular form into his design writings. His substantial personal research library, featuring hundreds of anthropological volumes, such as *Eskimo Artefacts: Designed For Use, Japanese Spoons and Ladles*, and *The Tewa World: Space, Time, Being and Becoming in Pueblo Society*, underpinned his knowledge of 'alternative' ecologies of design. He made extended visits with indigenous cultural groups, observing objects and aesthetics in everyday lives, and he filled his own home with anthropological objects from Balinese masks to Buddhist statues (see Figures 3.1, 3.2, and 3.3).[6]

This avid interest in anthropology was part of a broader popularization of the field of study in the 1970s as folk historians, archaeologists, and anthropologists used critical comparison with alternative cultures as a means of bringing into question the assumptions around contemporary life and values. Indigenous objects offered an unproblematic source for critical reflection on Western culture, an approach that frequently omitted the complexity of the indigenous cultures themselves, in favor of a romanticized vision of 'the other' as non-complex, untainted, and inherently authentic.

But what made Papanek's enthusiasm for the anthropological object particularly effective was his ability to apply similar principles of analysis to the objects of his own culture. Under the titles "Let Them Eat Fakes," "Road Maps to Hell," and "The Chrome-Plated Marshmallow," in the 1960s, Papanek hosted a US television series, *Design Dimensions*, for an educational channel exploring the design 'exotica' of Western consumer culture. This series was later developed into a

---

6. The archive and library of Victor J. Papanek was acquired by the University of Applied Arts Vienna in 2010, including a collection of Papanek's indigenous objects, and forms part of the Art and Design Collection of the University of Applied Arts Vienna.

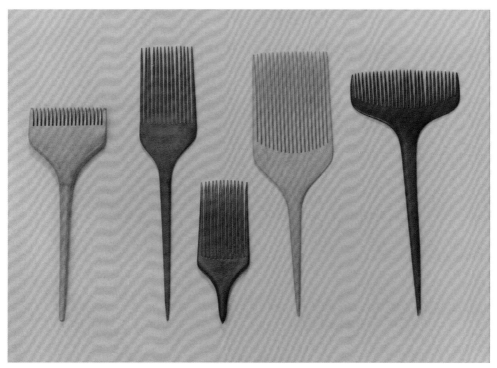

3.1 A set of wooden Japanese combs collected by Papanek as exemplars of indigenous design tied to cultural ritual and evolved ergonomics (in this case the elegant aesthetic of Geisha hairstyling). *Victor J. Papanek Foundation, University of Applied Arts Vienna*

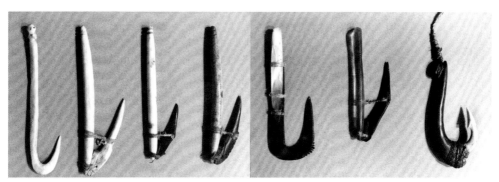

3.2 A collection of fishing hooks from Papua New Guinea, used by Papanek to show design development within indigenous cultures. *Victor J. Papanek Foundation, University of Applied Arts Vienna*

3.3 Victor Papanek and his wife Harlanne in their Copenhagen apartment 1973, with a backdrop of indigenous artifacts. *Victor J. Papanek Foundation, University of Applied Arts Vienna*

commercial TV series titled *Pop Culture* that explored the nuances of advertising, popular culture, and its human consequences.[7]

Papanek combined a nuanced understanding of indigenous material cultures, from Native American to Japanese, with a studied fascination for his culture's own 'exoticism.' He delighted in collecting 'idiot-gadgets' and socially useless products; an ethnological-style collection of absurd Western industrial culture strongly informed his critical writings around design and consumer culture. The foibles of designs such as a "Human Washing Machine" developed by Osaka's Sanyo Electric Co., priced at US$6,600 ("out of reach of all but the filthy rich," noted the TIME magazine 1972 clipping Papanek saved for his 'pop culture' archive), substantiated his lament of contemporary industrial design. Similarly, clippings such as an advertisement for a dog's "Santa Claus outfit" (under the title "Have a Living Christmas Ornament in the House") provided a fertile source for his quasi-ethnographic approach to the contemporary everyday (see Papanek 1971, 1973). His 1977 co-authored book *How Things Don't Work* was a culmination of this quasi-ethnological perception of Western material culture. It positively reveled in observations of the absurdity of everyday design malfunction, from ineffectual bottle openers to hazardous lavatory bowls (Papanek and Hennessey 1977).

The appropriation of vernacular, popular culture and anthropological objects by designers had its precedence in the decades of late Modernism. In 1955, Charles Eames made a film from Alexander Girard's MoMA exhibition *Textiles and Ornamental Arts of India*, which revolved around an imaginary bazaar filled with an array of brightly colored indigenous fabrics and artifacts. The Eames' fascination with cross-cultural material culture resulted in their being commissioned to write the "India Report" for the Indian government, in which they looked at ways to protect traditional design cultures from the impact of Western technologies. Funded by the Ford Foundation, the Eameses spent three months immersed in Indian culture; collecting artifacts, recording landscapes and rituals. They singled out specific objects of study, such as the *lota* (a traditional vessel) for in-depth research, the findings feeding directly into their studio work (Albrecht 1997: 3).

Similarly, their widely known and well-documented appropriation of the vernacular, as "functioning decoration," relied on their extraction of objects from their original cultural context, re-juxtaposing them to generate "extra-cultural surprise" (Kirkham 1995: 143). According to design historian Pat Kirkham, the mixing of objects of authentic origin and popular culture had enormous influence on both Eames' work and the contemporary culture of design:

> [The Eameses] changed the way people thought about objects, largely by presenting them in new ways and by encouraging different ways of perceiving, grouping, and displaying them . . . they used toys and everyday objects to illustrate design principles . . . and they emphasized the need to understand the contexts in which material culture was produced and used. (Kirkham 1995: 143)

---

7. The twelve-part series premiered on WUNC-TV as *Pop Culture: Essays in the Mass Media* when Victor J. Papanek was head of the Department of Product Design at North Carolina State University in the 1960s. The series originated from an educational television channel (WNED-TV) in the Buffalo, New York, area titled *Design Dimensions*.

In their films, their personal home and studio interiors, and their exhibits, the Eameses consistently drew upon the aesthetic of the everyday and the indigenous object (found pebbles, kitsch trinkets, Mexican pots, toys, textiles, etc.). Their meticulously cataloged slide collection of around 350,000 images and their films including *Glimpses of the USA* with 2,200 images of everyday America from supermarkets through to skyscrapers (made for the 1959 American National Exhibition in Moscow) are well-known legacies of the Eames' tireless engagement with material culture from the perspective of a participant observer's eye (Albrecht 1997). Under the title "Design Is a Method of Action" (a phrase coined by Charles Eames to describe this object-based design methodology), design historian Donald Albrecht summarizes the method thus: "the studied contrast between old and new, rich and humble, foreign and familiar, mass-produced and hand-crafted— became the Eameses' signature" (Albrecht 1997: 22).

The Eames' celebratory approach to everyday material culture belongs to a broader post-war cultural politics exemplified by the work of Eduardo Paolozzi, co-founder of the Independent Group (1951), and his well-known Krazy Kat archive of popular culture, everyday, and 'found' objects/images.[8] This self-conscious embracement of the everyday objects of consumer culture as a form of 'exotica' inverted the power relations of traditional anthropology, retraining the critical gaze to follow the flotsam of Western culture as a form of cultural authenticity. While the appropriation of an anthropological guise in the post-war period had been ostensibly concerned with challenging the boundaries of aesthetic valuation and 'high' and 'low' culture, the 1970s 'anthropologized' object had a more overtly political role to play in design.

Re-Appropriating the Commodity

In 1976, the same year that the Cooper Hewitt National Design Museum launched their inaugural *MAN transFORMS* exhibit, Victor Papanek and designer Gui Bonsiepe met at the *Design For Need* conference organized by the International Council of Societies of Industrial Design (ICSID) at the Royal College of Art, London (Bicknell et al. 1977). Bonsiepe and Papanek debated the role of design in 'countries of the periphery' (a term Bonsiepe preferred to 'non-developed' or 'Third World'). While Bonsiepe and Papanek differed slightly in their approaches, they were united in making 'peripheral' economies a key concern of socially responsive design. Most significantly, working with organizations such as UNESCO, Papanek strove to understand design from the indigenous or 'user' perspective.

The "before" (see Figure 3.4) and "after" (see Figure 3.5) images of a "radio receiver designed for the Third World" featured in the chapter "Design Responsibility" in *Design for the Real World* show the re-enchantment of materials, such as a tin can, dried cow dung, and paraffin wax. The "after" version of the design was "decorated with colored felt cut-outs and seashells by a user in

---

8. The Krazy Kat collection, now housed in the V&A, London, was an integral source for The Independent Group protagonist. See Robbins 1990.

3.4 Tin Can Radio: radio receiver designed for use in the developing world at 9 cents a piece. By Victor Papanek and George Seeger at North Carolina State College. *Originally published in Victor J. Papanek,* Design for the Real World *(New York: Pantheon Books, 1971), 163. Victor J. Papanek Foundation, University of Applied Arts Vienna*

Indonesia." "The user," Papanek reiterated, "can embellish the tin can radio to his own taste."[9] The neglect of design, as a transformative activity, ideally positioned to readdress material inequality and generate inclusivity, was lamentable to Papanek. But he considered it an inevitable outcome of a practice immersed in the schema of consumerist design: "The action of the profession [of design]," he wrote, "has been comparable to what would happen if all medical doctors were to forsake general practice and surgery and concentrate exclusively on dermatology, plastic surgery, and cosmetics" (Papanek 2004 [1984]: 241; quoted in Whiteley 1993: 99).

9. Papanek 2004 [1984]: 225–26. The radio was designed with George Seeger at the North Carolina State College.

3.5 Tin Can Radio receiver decorated with colored felt cutouts and seashells by a user in Indonesia according to their own taste. *Originally published in Victor J. Papanek,* Design for the Real World *(New York: Pantheon Books, 1971), 163. Victor J. Papanek Foundation, University of Applied Arts Vienna*

In 1973, the International Design Center (IDZ) Berlin ran an exhibition titled *Design it yourself: Möbel für den Grundbedarf des Wohnens* (furniture for basic living) with designs by Papanek, who was described in the accompanying literature as a "UNESCO expert." This 'do-it-yourself' spontaneous design aesthetic challenged the supremacy of capitalist standardization and democratized the idea of design; de-professionalizing the practice and the very idea of a connoisseurial design elite. As part of a broader discourse of alternative culture, the exhibit promoted the idea of self-empowerment by the adoption of low-impact appropriate technology: a set of basic design instructions and a simple set of tools (Hennessey and Papanek 1973; 1974). Self-assembly furniture and the new "Low-Tech-Kultur" were intended as an overtly political statement (Eisele 2005; 2006).

The ambitions of critical designers to make an impact on a broader socioeconomic level, and effectively 'change the system,' might seem naively utopian in retrospect. But who better than designers to radically re-think the commodity form in a post-Fordist age? When New Left thinker André Gorz published the English edition of his treatise *Ecology as Politics* (1979), he envisaged a world in which non-material exchanges (of time, labor, services) undermined a capitalist-driven economy of profit and an endlessly accelerated circulation of commodities.[10] Gorz's work outlined the significance of environmental issues in re-thinking the socialist agenda and revealed the extent to which the popular discourse around media such as the *Whole Earth Catalog* was underpinned by a serious politics of social change.

The linguistic and symbolic appropriation of the 'tool' as word and object (as seen, for example, in Hollein's *MAN transFORMS* and the *Whole Earth Catalog*) played on Marxist definitions of 'use' and 'exchange' value, reducing the capitalist commodity form to one of instrumentalism rather than artificially manufactured value.[11] It also drew heavily on the period's theoretical shift to phenomenology within social science and architectural practice. Kenneth Frampton's widely read essay, "On Reading Heidegger," in the 1974 edition of the cutting-edge architectural journal *Oppositions* proved highly influential among architects. But within design it took the Italian avant-garde design and architecture group Superstudio to push the notion of the 'tool' as part of an anti-design discourse to its contemporary conclusion.

In 1972, a groundbreaking MoMA exhibit, *Italy: The New Domestic Landscape*, placed Italian industrial design at the forefront of an ideological shift in design practice. Its curator, Emilio Ambasz, showcased the lush consumer designs of cutting-edge Italian designers,[12] nevertheless proclaiming that

> *for many designers, the aesthetic quality of individual objects intended for private consumption [has] become irrelevant in the face of such pressing problems of poverty, urban decay, and the pollution of the environment now encountered in all industrialized countries. (Ambasz 1972, quoted in Lang and Menking 2003: 56)*

In the accompanying catalog, Ambasz identified several distinct approaches to the dilemma of Italian design of this period: Conformist designers conceived of design as an autonomous and apolitical activity, while reformists were "motivated by a profound concern for the designer's role in society" (Ibid.). A further group was being "torn by the dilemma of having been trained as creators of objects, yet unable to control the significance of the uses of objects" (Ibid.: 57). Other disaffected designers asserted that "making objects of any kind is a chimera," while a more interventionist set were identified as "those who engage in object design as an active critical participation"

10. André Gorz's *Ecology as Politics* was first published in English in 1979; however, it was based on two earlier German books he had authored in 1975 and 1977.

11. See Fry 1992: 41–53 for a related discussion of "need" within design theory. See Harman 2002 for a discussion of phenomenology and tool analysis.

12. The exhibit included designs by Gaetano Pesce, Joe Colombo, Richard Sapper, Marco Zanuso, Vico Magistretti, Ettore Sottsass, Superstudio, and Archizoom, among others. See Ambasz 1972.

(Ibid.). The emerging anti-design movement was desperately fragmented in its attempts to reassess the role of the commodity in society.

The radical design group Superstudio, founded in 1966, epitomized the contradictions and dichotomies of 1970s design. For the MoMA exhibit, they created a catalog presentation *Micro-event/Microenvironment*, provocatively subtitled "Critical Reappraisal of the Possibilities of Life Without Objects." With no intended irony, their "passiflora" plastic floor lamp was featured in the luxury product section of the same exhibition (Ibid.: 61). The move toward the immaterial, with design reduced to 'tools' or systems for political change, co-existed with a thriving 1970s consumer product culture the radical designers appropriated as another form of 'evasion design' project. Far from being mere commodities, claims historian Ross Elfline, these objects operated for the radical Italian architects and designers as a "form of domestic insurrection, meant to disrupt the delicate cohesion of the sort of total design planning epitomized by their International Style forebears" (Elfline 2016: 60). If designers, according to Superstudio, were fated to generate objects "they were going to create difficult, even obstructive ones that would critically, even virally, interrogate domestic life" (Ibid.: 62).

In 1973, a group of leading Italian designers and architects (including members of Super-studio) appeared on the front cover of the design magazine *Casabella* announcing an initiative dubbed "Global Tools." Designer Alessandro Mendini, editor of *Casabella*, used the publication to propose a system of collective "open" laboratories networked across Italy, fostering an anti-paternalistic, educative approach to design thinking.[13] This initiative, which began in the same year as the international oil crisis, chimed with the sentiments of the Club of Rome think tank and its related publication *The Limits To Growth* (Meadows et al. 1972), which warned of worldwide overpopulation and diminishing resources.

From 1973 to 1975, Global Tools promoted the notion of products as 'collective tools': objects stripped of artifice and re-instrumentalized through an essential relation between materials, technique, and relative behavioral characteristics (see Figure 3.6). Recapturing the innate creative knowledge previously suffocated by the Western 'craze for efficiency,' Global Tools laboratories were envisaged as a type of consciousness-raising network, harnessing collective and informal creativity for purpose rather than profit; design re-humanized as a politically empowering force (Clarke 2016a).

The Global Tools initiative remained a provocative but largely unrealized project. However, the turn to the 're-enchanted object' or 'tool' exerted tremendous influence in other aspects of Italian design education. In 1974, under the auspices of the *Cultura Materiale Extraurbana* (Extra-Urban Material Culture) course at the School of Architecture at the University of Florence, Superstudio members Adolfo Natalini and Alessandro Poli directed students to the significance of folk tools and indigenous objects. Courses such as "The Galaxy of Objects, Objects of Simple Use" widely incorporated

---

13. "Global Tools" participants included Gaetano Pesce, Alessandro Mendini, Ettore Sottsass, and members of the radical architecture and design groups Archizoom and Superstudio.

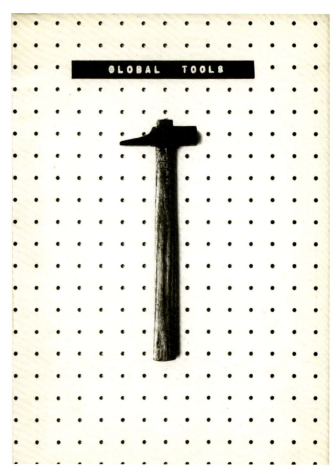

3.6 Front cover, *Global Tools* bulletin no. 1, design by Remo Buti, Edizioni L'uomo e l'arte, Milan, 1974.

anthropological techniques of observation and analysis. The intention was to subvert formal mechanisms of design knowledge, thus "erasing the dominance of a single middle class culture" (Lang and Menking 2003: 223). Students embedded themselves in remote regions of Italy to document and record diminishing Italian peasant cultures. Project Zeno—the complete documentation of a Tuscan farmer with his own material culture, from tools to farm shelters—acknowledged what Poli described as the "enormous heritage of knowledge to be found in this subordinate, marginal society in which we can trace not only the roots of our science but also the possibility of a different structure, an alternative way of living" (Poli 2010). Anti-design found solace in the innocence of the anthropological object, shaped by an embedded cultural relevance to social life and authentic social relations. Peasants in Tuscany existed outside the modern commodity culture vilified by Victor Papanek and Wolfgang Haug; their objects represented truer design—design generated by a delicate ecosystem fusing maker, user, and thing.

Concluding Remarks

By the late 1970s, design witnessed a clear "anthropological turn" as the broader remits of social science melded with those of the mainstream industrial design profession, resulting in the signing of the Ahmedabad Declaration in 1979 (Clarke 2016c). Within the framework of an ICSID and UNIDO initiative, tied to the soft politics of Cold War development, Westernized capitalist product design and the vernacular, indigenous and craft products of countries such as India and Mexico were thrown together in the guise of development policy making. Industrial design was seen as a vital means of forging "development and diversification of a developing country's industrial production by designing new products and re-designing old ones" (UNIDO 1979: 3).

This legacy persists, yet, as this edited volume suggests, there has been a seismic shift in the design culture of the last decades, whereby 'users' and methods of anthropological inquiry ranging from co-design to narrative storytelling have emerged as the key means of deciphering the nuances of object/subject relations (Clarke 2016b). Whereas once the policies of governmental agencies sought to appropriate local forms and modes of making for the furtherance of development agendas, over the last decades anthropology has been inculcated within corporate practice in the guise of a futurological brand of design anthropology. While the potentialities of design anthropology as a corporate practice have replaced the ambitions of the Ahmedabad Declaration in its cosmopolitical intent, critical reflection of the ways in which the 'anthropological object' and 'subject' come to be articulated remains a vital aspect of design anthropology.

References

Albrecht, D. (1997), "Design Is a Method of Action," in D. Albrecht (ed.), *The Work of Charles and Ray Eames: The Legacy of Invention*, 18–44, New York: Harry N. Abrams, Inc.

Ambasz, E., ed. (1972), *Italy: The New Domestic Landscape: Achievements and Problems of Italian Design*, New York: The Museum of Modern Art.

Attfield, J. (1989), "Form/Female Follows Function/Male: Feminist Critiques of Design," in J. A. Walker and J. Attfield (eds.), *Design History and the History of Design*, 199–225, London: Pluto.

Bicknell, J. and L. McQuiston (1977), *Design for Need: The Social Contribution of Design—An Anthology of Papers*, New York: ICSID, Pergamon Press.

Binkley, S. (2007), *Getting Loose: Lifestyle Consumption in the 1970s*, Durham: Duke University Press.

Clarke, A. (2012), "Actions Speak Louder: Victor Papanek and the Legacy of Design Activism," *Design and Culture*, 5 (2): 151–68.

Clarke, A. (2015), "Buckminster Fuller's Reindeer Abattoir and Other Designs for the Real World," in A. Blauvelt (ed.), *Hippie Modernism: The Struggle for Utopia*, Minneapolis: Walker Art Center.

Clarke, A. (2016a), "Survival: The Indigenous and the Autochthon," in V. Borgonuovo and S. Franceschini (eds.), *GLOBAL TOOLS: When Education Coincides with Life*, Berlin: Archive Books co-published with Istanbul: SALT.

Clarke, A. (2016b), "The New Ethnographers: Design Activism 1968–1974," in R. C. Smith, T. Otto, K. T. Vangkilde, J. Halse, T. Binder, and M. G. Kjaersgaard (eds.), *Design Anthropological Futures*, London and New York: Bloomsbury.

Clarke, A. (2016c), "Design for Development, ICSID, and UNIDO: The Anthropological Turn in 1970s Design," *Journal of Design History*, 29 (1): 43–58.

Eisele, P. (2005), *BRDesign: Deutsches Design als Experiment seit den 1960er Jahren*, Cologne: Böhlau.

Eisele, P. (2006), "Do-It-Yourself-Design: Die IKEA-Regale IVAR und BILLY," *Zeithistorische Forschungen/ Studies in Contemporary History*, 3 (3): 439–48.

Elfline, R. (2016), "Superstudio and the 'Refusal to Work,'" *Design and Culture*, 8 (1): 55–77.

Frampton, K. (1974), "On Reading Heidegger," *Oppositions*, 4.

Fry, T. (1992), "Against an Essential Theory of Need: Some Considerations for Design Theory," *Design Issues*, 8 (2): 41–53.

Gorz, A. (1979), *Ecology as Politics*, Boston: South End Press.

Harman, G. (2002), *Tool-Being: Heidegger and the Metaphysics of Objects*, Chicago: Open Court.

Haug, W. (1986 [1971]), *Critique of Commodity Aesthetics: Appearance, Sexuality, and Advertising in Capitalist Society*, Minneapolis: University of Minneapolis Press.

Hennessey, J. and V. Papanek (1973), *Nomadic Furniture 1: How to Build and Where to Buy Lightweight Furniture That Folds, Collapses, Stacks, Knocks-Down, Inflates or Can Be Thrown Away and Re-cycled*, New York: Pantheon Books.

Hennessey, J. and V. Papanek (1974), *Nomadic Furniture 2*, New York: Pantheon Books.

Hollein, H. (1989), *MAN transFORMS: Konzepte einer Ausstellung*, Vienna: Loecker Verlag.

Kirkham, P. (1995), *Charles and Ray Eames: Designers of the Twentieth Century*, Cambridge, MA: MIT Press.

Lang, P. and W. Menking, eds. (2003), *Superstudio: Life Without Objects*, Milan: Skira.

Meadows, D. H., D. L., Meadows, J. Randers, and W. W. Behrens III (1972), *The Limits to Growth: A Report for the Club of Rome's Project on the Predicament of Mankind*, New York: Universe Books.

Packard, V. (1960), *The Waste Makers*, Harmondsworth: Penguin.

Papanek, V. (1970), *Miljön och miljonerna: design som tjänst eller förtjänst?*, Stockholm: Bonniers.

Papanek, V. (1971), *Design for the Real World*, New York: Pantheon Books, 1971.

Papanek, V. (1971), "What to Design and Why," *Mobilia*, 193: 2–13.

Papanek, V. (1973), "Notes from a Journal," *Mobilia*, 219/220: 18–29.

Papanek, V. (1977 [1971]), *Design for the Real World: Human Ecology and Social Change*, St. Albans: Paladin.

Papanek, V. (2004 [1984]), *Design for the Real World*, rev. ed., London: Thames & Hudson.

Papanek, V. and J. Hennessey (1977), *How Things Don't Work*, New York: Pantheon Books.

Poli, A. (2010), "Nearing the Moon to the Earth," in G. Borasi and M. Zardini (eds.), *Other Space Odysseys: Greg Lynn, Michael Maltzan, Alessandro Poli*, 109–20, Baden, CH: Lars Mueller Publishers.

Robbins, D., ed. (1990), *The Independent Group: Postwar Britain and The Aesthetics of Plenty*, Cambridge, MA: MIT Press.

Stairs, D. (1997), "Biophilia and Technophilia: Examining the Nature/Culture Split in Design Theory," *Design Issues*, 13 (3): 41.

Teal, L. (1995), "The Hollow Women: Modernism, the Prostitute, and Commodity Aesthetics," *Differences: A Journal of Feminist Cultural Studies*, 7 (3): 80–109.

Turner, F. (2006), *From Counterculture to Cyberculture: Steward Brand, the Whole Earth Network, and the Rise of Digital Utopianism*, Chicago: The University of Chicago Press.

UNIDO (1979), "Design in India: The Importance of the "Ahmedabad Declaration Meeting for Promotion of Industrial Design in Developing Countries," aide-memoire, UNIDO Archive, Vienna, id.78-5076.

Whiteley, N. (1993), *Design for Society*, London: Reaktion Books.

4 Valuable to Values: How 'User Research' Ought to Change

Maria Bezaitis and Rick E. Robinson

In the early 1990s, in major research labs like Xerox PARC, Microsoft Research, and Bell Labs, technologists worked with social scientists incorporating the tools of anthropology to describe how people thought machines worked, to understand the interactions between people and technology, and the reciprocal impact of organizations, practices, and technologies on one another.

Introduction—The Immigrants' Tale

Neither of us is an anthropologist. Nor is either of us a designer, although one of us is left-handed. But both of us do, rather happily, self-identify with the 'design/anthropology' intersection around which this volume is organized. We work in this space. We've built networks here, we (mostly) think here. But when either of us attempts to tell anyone what it is that we do, we almost invariably start with the fact that we were trained in the social sciences or the humanities (respectively)— with where we *come from* as an introduction to what we *do*. We are, in a word, immigrants. And like most immigrants, our experience, as well as our expectations and outlook on the future, are blendedly influenced by both our originating contexts and our somewhat different understandings of the workings of the contexts we now find ourselves in.

One of the facts that makes this space an appealing one is that we are hardly unique in this. Among our immediate colleagues over the years have been anthropologists in some number, but also cognitive psychologists; sociologists; students of literature, linguistics, history, and criticism; people trained in the fine arts, theater, and performance studies; divinity scholars; art historians; and biologists. That leaves aside the similarly broad range of the disciplines that have historically worked in the design and development domains: engineers, designers, strategists, and so on. The design/research intersection seems to be a very appealing destination for folks trained in what were once unrelated fields. The reasons an immigrant has for leaving a well-settled home are always varied, but a constant across those variations is the idea that *the future could be different*—at an individual level, but perhaps more importantly for many, the potential to bring change to the world, to shift the ground, to alter the rules. It has been no different for us. Like many immigrants, we retain a good deal of where we come from in the ways that we think and in the values that we maintain, while at the same time trying to make as much out of the opportunities we came here to explore as we can.

We aren't writing a history of the 'user research' space; we are much more interested in a bit of prescriptiveness for the field as it continues to grow, but that prescription does depend on our articulating how we understand the 'somewhere' from which the trajectory starts. It matters to us that we are anchoring this chapter in the specifics of our own experience, because a big part of what we are trying to lay out here is the importance of the essential humanness of what we do: We are individuals situated in a field and in practices. We, and the organizations we work in and for, have very particular *values*. What we want to stress is not some abstract notion of how a practice develops, but that the *articulation* and evolution of practices and values matter to the quality and the future of this work. Working through that notion brought us to yet another story—perhaps less comfortable but equally crucial—that has to do with power and differentiation.

Each of us came to be doing what it is we do (notice how we neatly sidestep attaching a label) by quite different paths. In the decade gap between when Robinson left the University of Chicago and started at Jay Doblin & Associates and when Bezaitis left Duke University and began to work at E-Lab, the nature of the field and the opportunities for researchers had already changed significantly. In the decade or so since then, what both designers and scholars face is an altogether differently constituted field. We chose the immigrant figure deliberately: We want to emphasize that the work of design, development, strategy, and innovation was the place to which we and many of our colleagues came, bag and baggage. We don't think that there is a simple tale of assimilation here; it hasn't become a happy melting pot; our *unum* is still pretty *pluribus*. That's not to say that the work of design has been unaffected by the influx of new people, new terms, new methods, and new frameworks. In a fairly condensed period of time, these new arrivals have had a profound impact on the design world, have shaped and affected what had been a small intersection (that between research on and about people and the work of design) to the point where it is now a field itself, a recognized domain of both expertise and value. This development seems to have strengthened the attraction between the new territory and the wide range of disciplines new and old that came to it.

The other reason for working through the figure of the immigrant, however, is that it potentially characterizes not just our past but also our prospects. We do not believe that these blends of social science and design are capabilities that necessarily belong in any or every corporation. Nor do we believe that once they do they should necessarily become a permanent fixture. Companies become disposed to and in need of these capabilities for specific reasons in specific contexts. It is just as easy to imagine that these contexts will change, and in those changes corporations may cease to value what social science and design can deliver. In this sense, we've signed up for a lifetime of migration, and if that's the case, we, in all of our wonderful differences, had better be prepared to understand clearly the lessons to be learned from the various places we've tried to call home.

Over the past twenty years or so, the practices and values of the human sciences have added richness to a range of shared vocabularies and created, rather than simply altered, ways of working. Some of these ways of working refer heavily to the domains and disciplines from which they came; some not at all. Labels aside, the practices of the majority of the field are hybrids with a strong sense of 'hereness' to them. As the community grows, in both size and in range of roles, there is an understandable impulse to craft a singular identity, to find common labels for the 'we' and the 'work,' and to be able to train and support new practitioners without the same disruption between disciplinary training and professional identity that many of us went through in getting here. On the other hand, though, there is a peculiar way in which recourse to a common label allows us to ignore the realities of organizational terrain, politics, and growth. To recognize those realities moves (or should move) conversation around practice to a more fraught one that also deals with power. Power, organizational politics, and frank assessment of effectiveness are not often what gets discussed when we talk about the 'value' of this work. It should be. There is no 'canon' here yet; those other, original homes are far too valuable to the everyday work of this domain to ever be someplace we are no longer from. But we need more than method and process agreement to prosper. What follows is a discussion that seeks to surface the lessons and experiences that have got us where we are today so that we can move to a discussion of what should happen next.

Part I: How We Got Here

Only one of us went through graduate training with a non-academic career in mind. And for most of the senior researchers we know in industry, that accidental non-path seems reasonably common. A half a generation ago, there were few mentors, organizations, or communities that could have served as an inspiration to look outside of the academic track (leaving public and museum work aside). For our purposes, the careers we have each led are nicely emblematic, if not entirely representative, of the experience of many researchers involved in the emergence of this work.

While Robinson was in the midst of a post-doctoral fellowship, a major advisor (Mihaly Csikszentmihalyi, himself an immigrant from Hungary in the 1950s) introduced Robinson to Jay Doblin, the former head of the Institute of Design in Chicago who, with strategist Larry Keeley, ran a small design planning consultancy known at the time as Jay Doblin Associates. The expertise Doblin was looking for was explicitly methodological; what we later came to call "figuring out how to figure things out." Beyond the fundamental intrigue of methodology, the aspect of the work that was the most surprising, most engaging, was the practical aspect of it. The developmental disciplines (design, engineering, strategy) at Doblin were able to open up their work practices to engage with the research work, and this became an opportunity for a related, almost mirrored, need on the part of a researcher to pull apart the reasoning, the assumptions, and the processes that had become second nature in order to make research and theory a practical and useful thing in a setting where that value was not assumed. The point was to foster a dialogue between the researcher and the designer, and the goal in that interaction was to make research useful to design and to create for design a place from which it could reflect on its work. At that time, being a researcher in that context meant demonstrating a real difference to both process and outcome—to make the work of other professionals go better and to influence, through design and engineering colleagues, the making of very real things.

Robinson's first major project at Doblin provided an opportunity to work with anthropologists Lucy Suchman and Jeannette Blomberg and their colleagues in the Work Practices & Technology group at Xerox PARC. The idea that the folks at PARC were prodigiously credentialed in their various academic domains, active in professional societies, and yet worked for a copier company was something more than simply eye opening. That they existed and that the group was well-known and respected was a kind of validation, like finding other immigrants from home thriving in the new country. But more important was that their work, the breadth and catholicity of their methodologies, the intense collegiality of their practice, made a developmental space available, opened up the idea that new collaborations, different practices, and new applications were possible: a much different way of looking at an alternative career than simply seeing it as a slot in an organization that you perhaps did not know existed. This was something that could be built, and a trajectory opened up beyond one project, one problem.

With the PARC group very much in mind, Robinson, John Cain, and Mary Beth McCarthy left Doblin to form E-Lab, a multidisciplinary group with the explicit goal of delivering research that could be a basis for design. The emphasis was on developing the forms of research that could be relevant to many client audiences. E-Lab did not have the kind of 'productization' that market research had, didn't go as far toward realization as the product development consultancies, and did not have an MBA credentialed 'strategy' practice. Indeed, it was a struggle to find the language to describe what it was we were doing to prospective clients. Design effectively became the means to making the research useful. It was nice (and necessary) to have clients who 'got it,' but without providing those clients with ways to talk with their own colleagues, superiors, and funders, expanding the range of opportunities we had to work with was akin to making converts, one at a time.

With its concurrent emergence of important technologies and its intense, post-recession entrepreneurialism, the early 1990s offered a unique opportunity for the design field to enhance its role and expand its offer. Firms such as IDEO, Fitch, and Design Continuum had, earlier in the decade, merged multiple disciplines, particularly engineering and industrial design, and begun to change the way that business thought about the place and value of design. Around the same time, in major research labs like Xerox PARC, Microsoft Research, and Bell Labs, technologists had been working with communications designers, usability and human factors engineers, and, especially at PARC, social scientists who had started to use the tools of anthropology, linguistics, sociology, and psychology to describe how people thought machines worked, to understand the interactions between people and technology, and the reciprocal impact of organizations, practices, and technologies on one another. In the business world at large, there was something of a buzz about this kind of hybrid (the 'newness' of it, though, is debatable; Suchman 2000), and there were new channels for that buzz—publications like *Fast Company*, *Wired*, *Business 2.0*.

Outside of the corporate labs, doing research for hire meant finding a way to describe what kinds of benefits a company might garner from what was then an unfamiliar approach and then to put a price tag on it, which often meant to argue for relative worth in a zero-sum budgeting process. Much of the writing and speaking we did in design and management venues (see Robinson 1993, 1994a, 1994b, 1998, 2001; Robinson and Nims 1996; Robinson and Hackett 1997; Cain 1998) was in part a kind of marketing. The talks and papers were attempts to find common cause between market researchers, product managers, designers, engineers, and the small outposts of social and human scientists working (together) in industry. The language we were trying to find mattered *inside* E-Lab as well. Descriptions of the work had to make sense to all of the disciplines. It was important that both researchers and designers feel that the 'we' of the company was an inclusive 'we' rather than a one-sided one. The language of 'valuable' work, defined largely by distinctive methodologies and successful product outcomes, started when the field (and the company) was very young.

Shortly after Bezaitis joined, E-Lab came to focus on a synthetic moment—the development of 'a framework'—as the target for the fieldwork and the central output of projects. It was the explicit move to focus our discussions and value claims on the idea of frameworks—which we characterized as "useful representations of how experience is framed for the user"—which differentiated E-Lab's value in the market and the space in which the practice grew. The term 'frameworks' was a placeholder for the notion of distinct and specific analytic organizations ('frameworks' evolved to become 'experience models' in the course of E-lab's acquisition by Sapient in 1999) that linked data to questions. How those analytic organizations took their various and particular shapes was a function of the collaborations and multidisciplinary perspectives that sustained the work right across the range of projects.

Hallmark as a Case in Point

In one of Robinson's notebooks, dated 11/94 – 1/95, are notes on the first project that E-Lab did for Hallmark Cards. We had spent hundreds of hours in Hallmark stores—pilots of a new format—during one of their busiest seasons, and were now spending more hundreds of hours watching those tapes again, trying to figure out what was valuable to know, what was germane to the questions our clients were asking. They aren't field notes (which were kept in logged notebooks linked to the raw data), but rather a sort of laundry list of issues that might or might not have been important: "lighting," it says, and "vis. noise, blockage, interest, orient/nav." And in the midst of the list, "a theory of navigation and vis. orient is here somewhere." The note would have been more accurate if it had said, "is out there already." We were working on overlaying behaviors on to floor plans, trying to winnow the general from the specific, and the flat maps were stubbornly remaining two dimensional no matter how many arrows or colors we arranged over them. At the same time, co-founder John Cain was teaching a course in 'interactive media' at the Institute of Design, and using—as an approach to the issue of 'navigation'—architect Kevin Lynch's classic *The Image of the City* (1970). Sitting in our crowded technology/work room, John suggested that how Lynch's book framed orientation in the city might work for how shoppers saw the Hallmark stores, too. Lynch had looked at how people find their way around cities, both familiar and not, and had re-classed features of the urban landscape into a short set based on how people used them: paths, edges, nodes, districts, and landmarks (imagine the role of the lake in Chicago or of Central Park in New York City).

Many in this field like to speak of 'insights,' a term we find both empty and imprecise (Robinson 2009). Psychologist Howard Gardner and his colleague Joseph Walters, in their developmental studies of genius, creativity, and forms of giftedness, speak more specifically and usefully of 'crystallizing' moments: observations, ideas, connections, which are not complete in themselves, but which catalyze a well and richly prepared ground into a completely different way of seeing the world (Walters and Gardner 1988). The Lynch analogy was one of those—the final form of the idea did not flash, complete and pure, into the room. Rather, the concept needed to be worked against the data. We had to figure out a way to represent it, and we had to reframe the angle from which we saw the data—not shifting it in our heads onto two-dimensional maps, but seeing the three-dimensional topography as a visitor might have seen it. It worked brilliantly, but it was *work*, not a flash of insight. That merging of disciplines, the value of that move from rich, high-quality data to a simpler but more useful representation of how experience is organized for the user, became one of the central tenets of E-Lab's work and practice.

In the growing field of design research, that particular philosopher's stone eventually converted 'ethnography' and 'design research' to shorthand terms for a larger process. In much of the business discourse, the assumption driven by this terminology—and by many of the claims of design and research consultancies—was that field methodology defined the practice and value of ethnography. Even within our group, there were heated disagreements about the priority of technique versus theory or analysis or synthesis. And in retrospect, we see that our communications in every press contact, every pitch, conceded this ground.

As the use of terminology like 'user-centered research' became widespread, so the meaning of 'ethnography' became both broader and looser. The market-facing vocabulary of product development and marketing linked the growth of many different practices and intentions to a single measure: the success of the product at the end of the process, linking research with design in the case study format. The case study is perhaps *the* staple format of business education and development, the *lingua franca* for communicating the general or the applicable from the specific and the protected. The case study tied work to a narrative of how the thing made became better or more valuable after the application of a research or design or innovation process. It demystified the role of research in development, providing a way to connect the before to the after. It implicitly made the product the thing that was moving ahead, changing, getting better. But in doing that, the arcs of research came to tiny ends with each project finish rather than building and accumulating across instances, clients, and careers.

In much applied ethnographic work of the past decade or so, that difference has ossified somewhat; it has become embedded in the general discourse of the field, allowing the term 'methodology' to be widely used as a shorthand description for an enterprise's larger research approach, and much more insidiously, allowing discussion to skate over the surface of an organization's intentions, politics, and values. What conversation there is about the value of work like this came to be couched in production-like terminology; outcomes, findings, 'insights' as products, winding their way through a complex process, to which particular disciplines 'add value' through understanding, innovation, or skill. As hybrid work moved out of research labs and 'advanced concepts groups' and into product development organizations, the direct dialogues between researcher and designer became process interactions between research and design functions, with all of the politics, tradeoffs, and—to be fair—advantages which that entailed. The ideal that motivated the relationship between researcher and designer in the Doblin context, at PARC, and many others gave way to a different set of organizational and corporate values, processes, and mandates, which complicated the initial motivation to create a basis for reflection and to make better products for people. Not necessarily a bad thing but one requiring more attention than we, as a field, have given it.

Part II: Practice and Power

The 1990s ended with tremendous success and what seems to us now a calcifying disingenuousness. Collectively, we worked to address the demand we created in part by training new researchers from a huge range of backgrounds but also by trusting that tools and processes would compensate for uneven foundations or variations in skill. As a community, we glossed over the differentiations and power relations inherent to the value we worked so hard to produce. The ultimate effect was that one approach to research—one that privileged the fieldwork's technical side and immediate insights—became widely understood, almost expected, as *the* way to do user research, among practitioners and those who consume research in various parts of the enterprise. There were multiple important consequences. The labels of ethnography or user research, already interchangeable, came to stand for much less than they really should have. Consequently, we were less prepared as a community and as individuals to deal with the realities that were lurking right around the corner.

The difference between descriptive work and research that reflects an analytic organization is one of the persistent lines of distinction that characterizes ethnographic research not only from market research, but also from any work that attempts to locate its value in the technical act of collecting data *in situ*, from real people in real places. E-Lab's move to try to focus on frameworks was a struggle even inside the organization, largely because developing a framework is not a straightforward or easily transferable expertise. Finding that central meme, à la Geertz's 'deep play' in the Balinese Cockfight (1973), requires not only observational and analytic skills, but also an affinity for the work of abstraction and a considerable stock of relevant theory. Some people are better at this than others. Some people are better trained for it than others are. Some people are more interested in this kind of analysis than others are. This is true of any disciplined field, we would argue. The expertise involved in the development of a framework or an experience model established the high-value end of the work and, in a practical way, divided the community. In the consulting context, in particular, frameworks represented a level of strategic and organizational value and the capital associated with them. It was the development of frameworks that made ethnography relevant to the strategy arms of the organizations that contracted the work. In this sense, E-Lab was a microcosm of a phenomenon that would trouble the entire community going forward. What kind of work is strategic and what is not? What does that mean for value? Do we share the same skills? Should we?

At the close of the 1990s, the field was understood to be a valuable one, with a rather fuzzy outline starting to take shape at the intersection of the human sciences and design. There was a demonstrated ability to be responsive to a wide range of conditions. The strength of the field was evident not only in the number and range of businesses that populated this intersection but in the ways in which the client side—advertising agencies, consumer products manufacturers, retailers—began, broadly, to bring the expertise in-house. But it also showed signs of division and fracture that it continues to struggle with today. New demands of scale and speed, as well as simple maturation, brought out our organizational inexperience at E-Lab. We were not managers by training and avoided the kinds of confrontation and disappointment that addressing differences in value entailed. We let the differentiation (and its associated power relationships) inherent in multiple sources of value remain ambiguous. But that had to change, eventually, and it was the move to working as part of global corporations that provided the ground for lessons about growth and success. These were very different from how to talk about, how to 'sell' ethnographic work. In many important ways, the fact that the dot-com crash resulted in a diaspora, in a proliferation of practices, rather than any sort of diminished importance, is a testament to the effectiveness with which that first round of lessons was learned. Corporations have come to expect 'design research' or 'user understanding' in a far broader range of instances and settings than most of us foresaw.

But, unlike the early 1990s, when the definition of 'ethnographic' work was often in the hands of the people who had started practices, groups, or companies, by the early 2000s, there were expectations and established territories everywhere. For many researchers who arrived from practice-focused startups, as if from the provinces to the big city reality of multinational corporations, the different environment was a shock. The immigrant's process of adjusting and learning began again. The new world was inside corporations with established corporate cultures, rewards systems, and business processes. Organizations at the scale of an Intel (Bezaitis) or GfK (Robinson) or IBM or Microsoft are awash with realities that have nothing to do with experimentation and discovery, some of the values that marked E-Lab's and other early firms' defining moments. But these realities are crucial to succeed at the heart of big companies who have survived for quite a long while without ethnography and design.

In those big companies, well before the dot-com bust, social scientists of many stripes had already arrived and begun to work through (and around, in some cases) their organizational realities. The People and Practices Research (PaPR) team at Intel, launched in the mid-1990s and developed through persistence and struggle internal to itself and relative to the rest of the company, is one such example. The individuals who started there—Tony Salvador, John Sherry, and later Eric Dishman, Genevieve Bell, Ken Anderson, and others—had less experience overall with the startup as a path into applied work. Their early modalities of work at Intel were marked as much by working under the radar as they were by a corporate culture that rewarded brilliant individuals. PaPR's interlocutors were not designers but engineers, computer scientists, strategic planners, and marketers. The notion of teamwork at Intel included the business groups with which PaPR researchers worked. Nested inside an organization of scientists, individual expertise was an established path to success, precisely what had been overshadowed by E-Lab's emphasis on multidisciplinary experimentation and collaboration. Between 1998 and 2005, PaPR researchers demonstrated a savvy ability to adapt to their setting, and in a corporate reorganization in 2005, Salvador, Sherry, Dishman, and Bell moved into three business groups to lead groups of social scientists and designers in product group settings. Between 2006 and 2010, thanks in no small measure to the paths blazed by PaPR's first wave of researchers, PaPR became a bona fide R&D group rather than an organizational experiment.[1] In this timeframe, its charter was to conduct exploratory research at a global scale without the requirement of research questions that speak to the immediate and short-term needs of the business groups. This positioned PaPR in a manner that was distinct and complementary to its colleagues in the business groups, who are tied to their organization's focus on a product roadmap. Individuals in PaPR were hired for their demonstrated expertise because expertise is a requirement in a culture that fundamentally values science, but also

---

1. In 2010, PaPR was absorbed in its entirety by a larger investment inside Intel Labs called Interactions & Experience Research.

because that expertise enables them to change the terms of the work in applied settings. Demonstrating expertise is not the end game, it is a precondition for powerful exploratory research, and it is a precondition for practice in the real world (Bezaitis 2009). Deep domain expertise rooted in disciplinary history and training is that which allows a domain's fundamental terms to evolve into something new.

The slow shift away from a star culture in PaPR, where programs, as opposed to individuals, are the first and foremost highlight, was a difficult one, with both personal and professional origins. Academic training, for example, does not necessarily cultivate the values of collaboration, teamwork, and multidisciplinary exploration. Corporate cultures, particularly those indebted to scientific models for research, are guilty here, too. Reward and promotion systems still privilege the contributions of the individual scientist over the role played by an individual in the context of a group that works toward a shared set of program-level goals.

Individual expertise and collective practices both matter. Survival as an independent business or as a group inside a large corporation like Intel is a function of making one work well with the other. In small and in large corporations, individuals have to be visible as experts. Without experts, companies of any scale can't grow in new ways. Growth does not simply emerge from the messiness of practice. Messiness doesn't scale well. It is messy! Growth happens because individuals relinquish themselves to new influences and to the hard act of co-creation, but it also happens when individuals surface as leaders. Evolution in the value and role of a particular domain in an applied setting happens because the assumptions and values of that domain find new purpose and direction given their present circumstances. It is fair to say that expertise is a prerequisite to this kind of disciplinary evolution.

We are writing this at a time when ethnography's role inside many corporations and consultancies has an articulation that has been developed in the contexts of its application over the last two decades. 'User Experience' has become the expected and pervasive reference for the processes and techniques that feed qualitative, observational research into productive development processes. As the value of this kind of research has been linked to key deliverables and processes, business groups allow for much less exploratory work and become committed to—indeed reliant upon—known ways of doing the work. New drivers—efficiency, cost-savings, the native language of the business group—begin to surface as priorities over the need to use the human sciences to discover the right terms, tools, and theories for doing the work over time as these same businesses change. This is not just a question of new techniques generated by the truckload by design and innovation consultancies and presented annually at conferences like EPIC. This is a question of fundamental disciplinary evolution that accompanies the changing business climate, shapes it, and is shaped by it. These are questions of survival, and if we do not pave the way to what happens next on our own, corporations will take the liberty to do it for us. If history provides any lesson here, they will do it by continuing to absorb and to reproduce the 'best of' and do away with the rest.

We need to begin to scrutinize the constraints in which we work now and to consider explicitly how these contexts will continue to shape the value of the human sciences in industry. Just as importantly, we need to ask ourselves what are the values that are at the core of our practices, individual and collective? Good questions, obviously. But how to start?

Part III: Errant Sons, Wayward Daughters

Broad acceptance of 'ethnographic' work and the 'user-centeredness' of design and innovation means that demand, which was formerly a struggle to create, is now seemingly entrenched across companies large and small. The work of inventing a field seems to have given way to the yeoman-like application of method, and the trend away from an idealist stance toward a practical one seems to have accelerated. Outsiders have become assimilated. Of course, this demand won't stay entrenched for long if the field does not develop. Easy, oversimplified approaches will continue to evolve toward commoditized tool kits and lose any critical differentiation they have from other market and consumer research approaches. Like many established immigrants, we worry about the future of our inheritors; we worry about losing the old ways even as we celebrate the success of the next generation.

In the first part of this chapter, we talked about the role played by the early and realistic need of the field to explicitly connect the work we do to real outcomes and literal value. We did not argue that this was a wrong turn but that we are probably now at a point where we need to explicitly counterbalance it with a new emphasis on values, on purpose, on 'good work.'

In the second part of the chapter, we reflected on another phenomenon that seems to us broad but unacknowledged: the touchy and difficult issue of differentiation of skill and expertise among practitioners, and how moving the locus of expertise off of individuals and onto methodology perhaps ameliorated the tension that comes with connection of organizational influence to stratification of expertise. As strange as it may seem, these two very different impulses have together enabled a kind of conceptual drift in the purpose, values, and dynamic of applied interpretive social sciences. We'd like to see a correction to that course.

We propose to start with two practical but overarching organizing principles here, each fundamental to redirecting the growth of our field. The first is the need to acknowledge distinctions in kinds and levels of expertise. The second is the need to articulate the values of organizational entities, practice groups, and individuals explicitly.

The first depends in large part on the externalization of knowledge and the difficult recognitions that doing that well will entail. In our working practices, across two decades and seven major, growing practices, the hardest transition for a social scientist or humanities-trained researcher seemed to be the externalization required in a high-communication, multidisciplinary practice group. From fieldwork through to the creation of audience-destined materials, this is a very public process and setting. But making personal knowledge public is what makes the work work. And it also becomes the ground on which distinctions of contribution, fit, and expertise are played out. It is, in fact, a risky place to work, and mistakes or missteps are often high profile and high consequence. We think some practices have managed to inculcate these habits of public work and community very well. And we think that as a field, we can collectively examine what works toward this end and what does not. That would be far more profitable, eventually and to all, than ever more case studies claiming the invention of new methods.

The second, the values question, is one that we think has not been addressed. But the corporate tide around the issue is turning, and it will become not only easier, but likely incumbent on practices to be clearer and more explicit about what they are doing, to what end they use their various methodological and analytic tools, who they speak for, and to be able to explain the choices they have made, and how their work delivers on the expectations entailed by the values themselves. Corporate social responsibility, hard choices about environmental and social consequences, has made values in and of organizations a critical topic, though still quite difficult to address. And at the individual level, the recent emergence of studies in positive psychology on the notion of 'good work' has shown that innovative, complex responses to wicked problems are more likely to come from a kind of engagement that can only come when individual values are an explicit part of the activity (Csikszentmihalyi, Damon, and Gardner 2001).

Part IV: Expertise and Practice

As a manager of a practice, responsible to senior management for the effectiveness of groups, questions of expertise and practice abound: How do we take advantage and build momentum around inventive experiments by individuals? How do we create space for individuals to flourish and survive in the settings in which they work? How do we apply expertise to shape practice in the settings in which we operate? How do we acknowledge different kinds of strengths and deal directly with the ways in which corporations value these strengths differently?

Reflected in these questions are a very wide range of purposes and intentions that span the personal goals and commitments of an individual leader to the interests of the corporation to the growth of a field that exceeds the boundaries of any one place. This returns us to the importance of individual expertise, domain training, specialization, and individual contribution. The point here is not that it never matters. There is space for experts and expertise. But a collection of individuals with lots of expertise doesn't constitute a practice, and in such an absence, there's limited basis for the evolution of the work. All you can hope for is that new experts will come to replace the old expertise that is no longer needed, which is the blueprint for a model of work that many of us left in the first place. If we intend to stay in some form in the world of applied, industrial research, focusing on practice is a matter of survival.

A key challenge then is to work that balance out, the balance between individual training and knowledge, and that of the work created across a group of individuals in a business—the two key characteristics of the 'hereness' of our work. Expertise itself is balanced against the commonality and identity that is forged, again in very particular senses, in practice. Across disciplines, practice emerges. Over time, practice grows. Across practices, the field can grow; but only if knowledge is shared, sources are acknowledged, individual threads are recognized, and the collective effort is seen in both its parts and as a whole. This is how we create a history. It is this history that helps us decide, actively, where we go next.

Part V: The Value in Being Explicit about Values

Finally, we need to come all the way back around to where we started: the connection between the work we do and the 'places' where we have come to do it—the worlds of design, engineering, product development, brand, and business strategy. The purpose of these disciplines and divisions is to create new 'things' (a term we use broadly to include material as well as non-material entities such as 'identities'), and the initial impulse to find research that could provide a more instructive basis for making those things comes from those disciplines. So the research work has always had, in this venue, an instrumental end, no matter how idealistically any individual researcher may have framed the larger intent (us included; see Robinson's *Capitalist Tool* apologia during the height of the boom, 2001) of understanding behavior, experience, work. This history is crucial: for, as the field expands, interested researchers continue to arrive, unaware of this fundamental responsibility to getting something new made, to making some sort of change take place, and begin to work as if it is enough to do research. The point is that this was never enough.

That is not a bad thing. One way of understanding the work that we do, in all its variations, is that we look at a present set of 'what is' conditions and develop a knowledge-supported imagination of what "could be." The truth of good design work has always been somewhere between complete invention and acknowledgment of inevitability. Probably the wrestling with inevitability, and getting around it, is the impulse that most directly connects design and research. It seems to us that the early phase of the rise of human-centered design, design research, and ethnography in applied settings gave us a more nuanced, more complex understanding of the 'now.' It established in industries the idea of understanding the individual, social, and cultural influences on why people think the way they do, why they use what they use, and why they need what they (think they) need as important bases for good design.

Less obviously, the hand-in-glove work between the two fields makes researchers complicit in a conscious attempt to shape the future, not just in understanding the present. Design, by definition, involves an alternative, always somewhat subversive (Marcuse 1978) plan for the future. When research is twinned to that effort, when—to stretch the application of Jean Piaget's famous title—understanding is invention, the research that informs the design bears a significant part of the responsibility for those options and those limitations. If the work we do makes a particular alternate future more likely, that means directly affecting other folks' choices. We have made a choice about what others 'ought' to do, which is exactly what we sign up for when we undertake to do ethnographic research in applied settings. So, we have a responsibility to articulate why we are making those choices. How and what we have weighed in providing that framing advice to our development colleagues.

We use the term 'good design' almost reflexively as evaluation and often as explanation. When something is tabbed as 'good design' (by a magazine or an award from a professional association), we agree or not in the instance, but we accept, usually tacitly, that good design is different from indifferent design or bad design. Despite that, we do not usually think of 'good' in its moral or ethical sense, as in 'good versus evil' (unless we are from Google). Positive, thoughtful, or responsible design has included in it not just a final function or form, but a large number of distinctions understood and choices about those distinctions made in a particular light, with particular reasons for them. A child's toy, perhaps, can be safe or unsafe, educational or mindless, responsibly made or using the worst but cheapest materials available. It is not a toy made to be bad, but in each of the moments where choice matters, the choice made has been, in the current context at least, toward something less than as good as it could have been.

So the values that shape the making of things are not simply those of the individuals involved in the project(s). Corporations like to act as if these choices are not personal, which makes it easy to ignore the idea that values are being expressed throughout a seemingly 'rational' process. That does not mean that the issue of responsibility goes away. But where and how do we get values back into the work, especially if that might just mean conflict with the disposition of value in a business process (such as innovation, product development, communications, or business strategies)?

Just as a practice is an important locus for the externalization and evolution of expertise, it is also, we think, at the right scale and locus to ask, forcefully, "to what end are we doing this work?" with an emphasis on the "we." There are, of course, broad issues such as privacy standards where the articulation of values needs to take place across the practical manifestations of the many institutions (corporate and academic) that inform applied work. But clearly articulated values also provide the basis that a particular practice at a particular intersection of knowledge, individuals, intentions, and possibilities can use to orient locally, to nurture identity, and to push back against the limited and often narrowly construed sets of goals that a larger enterprise 'wants' in any given year. Of course, the answer to the question "to what end are we doing this work" changes as a function of the audience and the location of the audience—management versus development, for example. This has deep implications for the kinds of stories that we tell and how values must necessarily shift to address specific individuals who are responsible for different kinds of decisions.

We are not arguing here for any particular set of values, only for the conscious and explicit articulation of them in, by, and for working practices; an explicit awareness of what we are doing, with whom, and for what end. We believe that this notion is supported by a distinct push toward explicit values and away from a sort of corporate agnosticism afoot in some of the most interesting work in areas such as corporate social responsibility and environmental and social activism. The World Wildlife Foundation's Tom Compton, in a 2008 report entitled *Weathercocks and Signposts*, eloquently critiqued the predominant "marketing approach" to "motivating environmentally-friendly behaviour change" by arguing that "any adequate strategy for tackling environmental challenges will demand engagement with the values that underlie the decisions we make." Compton makes a nice distinction between the figure of "weathercocks" ("weathervanes" to American English speakers), or indicators of where or how things are going in the present (e.g., percentage of households recycling), with the figure of the "signpost," which tells us where to go, and often, how far it is or how difficult it is going to be to get there. Giving us guidance on getting somewhere is more important, and more difficult, than telling us how we are doing now. In the basic notion of design as the work of planning, how to get to 'next' from 'here,' we believe that values, as much as 'additional value' or 'experience,' should be the forward anchor of that arc.

The conceptual figure of 'signposts' is something that may have the potential to become part of how any research practice materializes its work, much in the way that 'frameworks,' 'experience models,' or 'customer journeys' have become boundary objects for ethnography and design. Creating signposts entails more active constructs than the more generally descriptive idiom of EPIC-type work usually affords a research practice. What makes a particular direction or evolution for any new 'thing' better than another is not an inquiry that can be bracketed out of a primary research question. Most applied ethnographic work brackets questions of form, engineering, marketing, and distribution in the pursuit of interesting models of how things work now. But when we take what 'ought' to happen into account, where a product or a techno-human 'ecology' should go, and the role the inquirers have in marking that way, become primary research objects themselves.

And in this is the connection between our two bits of proselytizing. The importance of rethinking the work as the creation of both a body of knowledge and an engagement with what that body of knowledge might be used for. Not to claim that all outcomes are foreseeable, but that they cannot be managed unless you are clear as to what the practice is after. This clarity needs to live at the heart of our commitments inside the organizations in which we work.

Immigrants' tales often hinge on the connections and differences between generations, and on the ways in which values are maintained or how they change. What it means to fully inhabit a new country is in the new ways of realizing the original 'things could be different' impulse. The first decade or so of concentrated work has made a next generation of work possible. But techniques and methodologies are not the best measure of change, nor the standard of innovation; they are a means to measure our ability to sustain ourselves in the present context, a component of necessary expertise. If we bound the field (or a practice bounds itself) by how it does its work rather than by what it is trying to accomplish, we have missed the point, and the opportunity.

In social as well as business contexts, values have always driven change. Deep humanism underlies both the work of social and human scientists as well as our colleagues in design and development disciplines. But we cannot assume their nature or their applicability. Values, like all human frameworks, are tractable things, and they are changed by the things we make and by the way we make things. Researchers and designers can, by making articulation and externalization an everyday part of their practice, keep the goal of making things better a realistic ideal.

References

Bezaitis, M. (2009), "Practice, Products, and the Future of Ethnographic Work," in M. Cotton and S. Pulman-Jones (eds.), *EPIC 2009: Taking Care of Business. Proceedings of the EPIC 2009*, 92–107, Washington, DC: American Anthropological Society.

Cain, J. T. (1998), "Experience-Based Design: Toward a Science of Artful Business Innovation," *Design Management Journal*, Fall: 10–4.

Compton, T. (2008), "Weathercocks and Signposts: The Environment Movement at a Crossroads." World Wildlife Federation UK. Available online: www.wwf.org.uk/filelibrary/pdf/weathercocks_report2.pdf (accessed February 2, 2016).

Csikszentmihalyi, M., W. Damon and H. Gardner (2001), *Good Work: Where Excellence and Ethics Meet*, New York: Basic Books.

Geertz, C. (1973), "Deep Play: Notes on the Balinese Cockfight," in C. Geertz (ed.), *The Interpretation of Cultures*, 412–53, New York: Basic Books.

Lynch, K. (1970), *The Image of the City*, Cambridge, MA: MIT Press.

Marcuse, H. (1978), *The Aesthetic Dimension: Toward a Critique of Marxist Aesthetics*, Urbana & Chicago: Beacon Press.

Robinson, R. E. (1993), "What to Do with a Human Factor: A Manifesto of Sorts," *American Center for Design Journal: New Human Factors*, 7 (1): 63–73.

Robinson, R. E. (1994a), "The Origin of Cool Things," in *Design That Packs a Wallop: Understanding the Power of Strategic Design. Proceedings of the ACD Conference on Strategic Design*, 5–10, New York: American Center for Design.

Robinson, R. E. (1994b), "Making Sense of Making Sense: Frameworks and Organizational Perception," *Design Management Journal*, 5 (1): 8–15.

Robinson, R. E. (1998), "A Cure for the Black Box Blues," *Perspective*, Summer.

Robinson, R. E. (2001), "Capitalist Tool, Humanist Tool," *Design Management Journal*, 12 (2): 15–19.

Robinson, R. E. (2009), "'Let's Bring It Up to B Flat': What Style Offers Applied Ethnographic Work," in M. Cotton and S. Pulman-Jones (eds.), *EPIC 2009: Taking Care of Business. Proceedings of the EPIC 2009*, 92–107, Washington: American Anthropological Society.

Robinson, R. E. and J. P. Hackett (1997), "Creating the Conditions of Creativity," *Design Management Journal*, 8 (4): 10–6.

Robinson, R. E. and J. R. Nims (1996), "Insight into What Really Matters," *Innovation*, Summer: 18–21.

Suchman, L. (2000), *Anthropology as "Brand": Reflections on Corporate Anthropology*, Lancaster: Lancaster University.

Walters, J. and H. Gardner (1988), "The Crystallizing Experience: Discovering an Intellectual Gift," in R. Sternberg and J. Davidson (eds.), *Conceptions of Giftedness*, 306–31, Cambridge, UK: Cambridge University Press.

5 Poetic Observation: What Designers Make of What They See

Jane Fulton Suri

From designers we ask for a designed world that has meaning beyond the resolution of purely functional needs. We ask for poetry and subtlety that make sense—not just by fitting in with the culture and environment—but by adding a new dimension to it.

Design and Observation

What does it mean to bring a design sensibility to looking, noticing, and learning about people, places, and things in the world? This chapter is about the importance of ensuring that design teams make time and space for designers to explore, to see, and otherwise sense the world in their own way, without the limitation of adhering strictly to some formal process or plan of 'research.'[1] It begins to explore answers to the question: What is their own way?

Design and innovation are creative endeavors that defy entirely rational and linear processes. Human intelligence, skill, and leaps of imagination are required to grapple with multiple variables and uncertainties to make future sense. And, as designers, we care about this future sense in more than a pragmatic way; we care also about its poetry.

---

1. The author is grateful to clients of the projects, design team members, and other colleagues who reviewed and helped refine this text, and especially to the featured designers for sharing their inspiring stories.

Social Science Perspective

Twenty years ago, it was rare for designers to even talk with human and social scientists, never mind to employ their theories and methods. These days, it is not unusual to find psychologists and anthropologists among designers, sharing and adapting methods, integrating insights, generating and evolving ideas and implementing them. Many progressive organizations, ranging from Nokia to Nestlé to the US Centers for Disease Control and Prevention, have embraced human-centered design research in addressing business and social issues.

As a result, the practice of observing and interviewing people in their natural habitats has become widely established in design. So much so that nowadays it is the social sciences—with their focus on people, context, behavior, and subsequent insight about motivation and meaning—that largely dominate the conversation about how observation informs and inspires design. Known in business circles as 'ethnographic-style research,' this practice of observation has become familiar to buyers of design services as a valuable form of 'consumer insight.' As *Business Week* noted in "The Science of Desire":

> *Now, as more and more businesses re-orient themselves to serve the consumer, ethnography has entered primetime. [It] provides a richer understanding of consumers than does traditional research. [Closely] observing people where they live and work, say executives, allows companies to zero in on their customers' unarticulated desires. (Ante and Edwards 2006)*

Certainly ethnographic-style observation can provide inspiration and grounding for innovation and design. It increases our confidence that ideas will be culturally relevant, respond to real needs, and hence be more likely to have the desired social or market impact.

But for design and designers there's much more to observation than that.[2] As we shall see, successful designers are keenly sensitive to particular aspects of what is going on around them, and these observations inform and inspire their work, often in subtle ways.

Now feels like a critical moment. As businesses and organizations increasingly embrace design thinking and human-centered approaches, it feels important to understand more about how observation really works in design. Am I arguing that a human/consumer-oriented focus is not important? Far from it. But there are other equally important, less celebrated, and less obviously logical ways that observation contributes to design. Being less predictable, less direct, and more subtle, there is a risk that the opportunity for some kinds of observation will be neglected in the planning and conduct of design programs and in our appreciation of designers.

---

2. The mirror image for anthropologists is that there is much more to ethnography than looking at people in context to provide insight about their needs and desires.

Myriad Ways to Look and See

At the outset of many projects we do not even know what we need to know or what we are looking for. We know only that we need to fulfill our promise to find or give appropriate shape to opportunities—whether that is for product, service, space, strategy, media, or organization. Even so, design teams often find themselves pressed to create and follow a detailed plan for research and exploration. There is no doubt that design projects benefit from constraints, including constraints on the time to explore, to hone intuitions, to seek inspiration. But following too tight a prescription for exploration can be counterproductive.

One can make good bets about fruitful activities: "Let's map the competition, explore metaphors, interview extreme users, consider connotations of the brand, examine cultural context, visit the factory and saleroom, observe production processes." But these activities, often built into 'the design process,' are valuable to the extent that they inform and inspire the imagination of designers. Designers need to interpret what they see (and otherwise sense) in ways that will lead to design outcomes. They need to be able to 'make something' of their observations, whether design strategies, principles, or concepts relevant to the project brief.

Interpreting what we see is both a personal and a social process. In our own individual ways, all of us pay attention to what is meaningful and interesting to us. While we might guess that certain activities will be fruitful, not everyone sees the same things or finds them equally useful. When working in a team, what is inspiring and relevant to some will be less so, or not at all, to others. This diversity and richness of perspectives is in itself powerful. Exploration in design is not a search for absolute truth, but for insight about the nature of the challenge and for generative ways to frame it. Indeed, one of the benefits of diverse perspectives is that they can help others see situations in a new light, challenge conventional interpretation, and reveal previously unappreciated possibilities.

Many factors play a role in determining what individuals notice in the world. Everyone's outlook is unique, but one factor shaping it is the cultural lens shared by people from the same discipline—each with its own traditions of perspectives and frameworks for looking. George Nelson's primer *How to See* (1977), for example, presents a collection of photographs with the explicit intent of helping us to appreciate visual design qualities of the world around us; *Everyday Engineering* (Burroughs and IDEO 2007) invites us to view our surroundings through a particular kind of engineering lens. Flickr and other Internet photo-sharing services offer representations literally through a variety of individual lenses. Similarly, visual blogs allow individuals to post what is observed and interesting to them in their everyday world.

These examples express particular and personal ways of appreciating and looking at the world. But how do such perceptions influence design output? Here follow four examples in which designers have seen the world in their own ways and brought that perspective to their work.

1. Inspiration Everywhere

The first example illustrates a particular sensibility about objects and their context. My colleague Gen Suzuki is an acutely perceptive industrial designer, internationally recognized in his native Japan as well as in the United Kingdom and in the United States. For Gen, the relationship of objects to their context is not only a source of fascination, influencing what he notices in the world around him, but also a source of design inspiration, affecting how he approaches the design problem. Gen captures, and is captivated by, instances of interesting or unusual, even humorous, juxtaposition and congruence between things.

These are examples of what Gen notices and observations that he finds personally inspiring. His perceptions are not related to functional attributes; the connections have a whimsical, playful quality. They are not instances that support a preconceived theme (see Figures 5.1 and 5.2). Gen said, "I took the photo of the subway wall before knowing what it might mean. I thought it was beautiful, but I didn't know why I thought it was good."

5.1 Billboard without an advertisement. This caught Gen Suzuki's eye as he passed it in a Tokyo subway station. He understood later that what intrigued him was the boundary between the object and its environment. © *Gen Suzuki*

5.2 The coffee Gen Suzuki was served on a summit in the Alps; the whipped cream on top was the shape of the mountain he had just climbed. © *Gen Suzuki*

Gen's pictures are reflections of his outlook, his observations, and thoughts at play independent of specific project work. His appreciation for these moments is instantaneous, and the subtle influence on his approach to design essentially intuitive. But, as he has reflected upon them and why they are personally inspirational, he has come to understand how this lens influences his approach to design execution. What is significant for him in both these images is the awareness of the object (the advertisement, the cup of coffee) in the context of its place and in relationship to other things around it. He is almost unconsciously attracted to what he calls "blurring boundary" in which objects possess a quality (material, visual, or spatial) that connects them in a meaningful way to other objects or the environment around them.

As a designer, he is excited by the opportunity to create new objects that live in more intentional harmony with their surroundings. For example, his pen stand was inspired by a similarly incidental observation of pens on his friend's worktop held in a stack of tape (see Figure 5.3). Gen's pen stand is conceived not as a container in isolation, or even just in relation to pens, but in relation to other objects on the desk whose form and negative internal shape stack to create a container of perfect dimensions. Gen refers to his pen stand approach as "overlapping boundaries."

5.3 Gen Suzuki's design for a pen stand was inspired by his observation of rolls of tape stacked on a friend's desk. © *Gen Suzuki*

At a functional level, this is an effective solution but, more than that, it embodies an emotional relevance. It is a design that elicits a smile, a sense of recognition and rightness, from the subtle harmony between the object and its context.

This example illustrates the value of an approach to observation that involves respecting and reflecting upon a personal and intuitive point of view. By noting instances in the world that capture his imagination—valuing and sharing them simply because he finds them beautiful, intriguing, or amusing—Gen enriches his design intuitions. By observing in this way, he learns about how particular qualities evoke a sense of beauty, intrigue, and amusement. He brings this sensitivity to his designs, evoking such experiences for other people.

2. Crystallizing Insight

This second example is about an unplanned observation that helped distill a set of design principles, in this case for a new bank space and service concept. The client company, a global financial institution, wanted to redesign bank branches to support a desirable experience for their customers in Central and Eastern Europe, where many citizens either saw no value in using banks or had a history of unpleasant interactions with them: "What would make people walk into a branch, and how could their visit feel like a positive one?"

This was a project where it clearly made sense to observe interactions between bank staff and customers. This would help to uncover culturally appropriate ways to encourage the desired relationships and experiences. Indeed, the design team met with customers and staff in ten cities and observed their behavior in twenty-five branches and fifty-plus analogous sites. These observations revealed how staff behaviors and spatial cues had given rise to an unwelcoming feeling for banking customers. Ultimately, what was learned led to a radically new concept for the branch layout and service model to better support staff and customer interactions. All this sounds as if the design emerged by following a predictable and rational plan, but Annette Diefenthaler, insightful and culture-curious design researcher on the Munich-based team, recalled (see Figure 5.4):

5.4 This image of a shoe store in a Russian mall became a powerful metaphor for the simple and honest 'old world' offering to Eastern European consumers. © *Annette Diefenthaler*

We were in Nizhny Novgorod and had had a late interview. On the way back, I asked the cab driver to drop me at this low-end shopping center that we had been passing by. I was just curious to see what that'd be like.

What I saw was a multistory hall with many small stalls. It all looked rather improvised. What amazed me was the way things were sold there: One stall sold only blue jeans. The next one sold only black pants. The next one had light colored skirts; another one had black shoes only. The way the goods were presented was incredibly straightforward: wall, hooks, black shoes. No frills. Now, we had been looking at many shopping centers that were all full of Western brands, creating all sorts of experiences around products. That was the new world, the new Russia.

And then there was this. And while at first sight you might dismiss that as depressing or boring, I realized that there was something very honest and straightforward in this way of selling goods. Customer experience? Not here. You want black shoes? You get black shoes. No fuss about it. There were no additional promises around the product: A pair of shoes is a pair of shoes—a shape, a type of material, a color, a sole. That enabled customers to clearly evaluate and compare the product itself without any distractions. There is an element of empowering the customer to make an informed and focused choice. In contrast, many of the 'new world' shopping centers offered a shopping 'experience'—meaning that goods were not only goods, but were mixed with all kinds of promises around them. So it was not just about buying the shoes but the coolness of the model wearing them on the poster, the glamour of the brand, etc.

Telling that story back to the team and relating it to some interviewees' comments led to one of our big learnings about Eastern Europe: In their 'old' world, things were super straightforward. The 'new' world brought about all these experiences. But that's not necessarily what people wanted—they wanted an honest offering.

This insight very much informed our thinking about what trustworthy and honest means in banking and translated into branch design: the layout, the service model, and in making suggestions about the product offer. It was the photo of the black shoes on the wall in our team space that kept reminding us.

Annette's chance observation was powerful. It helped the team make concrete sense of what they were discovering in a more abstract way in their interviews: Since people were already reluctant to even go to the bank, they weren't in for "an experience." Like the shoe store, the bank was a means to an end—customers were there either to make a transaction or to ask a question. As Annette put it: "They wanted the TV set, not the loan."

The team understood that the simpler the new branch experience was, the more it would engender a sense of trust. So in designing, their guiding principle was to make things visible, clear, and as tangible as possible. The new space is divided into two distinct parts—one for transactions and one for consultation—inspired by the idea of the visit as a means to an end. The new design also literally increases transparency, opening up a view of the branch interior from the street, so that passersby can see what is going on inside.

Annette's spontaneous curiosity yielded a dramatic observation that helped clarify an important design theme for the project. This was not random inspiration. Given the right catalyst, a designer's mind will process rich observations, stories, and insights from the field and crystallize these into design direction. What is important is to make sure we leave room in project plans, in daily schedules, and in designers' heads for this kind of intuitive curiosity to play its magic.

3. Contrasting Culture

At times, cultural immersion is the best way of informing design intuition. This example involves designers taking largely unstructured time to soak up an experience directly and multisensorially, using contrast and conversation to make sense of impressions.

Havaianas wanted to design a product extension for the brand. Their iconic flip-flops are enjoyed and revered around the world as a representation of Brazilian culture. They wanted to offer a range of other accessories that shared the same spirit, starting with a series of bags.

What would these bags have to look and feel like to be consistent with the Havaianas brand? The design team wanted first to understand the brand's tight connection to Brazil. Obviously, a good way to explore this was to go and spend time in Brazil. Less obvious was what Miguel Cabra, the exuberant and reflective Barcelona-educated design leader on the project, told me about the team's process:

"We had to go to India to understand Brazil," and "we really didn't talk to anyone about bags!" He explains:

Europe and Brazil are different in so many ways, from culture to social structure to weather; so much so that it was hard to learn deeply about Brazil because we didn't have anything to compare it to, and that's how the idea of India came. We thought it might be useful to visit another (but different) third world country just so we could figure out what really belonged to the identity of Brazil. We went to Bangalore because it's a rapidly emergent city. There are a lot of big companies, and they co-exist alongside a traditional and poor environment, and that reminded us of the contrasts of Brazil, where you can have the most amazing mansions next to a favela [slum].

To be honest, we had no idea how useful the trip to India would be; we went because we had an intuition. We did no formal observations whatsoever, but we did talk with a lot of people and observed with a very curious eye. It was after that trip to Bangalore that we could really begin to understand the essence of the Brazilian way of life. On the plane trip back we talked about the differences and similarities in what we'd seen in India and in Brazil. To our developed European eyes some things had seemed to be essentially "of Brazil" before we'd been to Bangalore, but were common to both cultures. A relevant example: One of the things that we saw a lot in Brazil was the "simple bag," a cloth closed by knotting the corners diagonally,

*two and two. But it turned out that this is just a general poverty-solution for carrying things—
you can see the exact same bag in Bangalore and São Paulo.*

*But there were differences; one was about color. Everybody knows that Brazil is a colorful
country. Warm countries tend to have less fear of colors than cool ones, and going to Bangalore helped us be much more concrete on how Brazil understands color differently. Color for
Brazilians is not only decoration; it's a way for them to make a statement of their hope, their
optimism, and their rebellion against their poverty. It's the cheapest way of showing their attitude and enhancing the places where they live and work.*

The team's observations of color in Brazil were captured in photographs that directly influenced
the color palette they curated in designing the bags (see Figure 5.5). And their observations of "the
Brazilian way" influenced not only elements of the design, but also the way the team worked (see
Figures 5.6 and 5.7):

*After we finished our research process we started as we normally do: ideating, brainstorming,
and sketching. But it didn't work, the results felt fake to us. We realized that in Brazil we had
seen that Brazilians don't 'design' if we understand design as the planning process before the
execution; they are much more intuitive about creating things, they don't sketch out a solution*

5.5 Images documenting observed uses and meaning of color in Brazil. © *Katie Clark*

5.6 The overloaded dolly; a typical sight in Brazil that inspired the idea of a bag that is not only a container but can also carry things bigger than itself. © *Katie Clark*

and then build it, they look first to what they have and build something out of it, and that is what prototyping is about. So we started to shift our strategy to a more "hands on" approach, which made a major difference. One of our design principles was 1 + 1 = 3, which is about taking two things that don't belong together, decontextualizing them, and building something completely new. This is how the "zip bag" was created—two "pockets" stitched together that create a third open compartment for your towel or yoga mat. A bag that can carry bigger things than the bag itself, which is also something we observed in Brazil—see my picture of an overloaded dolly.

Ultimately, for our things to feel real we had to adopt the way Brazilians approach creativity; we became non-designers, we became makers, and we substituted "brainstorm" for "hand storms." It was like being an actor in a way, like being Brazilian for a while.

5.7 The Havaianas zip bag embodying how expressions of color, gestures, and versatility play out in Brazilian culture. © *Katie Clark*

What the team learned about the Havaianas brand came about through a deep connection that the designers made with relevant aspects of Brazilian life. As Miguel says:

> When a brand blends so much with the culture of a country you can't just research around the people and the product, you need to really immerse yourself. You have to be there because, before you go, you don't know what you need to know or even what you can know.

In this kind of immersion there is process, though it's not strict:

> It's "look and think aloud about what you saw." So we notice the prevalence of color, materials, forms, and we ask ourselves: Is there a discernible pattern here? What are the similarities? If so, what are the formal rules behind it? Are there in fact patterns that you might call cultural design principles?

The process, the talking about it, proposing and testing the patterns you see, thinking about what that would mean for how we design, is probably more important than the input actually.

And there is design discipline about what to look out for:

Yes, curiosity about stuff like color, materials, marks that people make, and the behaviors that these encourage and oblige . . . but not to describe, rather to respond to with something new. To reinterpret. For instance, I'm interested in how particular objects oblige you to behave in certain ways that then characterize a whole body language and choreography for events or activities, and how these too have cultural meaning. So when we thought about bags, we could imagine a Scandinavian precision and economy of motion, postures, and gestures for putting things in a bag, snapping it closed, picking it up, positioning it on your body. This would affect the way you engage with it, wear it, carry it, take it off, put it down, that would be influenced by the materials of the body and strap, the enclosures, fittings, very differently from a Brazilian way. For Havaianas we created a rubbery strap making a bouncy bag that walks with you, with your stride.

4. Intriguing Essence

This example illustrates the power of a designer's eye for visual metaphor, and respecting such intuition despite the lack of an immediate rationale for its significance.

The resourceful and imaginative visual thinker and storyteller, Jason Robinson, was the lead industrial designer who developed a suite of advanced instruments for spinal surgery. Looking back on the project, he recalls two significant visual experiences that he had during the course of the project. Sharing his thought process, and wary of over-rationalizing, Jason begins by describing the second event:

In considering what materials and finishes to use, I was drawn to the look of surgical tools that were hand machined from stainless steel and anodized to withstand autoclaving. The clean precision of the matt silver metal was inspiring to me, and I wanted to explore how that would work with some of the forms I'd developed. At the same time, I was intrigued by the look of these tools in black—sophisticated and serious. Martin and I were at my computer reviewing the CAD [computer-aided design] models on the screen, looking at them first in silver. We wanted to see the same tool in black, and to avoid running a whole new rendering cycle—that would've taken too long—I selected a rectangular area and re-rendered only that part of the image. What we were looking at then was a matt silver tool with a black central section, where the rectangular area was projected onto the tool. Martin said, "that's cool!" It was.

It was an accidental result, and his reaction to it purely intuitive. Nevertheless, he felt it was something to explore further. As he developed the design, Jason remained intrigued by the tension between the contrast of that black element projected onto the silver semi-organic form: "But, why is that cool?" he kept asking himself.

I remember thinking, "It doesn't fit; it doesn't reference any other line in the form, like a part line or something. There's a conflict between this shape, the square, and all the other aspects of the form. All the other aspects and elements of the form were driven by logical and practical reasons, either ergonomic or to encase functional elements. The square exists on another plane. It's defiant!"

My mind went back to our first visit to the O.R. [operating room], the impressive scene of these dramatic operations, where surgeons were doing incredible things with absolutely no room for error. This was when I saw the connection. My mind made a link between the square and this epic thing that the surgeons were doing. It was the same link that I'd made between a pair of X-rays I'd noticed lying side by side in the O.R., and that had a very powerful effect on me.

The X-rays were of a spine, one before and one after surgery. The before image was anno-tated boldly with the surgeon's notes and decisive pen marks in red lines indicating that the spine should be set to this or that angle and where various bits of hardware should be placed. The after image showed the spine with all the hardware in place. It had a very strong graphic quality—anything metal really pops on an X-ray, so you see this burned-out white of the sur-geon's work wrestling with the X-ray soft gray and black of the organic form of the spine. Here was the soft curvature of this living, growing spine, with a will to grow in its own uncorrected way, and the surgeon's mark-ups that expressed the will and determination of science and tech-nology to correct it. That's what these tools are all about: going in and doing something that the body really doesn't want to do; and the surgeon is creating order and structure, straightness and rigidity. It was like the struggling of two wills. Defiant. So there it was: the moral of the story. It was there visually in that square element superimposed on the tool. It had that same sense of uncompromising dominance as the graphical characteristics of the X-rays.

What was striking for me was that there were lots of fascinating things all over that (oper-ating) room, but it was those X-rays, that dramatic diptych, which had caught my attention. I understood that they were important, I'd photographed and remembered them, but their significance really only emerged over time. Linking it to the black square projected on the rendering was not really a conscious process for me.

But then, after making that connection, and having it validated by other designers and the client, I felt confident that I finally had the components of the story that would explain why this apparently random black area was important to me and how it spoke of what was special about these tools. The design intent was to make these tools unique and stand out as world-class. We wanted to make them recognizable as high-end and communicate that they are "special tools, for special things, done by special people." It is a simple detail but one that pops out and says "something important and different is going on here."

What was initially a fleeting but conscious recognition of an interesting visual metaphor that he observed in the operating room ended up driving the signature look for the final design (see Figure 5.8). This kind of intuitive process is undoubtedly encouraged by the opportunity to observe but not guaranteed by any particular structured plan. "What was important," Jason said, "was to have the physical and mental space for all these things to be seen, and explored, and welded together over a period of time."

In Conclusion

What is common among these stories? Each in their own way, the four designers were inspired by their personal observation of the world and saw beauty, poetry, or meaning in something that

5.8 The final rendering for the surgical tool: It embodies the signature contrast of rigid and organic visual elements. © *Katie Clark*

others hadn't seen. At times, the inspiration was deliberately sought—by taking a trip to Brazil, to India, or to an operating room—while other times it came as the result of chance curiosity in a Russian shopping mall or while vacationing in the Alps. In each case, their insights emerged from activity and from thinking that was not part of a highly formalized research plan. But their approach was certainly not without discipline or rigor. Each case involved a similar pattern: a focused curiosity coupled with exposure to relevant contexts, attention to elements that invited intrigue, visual documentation and revisiting these records later, percolation and talking about what was significant with team members and clients, and storytelling and exploration of design choices and details.

Whether creating products, apparel, services, or spaces, these designers display a particular sensitivity to the physical, metaphorical, and cultural values inherent in context, forms, and materials and how these are experienced. Perhaps, as makers themselves, they have a heightened appreciation for the kind of elements in the environment that they can manipulate and control: formal relationships between sensory qualities, such as color, mass, layout, and texture, and dynamic qualities of feedback, rhythm, sequence, layering, and logic. This reflects awareness of both that things are made and how things are made, and of the choices and artistry that has gone into that making.

Firsthand exposure to people, places, and things seems to be key, but there is no formulaic method for observation of this very personal kind. Designers are enthralled by the world and the search for patterns and hidden rules that apply. But rather than observing it to describe what they see (which would involve seeing literally and objectively), their purpose is a generative and strategic one. Generative in the sense of a future orientation on what is observed—highly dependent on imagination and interpretation. And by strategic, I mean that their observations help in making deliberate judgments about the relevance and meaning of specific design choices.

Teams of designers, rather than individuals, allow more eyes to see more, and one would hope, differently. But in teams it is important to preserve the tension between multiple viewpoints and singular visions to allow the most powerful new perspectives to develop. Indeed, one of the most valuable contributions that designers make is to help others see situations in a new light, to see as yet unappreciated possibilities for how something (product, service, space, etc.) might look and feel as a future experience.

In attempts to make design and design thinking more widely accessible, there is increasing emphasis on teaching and learning about design process. This inevitably leads to attempts to formalize design activities and approach.[3] As interdisciplinary teams are encouraged to employ their collective observational abilities in uncovering problems, it is important to preserve flexibility, allowing for intuition and unstructured time to look and explore through a personal lens. On any

---

3. Recent examples published by IDEO include the open-source book *Human-Centered Design Toolkit: An Open-Source Toolkit to Inspire New Solutions in the Developing World* (IDEO 2011), The Field Guide to Human-Centered Design (IDEO 2015), as well as founder David Kelley and his brother Jim Kelley's (2015), *Creative Confidence: Unleashing the Creative Potential Within Us All* (Crown Business).

given project the pivotal inspirations and insights often come in unpredictable ways. Important seem to be the effort, focus, time, and judicious exposure to relevant (or even seemingly irrelevant) influences. Such is the ability of the human/designer mind to make connections and recognize (or create) patterns where—with a project brief as simultaneously filter and engine—inspiration and insight seem to pop out of the most random experiences.

It is important to understand this, to allow time and space for it to happen. This is not an argument for abandoning plans for structured research, just a warning to not be seduced into thinking that a predefined research plan is the sole basis by which individuals on a design team will absorb and articulate their understanding of the context for their work. Reflecting back on the examples, we might follow these principles to ensure that a design sensibility can prevail:

- Allow for chance and spontaneous exploration in design research plans.
- Remember to make time and space to satisfy personal curiosity and honor the intuitions that arise.
- Ensure time for immersion, documentation, and percolation to soak up what is relevant and inspiring.
- Encourage awareness and discussion about what is beautiful, engaging, and poetic as well as what is appropriate and functional.
- Recognize that quirky and personal perspectives enrich and catalyze group understanding.

Observation of the world is natural and essential to design. But ultimately, what matters is less what you look at, and more what you *see* and what you *make* of it. From designers we ask for a designed world that has meaning beyond the resolution of purely functional needs. We ask for poetry and subtlety that make sense—not just by fitting in with the culture and environment, but by adding a new dimension to it.

References

Ante, S. E. with C. Edwards (2006, June 5), "The Science of Desire: As More Companies Refocus Squarely on the Consumer, Ethnography and its Proponents Have Become Star Players," *Bloomberg/Businessweek*. Available at https://www.bloomberg.com/news/articles/2006-06-04/the-science-of-desire (accessed January 24, 2017).

Burroughs, A. and IDEO (2007), *Everyday Engineering: How Engineers See*, San Francisco: Chronicle Books.

IDEO (2011), *Human-Centered Design Toolkit: An Open-Source Toolkit to Inspire New Solutions in the Developing World*, Palo Alto: IDEO.

IDEO (2015), *The Field Guide to Human-Centered Design—Design Kit*. Palo Alto: IDEO.

Kelley, T. and D. Kelley (2015), *Creative Confidence: Unleashing the Creative Potential Within Us All*, New York: Crown Business.

Nelson, G. ([1977] 2003), *How to See: A Guide to Reading Our Man-Made Environment*, Oakland: Design Within Reach.

6 Prototyping the Social: Temporality and Speculative Futures at the Intersection of Design and Culture

Jamer Hunt

We can no longer be content with anthropology's 'hands-off' sensibility and design's 'more is more' mentality. There are simply too many complex, large-scale problems that now pressure our very existence . . . whether global warming, overpopulation, water and food shortages, economic inequities, or the worldwide adoption of an unsustainable 'American way of life,' real social transformation is urgently needed.

'Understanding the user' has become a mantra to corporate strategists—its late-arriving ubiquity only rivaled by its surprising obviousness. To facilitate this approach there has recently been what Ross Perot (homespun Texas billionaire who staged an independent run for the US presidency in 1992) might describe as a "giant sucking sound" as design consultancies voraciously add cultural anthropologists to their employment rolls. The reasons for this are myriad, but primarily stem from a relatively recent shift in design and business methods toward 'user-centered' design, a practice that foregrounds the needs and wants of the end-user as central to the development of new products and services. Large corporations such as Procter & Gamble and Intel have been hiring anthropologists and other social researchers to help them gain insight into user needs and desires with the ultimate aim of gaining greater market share and ensuring more predictable success with new product launches. Within design itself, the emergence of design ethnography, co-design, participatory design, and design probes—as well as other variously named design methods—further signals that designers are increasingly adopting the tools of social observation as resources for 'local knowledge' that better inform and inspire the development of new ideas.

This rather unproblematized incorporation of (often quick and dirty) ethnographic methods into commercial design processes continues unabated, leaving designers occasionally perplexed and anthropologists increasingly nervous about the commercial uses of their own hallowed practices. Most anthropologists would not consider one week of videotaping subjects brushing their teeth to be an ethnography, just as they did not spend six to ten years studying Durkheim, Mead, and Foucault with an eye toward convincing upper-middle-class new parents to switch diaper brands. In some ways, this confluence of corporate strategy and ethnographic processes is a shotgun marriage between an emergent industry need and a glut of social science doctoral graduates who have been facing a withering academic job market for over a decade. What often gets overlooked in the rush to consummate this affair, however, is the fact that these two practices—design and ethnography—represent dramatically different orientations toward change and time. More specifically, each practice configures its methods in relation to slightly incommensurable temporal frameworks, producing a disjuncture between them that is both revealing and potentially generative of new directions.

This essay will examine the role of the temporal within ethnographic and design practices. It will foreground each practice's engagement with the present by exploring design work that is speculative, critical, and experimental—work that leads to a questioning of cultural orthodoxies rather than to problem-solving and new product development. The emphasis throughout will be primarily on the meaning of anthropological methods to design, and not the inverse. And this is urgent. It is no longer sufficient for only a few in the academy to encounter the incisive work of anthropologists and for the vicissitudes of commercial interests to drive the work of designers. We can no longer be content with anthropology's 'hands-off' sensibility and design's 'more is more' mentality. There are simply too many complex, large-scale problems that now pressure our very existence to relegate these potential change agents to their past, more marginal roles. Whether global warming, overpopulation, water and food shortages, economic inequities, or the worldwide adoption of an unsustainable 'American way of life,' real social transformation is urgently needed. What does all this mean for the contested space at the overlap of design and ethnographic methods? Is it possible to prototype the social? Can a design process—rich with cultural insight—re-envision the social imaginary?

Temporality

In a simple sense, an ethnographic project attempts to illuminate the present by interrogating its (recent) past. Its methods are observational, descriptive, analytical, and interpretive. While not social historians, anthropologists do build up their interpretive snapshot of a culture by grounding their narratives in a series of flashbacks to recent events, occurrences, interviews, or observations. Put another way, ethnography is rarely projective; it does not speculate on what might happen next. Its focus is the present, built upon a series of past 'present' moments.

Design, on the other hand, is a practice of material and immaterial making, but its mode of being-in-the-world is generative, speculative, and transformational. A designer must project forward into a potential future to launch an artifact that will, if all goes right, transform a near present and rewrite our future. Whereas an ethnographer works in ever-greater detail to ensure that she has got the present 'just right,' the designer uses the present—and uses it often imperfectly—as a provisional leaping-off point for reimagining possible futures. Designers are often quite at ease basing a project on broad assumptions about the world: for example, "people are now nomadic, how can we design for mobility?" Social scientists, however, would want to know what is meant by nomadic, how nomadic, under what conditions, and by what criteria? Designers, by and large, use that assumption as a necessarily imperfect starting point, and getting things exactly right is not the point. The point is to move from that assumption into innovative ways of configuring future styles of living. What matters is the extent to which the project's outcome reconfigures our sense of future possibilities.

Tony Fry, a philosopher of design and sustainability, explores the vector between the present and the future differently. He challenges design to confront its profound ability to radically 'defuture.' For Fry, defuturing is the effect of our short horizon of investment and our reckless abandonment of the future. We prioritize the immediate over the long-term. He writes, "In our endeavor to sustain ourselves in the short term we collectively act in destructive ways towards the very things we and all other beings fundamentally depend upon. Such longstanding and still growing 'defuturing' needs halting and countering" (Fry 2009: 22). Defuturing is, for Fry, not simply the law of unforeseen consequences. Instead, it is a conceptual mindset inherent to a style of designing that privileges the instrumental over the social. Designers ignore—at our own and others' peril—the extent to which any act of design is an act both of prefiguring a future social milieu but also the erasure of multiple possible alternatives. Design, for Fry, both designs and keeps on designing. It is an ontology of prefigurement that destroys as it creates. When design does not fully comprehend the present, as is most often the case, it misdirects its outcomes toward self-annihilating ends. "The 'state of the world' and the state of design need to be brought together" (p. 4). Fry is calling here not simply for gentle course correction for design, but for a radical rethinking of its practices and premises: "Implied in the position outlined is that designers place the current needs of the market in second place to the politico-ethical project of gaining sustain-ability" (p. 46). To do this, Fry writes, "Design, in the first instance, has to be understood anthropologically" (p. 2).

Intervention

This temporal gap at the intersection of the two practices reveals another tension that is often involved as the two practices attempt to play nicely together. Designers are, by the nature of their training and modes of practice, comfortable with the need to intervene into the context they are exploring. Social, material, and technical transformation is always part of their working method. Design without both material and social impact in the world would not be design; designers must act in the sense that their outputs change the facts on the ground. Whether this is always done wisely, and with enough foresight, is precisely what is at stake. Our landscape is littered with what the architect Rem Koolhaas (2001) describes as "junkspace," the detritus that architects, product designers, interior designers, and others leave in their own wakes. There is an imperative to produce and make change in design, even if the consequences of this are not always fully considered.

Intervention, for anthropologists, is much more historically, politically, and ethically fraught. The Malinowskian model of 'participant-observer' does place an emphasis on 'participant,' but this does not mean that anthropologists have been comfortable with it in the way that designers are. Because of the discipline's dark history with colonial regimes and the subjugation of native peoples, many contemporary anthropologists recoil from an interventionist agenda. The pendulum has swung heavily to the 'observation' side of participant observation: Take only notes and leave only footprints. The ambition of most ethnographers has been to swoop in for a surgical, observational strike that produces new knowledge but not at the cost of altering the facts on the ground. That work is then turned into ethnographies that aim to produce knowledge for the sake of knowledge, and to allow that knowledge to circulate in the academy, first and foremost, and only later, perhaps, into more applied fields (such as development, policy making, business, and military affairs). The more applied fields of the discipline have continued to exist, but primarily as a marginal and politically tainted fringe of the profession. In 2007, a report on the front page of the *New York Times* about anthropologists working with the US government in Afghanistan and Iraq to sway the local population to support the US military incursions there led to a swift firestorm of protest within the American Anthropological Association, the official body of professional anthropologists (Rohde 2007). This extreme example has only reinforced the queasiness that most anthropologists feel when confronted with their own methodologies put to the ends of pragmatic intervention.

That contemporary anthropologists have generally recoiled from direct intervention does not mean that their work is irrelevant to our modern condition. What if that non-intervention was not what it appeared to be? Leaving aside the obvious fact that any anthropologist alters the situation she inserts herself into, an interesting line of argument opened up in the 1990s within anthropology, sparked in part by the publication of George Marcus and Michael Fischer's book *Anthropology as Cultural Critique: An Experimental Moment in the Human Sciences.* The authors argued that anthropology—far from discovering the essence of some faraway 'other' for the sake of building the encyclopedia of humanity—has always been more or less about ourselves, refracted through the lens of the other. The authors argue that the enterprise of ethnography has always had lodged within it a critique of our practices, albeit in veiled form: We do not study the other just to understand her better, but to reveal that our own ways are contingent, constructed, and transformable. Ethnography in this formulation becomes a lens through which to interrogate the seeming naturalness of our own customs. Deep analysis of the other is a form of cultural critique, they argue, and ethnography has always said more about us than about them. Marcus and Fischer describe the process this way: "The challenge of serious cultural criticism is to bring the insights gained on the periphery back to the center to raise havoc with our settled ways of thinking" (Marcus and Fischer 1986: 138). So, perhaps, the work of anthropology has always been less about knowledge production in a field that is far from home and more about delivering subtle, subterranean incursions into our own hallowed belief systems—about social hierarchies, birth rites, gender, death, wealth, or values—chipping away at their veneer of inevitability and permanence.

In part, the critical turn in anthropology (represented by the work of Marcus, Fischer, and others) recalibrated the field, shifting the focus of the ethnographic gaze from the exotic other to the exotic same. Whether financial traders, scientists, intellectuals, or social elites, many anthropologists looked upward and inward, turning their gazes closer to home. For anthropology in the wake of a critique of its colonialist roots and the power relations inherent within it, this was a turn toward exploring new ethnographic subjects. It was, in no small part, an explicit effort to preserve the ethnographic process while redefining what was understood to be 'the field.' Fieldwork—in this re-imagined form—could take place in laboratories, mansions, or central banks. Diasporic communities, large-scale migrations, and globalized development have fractured the discipline's focus on geographically isolated 'primitive' cultures. But while the field has evolved, the primary methodology has stayed the same. Despite a more explicit attention to the dynamics of power and agency in our own cultural milieus, this form of ethnography remains a practice of analysis and description, not intervention. Given the historical ambivalence of anthropologists toward intervention, can the critical gaze of the ethnographer shatter the glass wall and effect meaningful change? Or will its practitioners remain on the other side, nose pressed to the glass?

The Critical Turn

One innovative way of thinking through the merging of a design and an ethnographic practice around the notion of the critical emerges out of anthropology, but an anthropology that is focused directly on its temporal binds. George Marcus and Paul Rabinow, two of the anthropologists responsible for the 'critical' turn in anthropology in the 1980s, address this in a set of conversations captured in (a not coincidentally titled) *Designs for an Anthropology of the Contemporary* (2008). In this discussion, Rabinow claims that ethnographic research must reorient to the present but struggles to reinvent itself. Borrowing from Nietzsche, Rabinow invokes the temporal construct of the untimely to trace the contours of a new ethnographic practice that could leapfrog anthropology out of its rearward gaze and into the immediate present.

The term [the untimely] is taken from Nietzsche's Untimely Meditations and used to mark a critical distance from the present that seeks to establish a relationship to the present different from reigning opinion. . . . We've always tried to teach students to think in a manner that leads to inquiry. We have given them concepts and methodological tools, which slow them down. Today, the pedagogic challenge is to rethink the established combination of fast and slow operations that remains at the core of what inquiry should be. One might say: "Let's go to Chernobyl, but don't leave Weber behind." Of course, Weber is not going to tell you directly what's going on there—that would be ridiculous to expect. But surfing the Internet is not going to tell you what is significant, either. For that we need other tools, other methods, and different ethos. (Rabinow and Marcus 2008: 59–60)

Here Rabinow is struggling to reposition the temporal framework of ethnographic practice (or inquiry, in his terms), away from a slow reliance upon preexisting explanatory models and toward a presentist orientation that emphasizes connections, nodes, and experiments. This is ethnography as a sketch, to put it into design terms. Surprisingly, this conversation wends its way to the conclusion that the design studio may be an appropriate model for the kind of inquiry necessary for an anthropology of the contemporary. As the moderator of the conversation, Tobias Rees describes it, "The conversations gradually come to consider the virtues and possibilities of the design studio, in which possible aims, concepts, and methods for the anthropology of the contemporary are developed, tested, doubted, improved, and left in their unfinished state for others to take on" (Rabinow and Marcus 2008: 11). This remarkable leap to the logic of a design method only makes sense if one is looking through the lens of temporality. As Rabinow goes on to argue, "Well, if anthropology is to remain pertinent to the contemporary world it must figure out how to speed up certain aspects of its practices of inquiry. Certain of the venues we come to are changing too quickly to allow us to do anything else" (p. 95). What design brings to this process is a way to challenge more effectively the means for grasping some of the loose threads of the present as they reveal themselves to the analytic gaze. It pushes the anthropologist into a more speculative mode of inquiry, one that is quite familiar to designers. In a passage that could just as easily describe what designers do, Rabinow states the challenge to anthropology this way: "The task is to invent concepts to make visible what is emerging. This needs a critical distance from the present" (p. 64).

This "critical distance from the present" is not a position that is easily achieved. The question for design, then, is if it actually ever achieves it? If design is a practice that grounds itself in the present while projecting scenarios forward into the future, is it a critical practice? Certainly, designers reflect on the present and offer alternatives that are forward-looking. In that sense, as in Fischer and Marcus's assessment of anthropology's critical edge, design does offer some alternative to the present conditions and is therefore critical—though only in a 'lite' sense. For what is it critical in the name of? Most ethnographies, especially those of the past few decades, have adopted a specifically critical position with regard to revealing the strictures and structures of power, authority, and discipline as it plays it in the lives of the subaltern. There is an ideological forward edge that attempts, to put it bluntly, to speak truth to power. Ethnographic practitioners have principally been wrangling with the politics of identity, postcolonial subjectivity, and processes of globalization; politically, these critiques align—softly or more obdurately—with the ideology of the New Left. Design, on the other hand, operates more in the name of a kind of commercial opportunism. Though it does take an oppositional stand in relation to present conditions, most often what drives it forward is either a marketing opportunity or innovation for innovation's sake. At its best, it is indeed problem-solving, but to claim that that is its primary objective is to overlook the vast amount of dreck that it produces in the name of the 'new.' Any copy of the in-flight catalog *Skymall* will instantly confirm this.

Critical Design

There is a fringe of design practice that does adopt a more ideologically driven position in relation to design's place in the world, and that work begins to point to a fruitful conjoining of critical social analysis and design. These projects envision design futures through the technique of scenarios. They stretch our current conditions to their logical extreme, extrapolating the present into the future. Like science fiction, these scenarios of a designed future foreground the politics of our current manias. In that way, they implicitly challenge our designed—and social and political—orthodoxies. The projects effectively aim to give form to emergent social practices, providing us with a distorting mirror through which to see our present. The scenarios, by and large, are social scenarios in which the material and immaterial built environment prompt new kinds of behaviors. Heather Frank's project *Neugenics*, for example, posits a not-too-distant future where genetic modification and re-engineering are so common that newborns are having pre-modified DNA samples implanted under their skin so that they can later have access to their 'original' self's genetic inheritance, should they wish to reset their genetic dials (see Figures 6.1 and 6.2). Frank surrounds the doctored imagery with collateral materials from a print campaign that situates the modification of our genetics as a basic consumer option, similar to picking out lipstick or getting a tattoo. In so doing, she is challenging us to consider the dovetailing vectors of both increasing genetic modification and increasing body modification, and what might be the logical next phase of our consumer culture. She lays bare the consumer mechanics of our present obsessions with redesigning the self but does so through suspending our disbelief at the mid-point between believability and incredulity. Her project thus depends for its power on both its ability to plumb our social milieu and its ability to futurecast that through an extrapolation into the future.

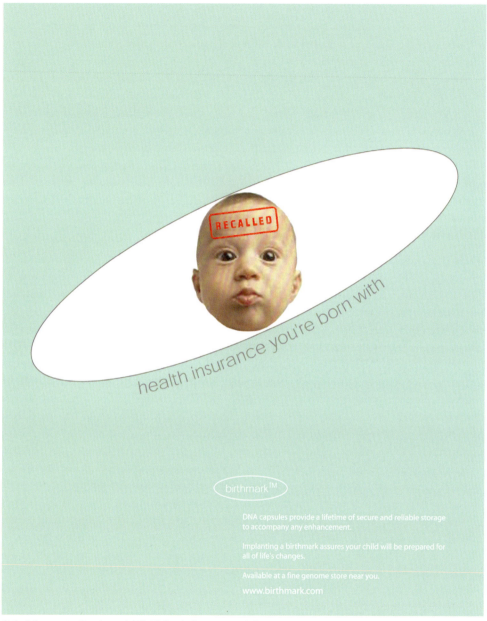

6.1 Neugenics Birthmark TM Heath Insurance Advertisement, 2002. Designer: Heather Frank.
© *Heather Frank*

6.2 Neugenics Birthmark TM Heath Insurance Advertisement, 2002. Designer: Heather Frank. © *Heather Frank*

These kinds of fictive social scenarios were pioneered, in our current era, through projects by the British designers Anthony Dunne and Fiona Raby (see Figures 6.3 and 6.4). Explicitly labeling their own work as "critical design," they constantly scan our cultural horizon, filtering for existing social technologies that range from our electrified domestic landscapes and bioengineering to security systems and robot helpers. From there, they build out future scenarios that amplify our anxieties and reveal the stakes of our current investments. Their landmark installation entitled *Is This*

6.3 Hydrogen Energy Future, 2004. Designers: Anthony Dunne and Fiona Raby.
© *Jason Evans*

6.4 Blood/Meat Energy Future, 2004. Designers: Anthony Dunne and Fiona Raby. © *Jason Evans*

Your Future? at the Science Museum in London (2004) illustrates the potential tensions between our current energy crises and the prospects for distributed energy production in the future.[1] Like a project for *Popular Science* gone slightly mad, they prototype a future everyday in which children do their part to contribute to our shared energy needs. But the scenario is not quite as harmonious as it first appears, as they depict the expanded role that children will have to play as energy producers in this domesticated economy. Will they become twenty-first-century child laborers, blithely subjugated in their uniforms and daily regimes? How far are we willing to go to sustain our thirst for energy, the exhibition is asking, and how much of our everyday are we willing to leverage to keep our junkie habit?

Knowear, a New York-based design and fashion firm, explores this same cultural fixation on addiction and its cost to our bodies and spirits in a series of projects that blend design, fashion, and body sculpting (see Figures 6.5 and 6.6). They fixate upon the increasing importance of brands both in our commercial landscape and in our own sense of personal identity. When we shop for new body parts (noses, lips, calves, breasts, hair, eye color, and on and on) with the same casualness that we shop for clothes, how close we will cozy up to the brands that seem to be more and more constituent of our own sense of selves? While we seem to be more skeptical of brandwashing by major corporations, at the same time we seem incapable of resisting their pitch. Knowear's projects Skinthetic Redux and BrandX push two sides of this obsession. Skinthetic Redux prototypes our bodies as sites for fashion's next line, merging flesh with the iconic pillowy texture made recognizable by Chanel. Brand X goes even further, transforming our seemingly harmless obsession into an eruption of skin brands. Channeling the original notion of brand (marks in the skin to signal ownership of cattle), Knowear excavates the contemporary and pushes it to an extreme. Brand icons press against our flesh until they become one with us, metastasizing into an outbreak of uncontrollable lesions.

As compelling as these projects are, it is clear that they will not, in and of themselves, effect large-scale social change. They are more speculative than interventionist. What each of these projects illustrates is a trenchant blend of a critical analysis of the present with a projection into a possible, prototyped future. But unlike more commercial design projects, they express an engagement with overt social and political aims—even though they sometimes suspend us in an uncomfortable place between reality and fiction. They compel us to reconsider how the present is futuring—to use Tony Fry's words—and how we may still have a chance to reconfigure that future potentiality. These projects slow down the future and its defuturing by prefiguring us in those future moments. They bring together the analytical incisiveness of an ethnographer's eye with the materializing vision of a designer. They are *untimely*, in Rabinow's terms, in that they "make visible what is emerging" (p. 64) by both slowing down the present and speeding us up to that present's future.

---

1. For Dunne and Raby's most recent speculations including a menstruation machine, a phantom-limb sensation recorder, and devices for food foraging see Dunne and Raby 2013.

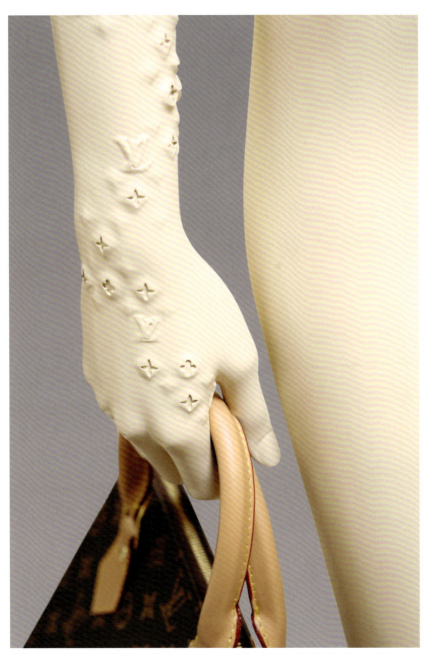

6.5 BrandX: Louis Vuitton Series Image #1, New York, 2007. Designers: Peter Allen + Carla Ross Allen. © *Peter Allen + Carla Ross Allen*

6.6 Skinthetic Redux: Chanel Series Image #4, New York, 2009. Designers: Peter Allen + Carla Ross Allen. © *Peter Allen + Carla Ross Allen*

References

Dunne, A. and F. Raby (2013), *Speculative Everything: Design, Fiction, and Social Dreaming*, Boston: MIT Press.

Fry, T. (2009), *Design Futuring: Sustainability, Ethics, and New Practices*, New York: Berg.

Koolhaas, R. (2001), "Junkspace," in C. J. Chung, J. Inaba, R. Koolhaas and S. T. Leong (eds.), *The Harvard Design School Guide to Shopping/Harvard Design School Project on the City*, 2, 408–22, Cologne: Taschen.

Marcus, G. and M. Fischer (1986), *Anthropology as Cultural Critique: An Experimental Moment in the Human Sciences*, Chicago: University of Chicago Press.

Rabinow, P. and G. Marcus with J. D. Faubion and T. Rees (2008), *Designs for an Anthropology of the Contemporary*, Durham: Duke University Press.

Rohde, D. (2007), "Anthropologists Help U.S. Army in Afghanistan and Iraq," *The New York Times*, October 4.

7 Consuming IKEA and Inspiration as Material Form
Pauline Garvey

Designers are 'creative brokers' in compiling, assimilating, and recombining knowledge economies in new ways. A creative broker synthesizes ideas from disparate fields and transmits them in novel ways, but one need not be a designer to engage in this practice: IKEA consumers describe themselves in similar terms.

Introduction

"No one does branding quite like the giant blue and yellow furniture company," announces *Form* magazine, the Nordic architecture and design publication for the Swedish Society of Crafts and Design.[1] This branding is resolutely hitched to what the magazine terms "Nordic display" featuring IKEA and several well-known department stores in Stockholm. In this issue, IKEA is not only a highly successful global brand, but also a poster child for Scandinavian display practices that have "moved beyond the mannequin" in cultivating a life filled with "surface, scenes and disguises" (Cirelli 2012: 59).

Since its launch of furniture retail in 1958, IKEA as a transnational corporation is variously described as either a purveyor of accessible design or standardized flat pack "monolithic tyranny of aesthetics" (Hartman 2007: 492). IKEA has been projected as an international icon of Sweden (see Kristoffersson 2014) or a new creeping manifestation of the international style, perpetuating homogenous domestic environments on a global scale. The corporation takes a highly publicized

---

1. Svensk Form (2012), *Form Nordic Architecture and Design since 1905* 5: cover page. Svensk Form, originally Svenska Slöjdföreningen (The Swedish Society of Crafts and Design), a not-for-profit association mandated by the Swedish Government to promote design in Sweden, was founded in 1845.

stance on waste and is a long-term advocate for sustainability.[2] At the same time it figures as a harbinger of recent retail trends in which furniture is increasingly deemed fashionable and disposable (Reimer and Leslie 2008). If brands operate on a series of dualities between, for instance, abstract sign and material biography, nowhere is this more apparent than in IKEA. Consequently, it is all too easy to lapse into descriptions of IKEA in abstract terms. Research respondents readily subscribe to this view, surfing the website of IKEA Malaysia to then compare the virtual experience to its equivalent in Moscow without pausing for breath. "IKEAization" we are told is "necessarily a disengagement with the collective sphere, a sense that the most beneficial work is carried out when one is sheltered from, rather than an active participant in, social reality" (Hartman 2007: 493). Bright and breezy IKEA merchandise, Hartman suggests, wallpapers over the fissures in contradictory self-construction and sociopolitical unrest. The collective is left behind in transitory, solitary fantasies.

Based on an anthropological study of Ikea consumption in Stockholm, this chapter offers an alternative perspective. In situating display techniques and shopping practices within the context of the IKEA flagship store in the southern suburbs of the Swedish capital, I argue that one finds a surprising congruence of sociality and inspiration as relational and materialized entities.[3] Inspiration is a dominant motif in IKEA sales rhetoric. Management opinion and in-house manuals valorize its importance, imputing it to the shopping public when given the necessary resources. To be inspired is thus suggestive of a linear process moving from external prompts to internal states, leading, one must suppose, to an eruption of fresh ideas and new purchases. As in popular renditions of the 'eureka' moment, this interconnectivity is often characterized as an asocial, abstract process. Following this logic, inspiration is buried deep in individual experience and prodded into consciousness by some random external event. In the following I argue that, conversely, inspiration is dispersed through aggregate experience, manifested in the concrete examples of Swedish design, and acquired through actual engagement with display tableaux.

In providing a canvas to consider ordinary interior conundrums, showrooms exhibit both the subjects and objects of domestic consumption. This emplacement of consumers as part of the showroom *mise-en-scène* is characteristic of IKEA display strategy, but the more general logic it suggests—the interpellation of experience as integral to shopping—conforms to archetypal transnational branding practice. Leading-edge companies across the globe recognize a vital progression from making goods to delivering services and staging experiences. They have consequently

---

2. IDEA Group Sustainability Report FY14, http://www.ikea.com/ms/en_US/pdf/sustainability_report /sustainability_report_2014.pdf.

3. Through an anthropological study of IKEA consumption, 48 interviews with householders were conducted in and around the world's largest flagship store located in Kungens Kurva (King's Curve) in the southern suburbs of the Swedish capital. Covering a staggering area of 56,200 m[2], the Swedish IKEA store is the engine behind the Nordic countries' largest marketplace in Skärhomen. My research aim was to follow furniture from shop floor to domestic setting in various locations in Stockholm and its suburbs.

valorized experience as central to brand recognition (see Foster 2005; 2008). Brands are now based on consumer activities, expressions of community and integrated into mundane actions of everyday life (Arvidsson 2006: 236). Consumers are heralded as an untapped resource for 'value co-creation' in contemporary business (cf. Arvidsson 2006; Zwick, Bonsu, and Darmody 2008). Value co-creation implies putting shoppers to work not only in obliging them to assemble flat pack furniture but also in absorbing and territorializing their expertise, skills, and creativity. In encouraging synergies between corporations and their publics, contemporary business logic, then, aims to co-opt the intellectual and affective work of shoppers in the development of brands and products. One way of doing this is to build relationships with consumers, such as encouraging them to identify with the brand; to consolidate as publics; and to innovate and supply new avenues for product development (Zwick, Bonsu, and Darmody 2008). The shopping environment is integral to this process. Already, by 1974, Kotler coined the term "atmospherics" to describe the physical backdrop of commercial outlets in order to emphasize the importance of the senses in retail (Kotler 1974, 48–64). Now "brandscaping" gives name to "lights, design, music and the demeanor of personnel to encourage consumers to co-perform a particular ambience" in retail centers (Arvidsson 2006, 80 in Manning 2010, 43–44). Store atmosphere should engage the olfactory, tactile, aural, and visual senses (see Hultén 2011), while "branding sociality" describes the corporate choreographing of distinct types of social interaction in shop environments.

Not purely a transcriptive strategy, however, Löfgren (2005, 2013) identifies a specifically Swedish articulation of global trends emerging between 1995 and 2005 in which rapid socioeconomic changes in line with growing informality were adopted in Swedish state agencies, corporates, and centers of cultural production. Local expressions of this 'new economy' can be seen in the packaging of products, places, and services in terms of novel and worthwhile experiences. Creativity and innovation were valorized in workplaces and playfulness and positive subjective experience was lauded as the route to selling goods. As part of a shift to the informal, a movement toward dismantling traditional hierarchies emerged across a spectrum of industries from biotechnology to cultural centers, while the performative and emotive dimensions of branding were embraced in commercial enterprise. So far, this emphasis sings the tune of international commerce but Löfgren points out that the particular flavor of informality, the focus on erasing traditional rules, and the specific emphasis on spontaneity lent an enhanced cadence to the adoption of the experience economy which "was both faster and stronger in Sweden than in most other European countries" (Löfgren 2005: 19).

It is clear that IKEA display strategy actively orchestrates a holistic experience, encouraging corporeal and affective engagement with showroom furniture in order to provide a tightly choreographed experience. The sensorial injection, underlying the "try me before you buy me" sales pitch, I suggest, serves to enliven the showroom merchandise through the activities of others. But while these branding strategies conform to international commercial practice, the IKEA flagship in Stockholm's Kungens Kurva is an interesting example because of its particular place in Swedish domestic design and cultural history. Specifically, some factors mark its local appropriation as uniquely distinct from the blanket assumptions regarding global retail. For example, twentieth-century Sweden witnessed significant alliances between design, domesticity, and state policy, such that "good design" made in Sweden "projects a powerful, concrete rendering of a sort of essentialized 'Swedishness' embedded in objects identifiable as emblems of nationalist pride" (Murphy 2015: 3). Characteristically for Scandinavian countries, the locus for quality of life is centered on the home. Until the 1990s, state housing provision entailed an explicit design dimension. Such design involved close measurement of domestic activities to facilitate the most efficient use of space. Other important housing conditions were based on access to direct sunlight, room climate, sound isolation, electric installations, elevators, building heights, and complementary buildings and patios (Eriksson 2000). In addition, precise measurements resulted from studies of domestic activities such as guidelines as to the heights or widths of kitchen worktops or distances between stoves and kitchen sinks. The result was a series of enforced architectural norms, not only endorsed by the state but proscriptive for the building industry to procure state (municipal) funding. Such efforts were directed to managing domestic spaces, standardizing sizes and shapes of rooms, and facilitating storage in tight spaces. Swedish domesticity, therefore, has long been purveyed, displayed, and scrutinized around organizations of domestic material culture that entailed far-reaching claims (Sandberg 2011; Garvey 2017). Here, design is not an adjunct to everyday life: it is the medium for active, political intervention with the promise of social betterment throughout the twentieth century (Lindqvist 2009; Kristoffersson 2014; Murphy 2015).

The IKEA Showroom

In marked contrast to conventional display strategies that "rely on eye-catching window displays that ratchet up the drama in an endless cycle of oneupmanship, Ikea does the opposite. Their sales strategy requires that customers recognise themselves and their homes in Ikea's displays" (Cirelli 2012: 68). Indeed, while more conventional department stores endeavor to catch attention through show-stopping window displays, IKEA substitutes the shop window with showrooms that "strive for the familiar" (Ibid.). On arrival, escalators carry shoppers directly to the third floor, where one must proceed back down passing a succession of *tableaux*, accessible staged rooms furnished to accommodate particular groups based on the local demographic. Nothing can be purchased here and frenetic accumulation is deferred to the basement area. Instead, the displays run in circles, while large glass walls allow the shopper to view lower and upper floors. One first encounters the living rooms, followed by other living spaces such as bedrooms, offices, and kitchens where one is provided with typical family scenarios. Inhabitants are continuously implied in large floor-to-ceiling posters, for instance two men cooking together under a sign "we live in 25m squared." Or more subtly, presented by photos of babies with young couples (suggestive of parents) or elderly women (the granny).

There are photographs of other fictional family members, too, knitting in bowls, and books on shelves (see Figures 7.1 and 7.2). Single individuals, couples with children, and typical household pursuits and/or hobbies are implied in these rooms. Specific interests—or target groups—are alluded to through car magazines on bookshelves or provision for adult leisure or learning. Children's play, too, is catered for through the placement of specific furnishings and suggested use of storage. The rooms are effective through their suggestion of absent presences, allowing shoppers to imaginatively emplace themselves within the *mise-en-scène*. A breakfast tray sits on the bed of one *tableau*, as if someone has just got up (see Figure 7.3), while a baby's cot stands in the corner. Distinctions between participating in the domestic-like environment and mere browsing meld as individuals interact with the furnishings or read the tags labeled "tips."

Consumers are both the subjects and objects of this visual and tactile experience. A man lounges on a sofa gazing absentmindedly at the television, switched off. After a while, he rests his

7.1 Family Photographs: IKEA showrooms encourage an impression of absent occupants. ©
Pauline Garvey

7.2 Knitting needles suggest domestic activities. © *Pauline Garvey*

arm above his head, deep in thought, as if settling down for the evening. Around him is the hum of animated activity: excited children and worn parents browsing and speculating, shoppers are sitting on sofas, opening drawers and gazing in mirrors, all immersed in the collective project of domestic contemplation. These individuals are not only viewing the rooms, they are placing themselves and, crucially, other people in these environments. One Dublin man—who has an interest in perusing high-end design magazines—finds this reiteration of inhabitants an unnecessary distraction in the IKEA catalog. "Get the people away," he says while browsing his catalog with me. He absentmindedly waves his hand about his head in irritation, as if swatting a bee or another annoyance to his concentration.

Mass interaction with domestic arrangements as one finds in IKEA is mistakenly branded as solitary. The rooms are uninhabited but the implied occupants of these living spaces are not entirely absent either. Rather, they are peopled in the presence of householders milling about,

7.3 Breakfast tray on bed in IKEA showrooms in Stockholm. © *Pauline Garvey*

touching, comparing, and otherwise providing the injection of 'family' that the scenes might otherwise lack. Parents refer to their children lying on beds in IKEA showrooms in amused tones, as if they are being transgressive. In fact, IKEA management does not just tolerate customers sitting on beds, sofas, or at tables but positively encourages it. In the Dublin store, customer interaction with showpieces is measured in color codes: The more people physically locate themselves in, on, and around exhibits the more successful they are deemed to be. Behind these practices is the framework of 'inspiration,' a nebulous idea based on the co-location of people and scene, envisioning oneself in these spaces, physically interacting with the furnishing, and emotionally responding to them. Trips to IKEA imply collective activity to such an extent that shop floor workers recounted to me, on my first day of in-store research, of occasional elderly visitors who visit the store every day simply to connect with people.

Social Life at IKEA

In Stockholm, IKEA merchandise and its various appendages are continuously part of one's peripheral vision, in both public and private spaces. From the small IKEA signature furnishings, such as lamps and bookcases immediately identifiable on arrival to homes, to blue and yellow bags that are convenient holdalls for laundry or bulky goods, IKEA is part of the sociopolitical weave of standardized housing and national imaginaries that make up recitations of the "typical" household.

Behind the scenes as well as on the shop floor, staff offices encourage an ethos of collectivity. In Dublin, in-house posters remind employees that IKEA "sides with the many." From early on, founder Ingvar Kamprad underscored the importance of family as a collective metaphor for staff—but also for his consumer base of 'store visitors,' constituting 915 million in 2016.[4] Nils Larsson, a manager in the marketing head office in Helsingborg, claimed that 80 percent of Swedes visit an IKEA store at least once a year. Similarly, the fact that it is directly linked to Ingvar Kamprad is of immense importance to the national market. An annual trust barometer compiled by academics at the University of Gothenburg charts public trust in national institutions.[5] For several years, IKEA has ranked among the most trusted institutions in Sweden, far surpassing confidence in the government or the media. Here, in the corridors of the retail service office, democracy or equality is the name given to this mass appeal. Elsewhere the normative potential of IKEA merchandise can pose a problematic balancing act.

While IKEA products are generally recognized by my research respondents as acceptable quality and good design, having too much 'IKEA'—often named as an abstract entity—suggests an inability to be an individual or show personal history. One woman expressed some embarrassment about having a living room planned by IKEA interior designers and completely outfitted with its furniture: "You shouldn't live the brand, you know," she says. Against this background, interviewees reiterated domestic acquisition as a non-solitary endeavor and emphasized the comfort of company over the loneliness of a solitary visit. Such comments were interspersed with references to hanging out, browsing, day-trips, or family outings to the store. And just as a 'day-trip' indicates both time and space devoted to leisure, respondents consistently point to the necessity of IKEA visitation with co-present others. Lucas, a thirty-eight year old father of two, suggested he doesn't go alone: "IKEA is a family thing, it's like an outing now." Other locals reminisced on trips as young teenagers, when they would pop in with friends for lunch after (and possibly during) school. Per, a ticket

4. "Worldwide Facts & Figures, September 2014–August 2015," graphic chart, IKEA. Available at http://franchisor.ikea.com/ikea-retailing-facts-and-figures-new/, accessed on January 26, 2017.

5. IKEA retains pole position with 78 percent indicating a lot/quite a lot of trust, and Ingvar Kamprad, the founder and outward face of the furniture giant, has precisely the same high result. The Trust Barometer is an annual measurement of trust in social institutions, parties, the mass media, and companies. The Barometer was designed by Lennart Weibull and Sören Holmberg, professors at the University of Gothenburg, in conjunction with the market research company TNS Gallup, 2008.

officer in the Stockholm underground, complained about everything being the same in IKEA, but commented that at least "everyone can be the same together." Finally, Berit, a middle-aged lawyer, described household shopping trips as a nice way to socialize with her teenage daughters:

Berit: But I like small things—take the girls and go for a late evening shopping for a few hours. It is a nice way to talk 'cause we know exactly what we want and what we look for, it is a way to socialize. If someone at work was to say I have my car today and I will go to IKEA for lunch, would someone like to join me, you would always fill the car because everyone would like to join, because it is a way of socializing.

Pauline: Is that different from other stores, where else might you go?

Berit: Well, no one would suggest that we go to a different store. No, no one suggests a different store. IKEA is not a store, it is a concept (laughs). IKEA is . . . IKEA.

But considerations surrounding collectivity extend beyond questions of normative domestic arrangements. Take Linda, for example. Linda is a woman in her mid-thirties who worked as a schoolteacher but had recently returned to third-level education when I met her. It was during one discussion that she expressed an issue that I began to recognize as common. It is not so much the store itself, or the lines, the maze-like channeling of people, or the size that she complained about. Rather, it was the potential to spotlight the quality of her own relationships that came under scrutiny. To explain her point she described some friends who had recently divorced and gone to IKEA, with some difficulty, to purchase furnishings for a new apartment. Referring to the ex-partner of a friend, she said:

Linda: He was feeling the same experience as I had of being single and not really enjoying it but having to get things that are only for one. It can be a nice feeling too because you can get things that you really want for yourself. But you have to be in that state of mind to enjoy it, especially in IKEA where people are holding hands and all lovey-dovey and planning for their future together. So it can be a major blow, I mean, if you are not quite "there" in yourself. I have actually brought my best friend a couple times to hold my hand and walk around a little bit. Which sounds ridiculous but it helps.

Pauline: So would you avoid going there if you were single and not quite happy about it?

Linda: I have never seen a single person walking around—I've probably seen single people but, you know, a person walking around by themselves in IKEA. It is always two and two, or you see people my age with a parent, like a guy with his mother. Women with toddlers, always in pairs, it is a very social thing. It can be hard to go in there if you don't feel . . . prepared for it.

Linda continued that at certain points in her own life trips to IKEA felt positively alienating. In discussing these emotional responses, she made no reference to the actual furnishing on show but described in some detail the people around her and the impact that their planning had on her. Interaction with in-store strangers would not necessarily alleviate this feeling, but she qualified that on exceptional occasions people can be "quite flirty" there.

Inspiration

Inspiration is free, the IKEA website declares. And it follows:

> Visit an IKEA store and sit, lie down, test, touch and try things out. Look inside our closets and under our beds. (Who knows what good ideas you'll find there.) Even if you walk away empty-handed, you'll be taking home a whole lot of fresh ideas.[6]

Within design studies and practice, the creativity of the individual is often valorized and fore-grounded, and industries associated with design are deemed "inherently innovative and creative" (Sunley et al. 2008: 677; see also Heskett 1980; Dorst and Cross 2001; Reimer and Leslie 2008). The designer-as-hero is reinforced, however, not only in popular culture, but through a range of design educational programs and dispersed through the design canon (Julier 2000: 38–39, quoted in Reimer and Leslie 2008: 150).[7] Despite this, there is little understanding as to how innovation operates in design industries, Sunley et al. assert. Replacing the designer-as-hero but underscoring individualized consumption, Hartman likens the lone IKEA consumer to a designer in fabricating a fictional self-as-hero in which the fantasy it engenders is an alternative to everyday realities. This fantasy is not "of actually *being* a successful young urban architect but the idea that one is *plugged in* to a world that consists of effortless modern design" (Hartman 2007: 487, emphasis in original). He suggests one might view the showroom *tableaux* as a medium to refract back desired identities over actual ones: "'I am not a bureaucrat but an artist,' says one; 'I am not a worker but a writer,' says another; and so on" (Ibid.). The struggle that Hartman identifies is in constructing an invention, a type of exploration and creation of desired-for identities that are unattainable in actual life. IKEA, he suggests, provides a gloss of fulfillment over real disenchantment. The sinister complement to this situation is that real social change is subverted. As an embodiment of the superficial and transitory, IKEA consumption, he contends, is more closely likened to "eating and excretion, rather than collecting" (p. 495).

Instead of focusing on products as the terminus of a creative design process, I follow Reimer and Leslie (2008: 150) in pitching design as rarely isolated but emerging from a network of diverse knowledges and relationships. According to this argument innovation and creativity are

---

6. "Ideas and Inspiration," IKEA, accessed November 3, 2015, http://www.ikea.com/ms/en_SA/the_ikea_story/the_ikea_store/ideas_and_inspiration.html.

7. Such as in the Steve Jobs Hollywood movie, released 2015.

not restricted to the individual virtuoso but spring from a spectrum of social or collective influences, and are recognized within a framework of social norms (Woodman, Sawyer, and Griffin 1993; Sunley et al. 2008: 685). Designers are "creative brokers" in compiling, assimilating, and recombining knowledge economies in new ways (Sunley et al. 2008: 685). A creative broker synthesizes ideas from disparate fields and transmits them in novel ways, but one need not be a designer to engage in this practice: IKEA consumers describe themselves in similar terms. In this matrix, showroom exhibits are, as with any designed environment, active arenas of "engagements and entanglements" (Highmore 2009: 3). As designed environments, these are material stages that carry more social purchase than unadulterated acquisition. In designating design as an active field, consumption spaces encompass both finished products as well as the practices that shape the world in multiple and complex ways (Highmore 2009: 3–4). The IKEA showroom provides an interactive space for the consultation, browsing, and occasional keen awareness of other domestic arrangements, other people, other couples, and families. Instead of a presentation of how one would really like to be, the warehouse experience reiterates collective domestic endeavor, through which one must negotiate a unique presence.

The suggestion of the comfortingly normative is very present in in-house IKEA publications. On the contents page of a publication aimed at members of 'IKEA family' entitled *IKEA Family Live* (2008) the shopper is urged to make small changes even if time and money are limited. The word inspiration features here and significantly refers to inspiration as channeled through other people:

> [S]ometimes the dream kitchens displayed in magazines are so removed from our own reality that attempting the change will feel hopeless. Perhaps you have bought the kitchen of your dreams just to discover that it does not work the way it should in your everyday life. That is what we at this magazine are hoping to help you with. To inspire and encourage the desire for change. Or to have another go at something that did not turn out very well. To suggest changes that are possible even with limited time and funds. And who to better inspire us than other people, all around the world, showing you how they have done things. If they can, then so can you![8] (Brandt 2008: 3)

Despite this valorization of the aggregate, for many a home decorated completely in IKEA merchandise—or smacking too closely as 'designed'—is named precisely as an example of *a lack* of personality. Indeed, in a best-selling Swedish novel recommended to me by interviewees, one finds

---

8. "Ibland kan drömköken som visas i tidningar vara så långt ifrån vår egen verklighet att det känns lönlöst att ens påbörja en förändring. Du kanske har köpt ditt drömkök bara för att upptäcka att det inte fungerar som det ska i din vardag. Det är här vi vill hjälpa till med vår tidning. Inspirera och ge lust till att påbörja en förändring. Eller ta nya tag i något som inte blivit bra. Visa på förändringar som är möjliga även om tiden och plånboken är begränsad. Och vem kan ge oss bättre inspiration än andra människor, runt om i världen, som visar hur dom har gjort det. Kan dom kan du!"

an example of an absence of personal interest in the home typified by the heroine's single visit to IKEA and her lack of consideration for her purchases while fitting out her apartment.[9] Such examples underscore how it is not necessarily nor essentially the actual IKEA furnishing that is at issue here but rather the consultative process, the manner in which furnishings are acquired and integrated into existent domestic forms that counts.

Part of this package springs from the circumstances that frequently surround home provisioning. IKEA shopping often centers on changes in key moments in one's life: setting up home for the first time, entering university, moving in with others, or occasionally in periods of marriage breakdown. Inexpensive furniture in the IKEA package is often turned to at such moments to fill the hole that a new domestic environment creates. Fulfilling this role renders IKEA ubiquitous in Stockholm, where even occasional television drama suggests romantic commitment through images of couples upwardly ascending IKEA escalators.

What emerges therefore is a mix of notions that combine the quality of inspiration and the process of consultation that is inflected through significant others. In recent decades and for various reasons, IKEA stores have personalized innovative or popular products by naming individual designers, bolstering an image of creative personages and on-going change. The canny solutions channeled into ordinary products are carried into domestic environments where reference is made to an aggregate of designers—'IKEA designers'—as a collective rather than as individuals. In other words, despite a process of design individualization by IKEA marketing strategies, my informants respond to inspiration as an environment and one that is constituted through collective presences. Moreover, these presences both imply co-present others as well as a set of design intentions materialized in goods. These intentions, such as storage "solutions," are purchased and carried through to domestic spaces where the design project continues. It is the nature of this dual experience that is inspiration, not inspirational.

Conclusion

As a transnational corporation with a global reach, it is all too easy to lapse into an assumption of IKEA as an abstract entity. And in the abstract one might gain an impression of specific shop floors as vacant spaces devoid of people. And yet many people cognizant of flat pack rationalization have also themselves experienced the milling about; the fingering, touching, and smelling; the lengthy queues; maze-like stores; and frustrating re-assembly. As Sarah Pink argues with reference to Wenger's work, the experience of knowing is "specific, engaged, active and 'experiential'" (Wenger 1998: 141; Pink 2009: 34). She continues, since knowing is experiential it is "inextricable from our sensorial and material engagements with the environment and is as such emplaced knowing" (2009: 34).

---

9. Stieg Larsson ([2007] 2011), *The Girl Who Kicked the Hornet's Nest*, Millenium series, translated by Reg Keeland (New York: Vintage Crime/Black Lizard).

IKEA design is not cutting-edge, but even by virtue of its attribution as design it implies a designating role (see Drazin and Garvey 2009). One of the ways in which this point is articulated is through the idea that IKEA is *Svensson*, for the Average Joe, or simply just for everybody. Here the seemingly 'everybody' is present in the milling about, moving and discussing, touching and comparing, sitting, testing, trying and viewing, which is carried through to a myriad of ordinary homes, hotels, community centers, and dispersed public buildings throughout the country. Inspiration in IKEA as a set of intentions does not have a separate reality from its canny solutions and human immersion.

In an advertising campaign launched in tandem with the 2008/09 catalog in Stockholm, an evocative image was used. The image in the advertisement represented a series of pixelated faces, which on close inspection were made up of hundreds of tiny images of IKEA goods. These ads featured heavily in metropolitan train and underground stations, and marked the diversity theme that was celebrated that year (Lindqvist 2009: 57). Within the framework of diversity, the image implies that IKEA creates a unifying cohesion from innumerable individual elements. A face here emerges from a carefully assembled confluence of tiny individual products, undermining any clear separation between unique persons and the myriad of consumer goods. In this poster, IKEA is a collection of people and things: the differences of the aggregate combine into a single vision of cohesion, an individual collective made from hundreds of small divergences. The constitution of ordinary people from diverse products so skillfully proposed by IKEA's promotional material enhances the collective feel of inspiration under nothing less critically normative than the rubric of democracy.

References

Arvidsson, A. (2006), *Brands—Meaning and Value in Media Culture*, London: Routledge.

Brandt, L. (2008), *IKEA Family Live*, summer edition.

Cirelli, J. (2012), "Facing the Street," *Form: Nordic Architecture and Design since 1905*, (5): 60–9.

Dorst, K. and N. Cross (2001), "Creativity in the Design Process: Co-Evolution of Problem Solution," *Design Studies*, 22 (5): 425–37.

Drazin, A. and P. Garvey (2009), "'Design and Having Designs in Ireland': Introduction to Anthropology, Design and Technology in Ireland," *Anthropology in Action* 16 (1): 4–17.

Eriksson, J. (2000), "Bostaden som kunskapsobjekt," in C. Enfors, B. Nygren, and E. Rudberg (eds.), *Hem i Hem i förvandling: Arkitekturmuseet, årsbok 2000*, 44–73, Stockholm: The Swedish Museum of Architecture.

Foster, R. J. (2005), "Commodity Futures: Labour, Love and Value," *Anthropology Today*, 21 (4): 8–12.

Foster, R. J. (2008), *Coca-Globalization: Following Soft Drinks from New York to New Guinea*, London and New York: Palgrave Macmillan.

Garvey, P. (2017), *Unpacking Ikea: Swedish Design for the Purchasing Masses*, Abingdon, Oxon: Routledge.

Hartman, T. (2007), "The IKEAization of France," *Public Culture*, 19 (3): 483–98.

Heskett, J. (1980), *Industrial Design*, London: Thames and Hudson.

Highmore, B. (ed.) (2009), *The Design Culture Reader*, London: Routledge.

Hultén, B. (2012), "Sensory Cues and Shoppers' Touching Behaviour: The Case of IKEA," *International Journal of Retail and Distribution Management*, 40 (4): 273–89.

Julier, G. (2000), *The Culture of Design*, London: Sage Publications.

Kotler, P. (1974), "Atmospherics as a Marketing Tool," *Journal of Retailing*, 49 (4): 48–64.

Kristoffersson, S. (2014), *Design by IKEA: A Cultural History*, London, New Delhi, New York, Sydney: Bloomsbury.

Larsson, S. ([2007] 2011), *The Girl Who Kicked the Hornet's Nest*, millennium series, New York: Vintage Crime/Black Lizard.

Lindqvist, U. (2009), "The Cultural Archive of the IKEA Store," *Space and Culture,* 12 (1): 43–62.

Löfgren, O. (2005), "Cultural Alchemy: Translating the Experience Economy into Scandinavian," in B. Czarniawska and G. Sevón (eds.), *Global Ideas: How Ideas, Objects and Practices Travel in the Global Economy,* Malmö: Liber & Copenhagen Business School Press.

Löfgren, O. (2013), "Changing Emotional Economies: The Case of Sweden 1970–2010," *Culture and Organization,* 19 (4): 283–96.

Manning, P. (2010), "The Semiotics of Brand," *Annual Review of Anthropology*, (39): 33-49.

Murphy, K. M. (2015), *Swedish Design: An Ethnography,* Ithaca and London: Cornell University Press.

Pink, S. (2009), *Doing Sensory Ethnography*, London: Sage Publications.

Reimer, S. and D. Leslie (2008), "Design, National Imaginaries and the Home Furnishings Commodity Chain," *Growth and Change,* 39 (1): 144–71.

Sandberg, M. B. (2011), "The Interactivity of the Model Home," in A. Ekström, S. Jülich, F. Lundgren and P. Wisselgren (eds.), *History of Participatory Media: Politics and Publics, 1750–2000,* New York, London: Routledge.

Sunley, P., S. Pinch, S. Reimer and J. Macmillan (2008), "Innovation in a Creative Production System: The Case of Design," *Journal of Economic Geography*, 8 (5): 675–98.

Wenger, E. (1998), *Communities of Practice: Learning, Meaning and Identity*, Cambridge: University Press.

Woodman, R. W., J. E. Sawyer and R. W. Griffin (1993), "Towards a Theory of Organizational Creativity," *Academy and Strategic Management*, 12 (4): 493–512.

Zwick, D., S. K. Bonsu and A. Darmody (2008), "Putting Consumers to Work: 'Co-creation' and New Marketing Governmentality," *Journal of Consumer Culture*, (8): 163–96.

8 "Erotic Needlework": Vernacular Designs on the Twenty-First-Century Market

Nicolette Makovicky

Crafts have gained their supposedly subversive edge not only by becoming the imagined antidote to the temporal and social experience of neoliberal capitalism, but also the antithesis of the archetypical capitalist individual: the entrepreneur. Does the rise of the "stringi" (handmade erotic lace thong) reveal a new approach to craftsmanship, born out of the necessity to adapt to a new, globalized market?

A pair of thongs is said to have saved the slowly dying art of lace making in Koniaków, Southern Poland. Since the interwar period, women in this mountain village in the Carpathian borderlands have been crocheting doilies, tablecloths, collars, and blouses, as well as ecclesiastical textiles and vestments in a delicate, floral lace. For over a decade, lace makers have also been producing bra and panty sets for private clients and retailers, and online shops in the United States, United Kingdom, Japan, and Germany.

In local galleries, bikinis and minimal underwear jostle for space with doilies and pictures of Koniaków lace being presented to Pope John Paul II and Queen Elizabeth II. While lace makers were finding it hard to sell their traditional products throughout the 1990s, the emergence of this form of handmade 'folk lingerie' reignited the public's interest in the local craft. Despite their enormous commercial appeal, the "stringi" and their producers have met with some resistance from official representatives of culture, as well as within the community itself. The National Artistic and Ethnographic Commission (*Krajowa Komisja Artystyczna i Etnograficzna*) has refused to grant the crocheted lingerie the official status of 'folk art,' seeking to assert its right to determine

8.1 Koniaków lace maker Marta Legierska sits by the window in her cottage making lace. She has worked as an artisan for over sixty years. © *Nicolette Makovicky*

8.2 'Stringi' on display for sale at the home of a lace maker in Koniaków.
Designer: Krzystyna Gazurek. © *Nicolette Makovicky*

and control "Koniaków Lace" as a brand (Grygar, Hodrová, and Kocárková 2004). Fueling the debate, the Polish and international media presented these tensions as the result of a liberal, young minority challenging an elderly, conservatively Catholic village population. The stringi have thus become a symbol of burgeoning modernity and secularism in the imagined space of traditional Poland.

Crafts have commonly been regarded as the precursor of the modern design profession, pressed out of the mainstream economy by the advent of industrial production and Fordist work practices (Heskett 1980). As a consequence of this division of labor, 'creativity' has been increasingly disassociated with the 'skill' of realization, and the idea of craftsmanship is commonly associated with manual virtuosity rather than design activity. Despite a recent resurgence of interest in professional studio crafts and craft theory as a subject of scholarly study (Alfoldy 2007; Risatti 2007; Adamson 2007, 2013), home or cottage industries such as the one found in Koniaków are often thought of as 'unselfconscious' or vernacular design (Alexander 1964; Jones 1992; Lawson 1997): a form of *bricolage* circumscribed by a limited toolset, readily available materials, and the strictures of stylistic tradition. This belief in the inherent conservatism of vernacular design has led it to be immutably tied to economies of affect and gifting in the post-industrial world, and to sweatshops, exploitation, and child labor in the developing world. In one case, vernacular design stands for cozy anti-modernity, in the other it has been appropriated as industry's running mate.

Stringi—and the craftswomen who make and sell them—fit neither description. Their appeal might be understood as part of a resurgence in interest in the handmade, crafts and craftsmanship amongst artists, designers, academics, and the general public since the millennium (Hung and Magliaro 2006). Exhibitions such as *Radical Lace and Subversive Knitting* (2007) at the Museum of Arts and Design, New York, and the revival of knitting as a public, group activity ('Stitch 'n Bitch') are evidence of a revaluation of craftsmanship and the handmade. Associated with a type of social agency based on collective inheritance and practice, crafts have also become a powerful tool for political commentary. Yet, the emergence of stringi in the early twenty-first century suggests that there might be different kinds of questions to be asked about contemporary crafts and craftsmanship—questions not only about tradition and community, but also about entrepreneurship, the individual, and the market. Their success is as much based on a reinterpretation of a nineteenth-century-style cottage industry as on the redesign of local tradition to suit the demands of the twenty-first-century market. Stringi, I propose, are not just subversive to traditionalists in Koniaków but also challenge the romantic figure of the craftsman that still haunts much theory and practice in the arts and design.

In the summer of 2003, Koniaków celebrated 200 years of local lace by throwing a festival honoring the craft. The owners and curators of local galleries and the village's lace museum hosted two days of exhibitions, music, food, dancing, and competitions.[1] It was at this festival and in the

---

1. While the anniversary was largely fictive—ethnographic studies suggest the local craft is closer to half that age (Poloczkowa 1968)—the impetus to organize the festival was primarily commercial.

gallery of the local entrepreneur Jerzy that the handmade, lace G-strings first appeared. Pinned on a wall beside lace doilies, tablecloths, and demure blouses, the colorful lace underwear was a novel—and provocatively skimpy—addition to the well-known repertoire of products turned out by the local cottage industry. As Jerzy tells the story, however, the stringi may never have attained fame (or infamy) without the aid of the press and photographers who visited the village to record the anniversary celebrations. Visiting his gallery, a journalist saw the G-strings for sale, inquired about their origins, and finally bought them. According to Jerzy, she then took them from one gallery to another, asking prominent local lace makers about their opinions of the new product. He seemed to indicate that the journalist was looking for controversy and ultimately found it at the house of the elderly, prize-winning lace maker, Danuta Kucharska. She is quoted as having reacted to the sight of the crocheted underwear with the words "it's a disgrace" (Domanska 2003). According to Jerzy, Danuta became angered by the new product because "she was an older woman—she didn't know that her own daughter went to church wearing stringi—she thought it was only "loose" women who used stringi. She, however, identified the moral hazards of the stringi to what she saw as their artistic inferiority: "They are just such thin strips, how can they show your virtuosity? I'm not against women making them, but let them be called Koniaków G-strings, not Koniaków lace."[2]

Virtue and virtuosity, shame and greed became the discourse through which tradition and modernity were discussed as the press feasted on the quaint story of village grannies crocheting racy lingerie. Through newspaper coverage such as by *Gazeta Wyborcza* and *The Wall Street Journal*, Koniaków and its lace makers came under the glare of the national and international media. Much was made of the contrast between the titillating nature of the product and the apparent piety of the Catholic village community; one German magazine dubbed the local production of lingerie "erotic needlework" (*Stern*, April 13, 2006). Danuta's quip that Koniaków lace once "covered altars, now they cover backsides" became shorthand for numerous light-hearted articles on the controversial new laces. According to media reports, women who made lace stringi risked being named and shamed at Sunday sermons, others being unsure of whether they were obliged to admit to their production of the skimpy lingerie at confession. Lace makers were widely reported to be ashamed or shy about their involvement in the new business of making G-strings—no one wanted to admit to the visiting journalists having their hand in the invention of the stringi, nor would they confess to owning a pair themselves. Basking in the attention the stringi brought him and his gallery, Jerzy clearly enjoyed playing devil's advocate by announcing that, in his opinion, stringi were as traditional as altar cloths. Danuta, on the other hand, was rumored to be visiting the lace makers of the village one-by-one, trying to convince them of the inauthenticity of the new fad.

---

2. Quoted from an interview undertaken by Eva Kočárková (2005).

8.3 An elderly lace maker sits outside her home working on a summer day in Istebna. ©
Nicolette Makovicky

8.4 Antique Koniaków lace from a bonnet (detail). Design attributed to Maria Gwarkowa. © *Nicolette Makovicky*

Despite Danuta's efforts to put a lid on the production of lingerie, the commercial success of the lace stringi became the impetus for a rapid transformation of commercial practice, apprenticeship, and established authority among local artisans and lace makers. Within the span of a few months, three new businesses selling lace and lace lingerie set up in Koniaków and the neighboring village Istebna. Although men ran two of these, it was the young lace maker Halina Wysocka who was granted the status of an innovative, groundbreaking entrepreneur by the press. Halina founded her company together with her brother, bought the domain www.koniakow.com, and started selling lace G-strings online. On the company's website, professional models show off the wares, posing somewhat provocatively on a background of tropical foliage and sandy beaches. Today, one can buy anything, from stringi to bikinis, hats, gloves, lace blouses, and even dresses made entirely of lace from Halina's company. With over thirty lace makers on her books, most of them on short-term or flexible contracts, she takes both retail and wholesale orders, and supplies several companies that run websites located in the United States, United Kingdom, Japan, and Germany. With all her items carefully copyrighted and labeled, Halina assures her clients that all the products are handmade, using authentic motifs and techniques—regardless of whether they are tablecloths, wedding dresses, or thongs. "We draw on tradition," Halina told me. "The flower (motifs) are traditional, but it is a contemporary form of art."

Newspaper articles covering the story of Koniaków's stringi have cast the young entrepreneur Halina and the socially conservative Danuta as stereotypes of Polish post-socialist society. They have turned the emergence and commercial success of the stringi into a metaphor for the post-1989 marketization and liberalization of Polish society. Stringi were made into the symbols of a new, capitalist modernity arriving to the village community. In the village itself, however, the authenticity of the lingerie was still up for debate. Lace makers were pleased that the commercial success of the stringi ensured that the demand for their products returned to that of the halcyon days of late socialism, when the state-run folk art cooperative "Cepelia" had secured a steady stream of orders. However, there was no consensus among lace makers on whether stringi could be considered (and marketed) as authentic and traditional. These doubts continued even years after stringi had become a staple of the local craft repertoire. When I first spoke to lace makers in 2007, the discussions about authenticity centered on whether technique or form took precedent. Some lace makers claimed that anything produced using crochet and local motifs could be called lace, while others maintained that utility and marketability made the stringi a purely commercial product only tangentially connected to local traditions. As one lace maker put it: "Yes, they are made with a crochet hook, but it isn't a tradition. Stringi—who sees them? If one makes stringi, it is so that one can buy bread."

For this lace maker, the rapid turnover and commercialism of stringi were essentially the antithesis of what she understood as traditional artisanship. She thus shared Danuta's opinion that there was a difference between Koniaków lace and Koniaków lingerie—a difference that lay not in technique or form, but in function and commercialism. According to Danuta, stringi stood apart through their offending utility (covering backsides) but also in the simplicity of their execution.

Often made up of 30 to 40 identical lace flower motifs strung together, they do not show off the rich variety of the local stylistic repertoire in the way a tablecloth does. Rather than being made with pride and care, such items were made for commerce—indeed, the fact that stringi can be made in a matter of a few hours, rather than the days or weeks needed for larger pieces, was to Danuta further proof of their low grade. According to Danuta, then, the morality under threat by the popularity of the stringi was not that of the Church or family, but the morality of good crafts-manship. This old-fashioned value, which sociologist Richard Sennett defines as "doing something well for its own sake" (Sennett 2007: 104, 2008), lies at the heart of her artisan identity and her measure of creativity and artistic authority. Her opinion was shared by the National Artistic and Ethnographic Commission, who declared that due to their utilitarian nature stringi could not be certified as 'folk art' (Grygar, Hodrová, and Kocárková 2004). The commission thus sent the message that crafts should be valued primarily for their representative qualities. For Danuta and the commission alike, folk crafts and crafted items were seen to gain their value through their symbolic display of overproduction. Their obligatory 'uselessness' stood in a direct relationship to the disproportionate amount of labor invested in them. Not only did crafted items have to be non-utilitarian, they must also defy the cost-benefit analysis applied to any other process of production or purchase in the market today. And this quality should be visually evident—craft appeals through the 'enchantment of technology' (or technique, in this case) (Gell 1992). As the lace maker said: "Stringi—who sees them?"

The privileging of the symbolic and representative value of lace by Danuta and the National Artistic and Ethnographic Commission reveals a pervasive prejudice toward crafts and the hand-made as 'quaint' and 'decorative,' which continues to mark Euro-American public discourse on the subject. Yet, it also touches on the potential of crafts and craftsmanship to present a critical alternative to the market and consumer society. Crafts like lace making display an alternative tem-porality not simply through their use of historical motifs and techniques, but through their very mode of production. The recent rediscovery of the joys of crafting and the handmade among art-ists, designers, and consumers has largely been based on this sense of craft as giving access to such a different temporality (Hung and Magliaro 2006). While designing and making something by hand is rarely cost-effective, it is this very inefficiency that has become a tool for social commen-tary and political activism in the last decade. The rise of 'craftivism' has seen feminist groups such as the Revolutionary Knitting Circle (Canada) employ the materiality of the mundane to pro-vide potent social and political critique of globalization, war, poverty, environmental issues, and women's rights.[3] Knitting, in particular, has found a new place in contemporary popular culture.

---

3. The Revolutionary Knitting Circle has campaigned for peace and community sustainability at events like the G8 Summit in 2002 and an action to end the Iraq War in Calgary on March 20, 2004. Other exam-ples of craftivism and knitting for social causes are the support of Doctors Without Borders by the group "Knitters Without Borders" and the collaboration between the Danish artist Marianne Jørgensen and Lon-don's Cast-Off Knitting Club to create the work "Tank-Cozy" (a World War II tank covered by a pink knitted blanket), a protest against Denmark's involvement in the war in Iraq. For more details, see Pentney 2008.

Publications such as *Stitch 'n Bitch* (Stoller 2003) have transformed this domestic craft—once associated with housewifely frumpiness and poverty—into a new form of humorous, subversive creative expression. Recipes for knitted cupcakes, bikinis, and dog coats now compete with recipes for sweaters, shawls, and socks. Moving out of the home, knitting has become a hobby practiced collectively by mainly young women meeting in public spaces of consumption—parks, cafés, and museums. Challenging perceptions of domesticity and femininity, the practice of knitting also stands as a rebellion against the tyranny of time management, efficient production, and flexible specialization (Parkins 2004; Minahan and Cox 2007; Pentney 2008; Myzelev 2009).

Richard Sennett's (2008) call for the adoption of craftsmanship as a model for working life comes from the same concern about the devaluation of human value in the context of the new global economy. He calls for the revaluation of skill, experience, commitment, and trained judgment, which he identifies as part of craftsmanship as an "enduring, basic human impulse, the desire to do a job well for its own sake" (p. 9). The craftsman is a person "engaged practically if not necessarily instrumentally" (p. 20) in the pursuit of "objective standards" and "the thing itself" (p. 9). Here, instrumentality has become the metaphor for the short-term, flexible, and insecure nature of most employment in a society where work as vocation has become a privilege (Bauman 2005). Sennett's argument that market competition does not create the conditions which foster quality echoes the statement that stringi are made only "for bread" while other forms of lace artifacts display truly authentic workmanship.

Although he would probably be reluctant to align himself with the narrow conception of craftsmanship advocated by Danuta and the National Artistic and Ethnographic Commission, Sennett shares with them a belief in crafts and craftsmanship as the product of an alternative political economy of time, knowledge, and value. Against this background, the popularity of crocheted, lace thongs from the hands of craftswomen in a small Polish village is unsurprising. Like the knitted cupcakes and breast prostheses ("Tit-Bits")[4] of radical knitters, Koniaków lace thongs are unusual and humorous in their unexpected combination of material, technique, and function. Yet, for all its critical potential, this humor fails to challenge the social and symbolic value of craft itself. The appropriation of craft as socially and politically subversive relies on a discourse on the handmade that is itself decidedly conservative, if not romantic. Craft and the handmade are seen as untouched by the pressures of efficiency, commerce, and politics, belonging instead to an economy of affect, to the domestic, and to the historical. Equally, defining craftsmanship as the disinterested pursuit of objective standards of quality suggests that norms regulating aesthetics, authenticity, and excellence are the 'natural' outcome of cumulative, communal practical experience.

While the art historian Howard Risatti (2007) warned that studio crafts are in danger of being absorbed by the fine arts world, scholars of the history of guild crafts, folk traditions, and indigenous arts alike have made a direct connection between the alleged traditionalism of crafts and the collective nature of their transmission and production. From the guilds of medieval Europe to the

---

4. See www.titbits.ca.

traditions of indigenous craftsmen and women from the peripheries of the industrialized world, community is seen as the context and medium of apprenticeship, aesthetic judgment, and stylistic coherence (e.g., Gell 1998; Sennett 2008). While today's subversive crafters may not dream of uniting the designer and craftsman in the manner of the British Arts and Crafts Movement, there is a definite sense in which both academics like Sennett and practitioners such as members of the Stitch 'n Bitch movement perpetuated the Arts and Crafts philosophy of work and life together through the creation of community. Within such collectivities, the imagined alternative political economy of time, knowledge, and value inherent in craft and craftsmanship can be enacted. In short, crafts have gained their supposedly subversive edge not only by becoming the imagined antidote to the temporal and social experience of neoliberal capitalism, but also the antithesis of the archetypical capitalist individual: the entrepreneur. The perception of craft as communal and essentially non-commercial is based on a particular model of culture as bounded in space and time—whether it is a workshop or the local community of a village such as Koniaków. It also advertises a certain form of social agency based in collective inheritance and action. Against this background, the emergence of the stringi and businesses like Halina Wysocka's appear to be an anathema. How can a community of practice also be a community of entrepreneurs? Does this represent a radically new approach to craftsmanship, born out of the necessity to adapt to a new, globalized market?

Trying to answer these questions, it is necessary to understand the way conceptions of folk culture and personhood have changed over time, as well as the history of lace making in Koniaków itself. And it reveals some interesting truths about the nature of vernacular crafts and their entanglement with industrial design, state ideology, and the market throughout the twentieth century. Just as the village communities all over Europe have undergone enormous sociocultural changes since the nineteenth century, neither did the craft of lace making nor the position of craftsmanship in Koniaków exist in a temporal vacuum. Rather, they changed in structure and purpose together with the modernization of Polish society and the fluctuating nature of Poland's national borders.[5] Along with other folk crafts, Koniaków's lace and lace makers found themselves appropriated by a succession of political discourses and changing ideological designs for life. In Poland, as in wider Central Europe, the late-nineteenth-century turn to the vernacular was an integral part of national romantic movements (Crowley 2001; Kinchin 2004; Szczerski 2005). With the country partitioned between the Russian Empire, Prussia, and the Austrian Monarchy until 1919, *fin-de-siècle* Polish intellectuals in search of a Polish homeland identified the Carpathian borderlands as the ancestral home of a national Polish character, language, and expressive style (Crowley 1992, 2001; Manouelian 2000; Dabrowski 2008). Villages such as Koniaków,

---

5. Poland was partitioned between the Russian Empire, Prussia, and the Austrian Monarchy in 1772. Koniaków fell under the Dukedom of Cieszyn Silesia, part of the Habsburg administration.

together with their highlander (*Górale*)[6] population and their material culture, became a Polish national "poetic space" (Smith 1991).

In the late nineteenth century, crochet lace began to be produced by women in Koniaków for the decoration of the front of the "czepiec," or a married woman's headdress.[7] It was not until the development of the nearby lowland village of Wisła into a spa town in the early 1930s that lace lost its exclusive connection to local, vernacular costume and became a commodity for outsiders, and domestic craft became a cottage industry employing the majority of the women in the village. According to local stories, the redesign of local lace into a product for bourgeois spa guests was aided by the collaboration of the Jewish owners of Wisła's haberdashery and a single Koniaków lace maker named Ana Rucka (see also Poloczkowa 1968). Ana is not only credited with working out a method for making lace in the round for the creation of doilies and tablecloths, but also with spreading the knowledge of the technique to other village women, who traditionally gathered in each other's houses on winter evenings to spin, sew, or embroider. As the demand for lace grew, women in Koniaków made oval, square, and rectangular tablecloths and doilies, and accessories like collars, cuffs, and gloves for sale in Wisła's hotels and shops.

After World War II, another local lace maker, Maria Gwarkowa, became responsible for the creation of a craft cooperative that employed several hundred local lace makers. A constituent part of the Katowice-based folk art cooperative ARW and run by the umbrella organization Cepelia, the cooperative supplied craftswomen with designs and thread, and sold the finished products through a network of national and international Cepelia folk art shops. The involvement of the socialist state in Koniaków's cottage industry, however, went far beyond that of reorganizing production and sales to suit the demands of socialist ideology. Throughout the Eastern Bloc, communist parties appropriated peasant crafts in order to underpin the legitimacy of socialist rule (Kaneff 2004). In this respect, Poland appears to have been no different. While the emphasis may have been on the 'folk' rather than the 'craft,' both movements also represented an attempt to reform vernacular crafts into a contemporary expressive medium (Makovicky 2009). The dominance of Stalinist socialist realism led to a revival of nationalist design philosophies after World War II and vernacular crafts came to play a leading role in the development of a new national industrial design aesthetic (Taylor 1990; Crowley 1994, 1998). As a form of culture that could be traced directly

---

6. The Górale—literally "highlanders"—were pastoralists inhabiting the Polish and Slovak High Tatras, as well as the Beskid mountain range spanning the contemporary borders of Poland, Slovakia, and the Czech Republic. Today, the inhabitants of Koniaków proudly claim Górale heritage and celebrate their history of pastoralism, characteristic folkways, and music.

7. There is no consensus on when women in the village started making lace; artisans claim that the tradition is as much as 200 years old. The most plausible is that the wife of a local schoolteacher taught the younger girls in the village the technique of crochet in the mid-nineteenth century as part of a general course in needlecraft and domestic economy (Poloczkowa 1968). Based on the skills taught at school, young women in Koniaków started producing and eventually developing an indigenous repertoire of abstract and floral motifs unique to the village.

to working class or peasant roots, crafts supplied the 'national form' for the 'socialist content' of Stalinist material culture. Under the direction of the staff of the Institute of Industrial Design (Institut Wzornictwa Przemysłowego) in the 1950s, peasant craftsmen and factory workers were encouraged to develop prototype designs that could later be advanced for production by trained designers. As part of this scheme, the designer Lidia Buczek reinterpreted Koniaków lace designs to create templates for decorative lingerie. Now forgotten, these ancestors of today's stringi were mass-produced in the textile factories of Łódź (Taylor 1990).

Ethnographers, art historians, and designers were brought together with craftsmen and women through the creation of Cepelia and the use of vernacular crafts for the development of 'politically correct' design at the Institute of Industrial Design. Despite the purported democratic nature of such collaborations, associations such as Cepelia and the lace-making cooperative run under its auspices tended toward an inflexible, hierarchical organization characteristic of socialist institutions. Although vernacular crafts were celebrated as embodying the "'common-sense' hegemony of the collective . . . over the creative individualism of the artist" (Crowley 1998: 76), the final approval and authentication of products laid with consultant ethnographers and the organization's professionally trained designers. This move placed artistic authority into the hands of academics and outside the local context of the village and the industry itself. Lace makers were invited to share this authority by working for Cepelia or applying for numerous competitions, prizes, and certifications granted by the National Artistic and Ethnographic Commission, but ultimately the state institutions that figured simultaneously their employers and their clients stipulated the criteria for authenticity.

Thus, there existed a tension between the politically espoused ideals of communal practice as design philosophy and the reality of a system that provided lace makers with the opportunity to create for themselves careers as 'folk artists.' The social and artistic authority of the cooperative founder, Maria Gwarkowa, and that of Danuta Kucharska—who opposed the labeling of stringi as authentic Koniaków lace—were bound to the commercial and political power of these institutions. Yet, since 1989, post-socialist, neoliberal economic reforms have meant that state institutions such as Cepelia are no longer practically or financially responsible for the production of lace in Koniaków. As before World War II, supply and demand are again being regulated by market forces. This dismantling of the state-supported cooperative system has cast uncertainty on the validity of the structures of artistic and social authority this system provided, leaving the question of tradition, innovation, and authenticity open for renegotiation by all actors in the local community. The inability of Danuta (and the National Artistic and Ethnographic Commission) to prevent the making and sale of stringi as authentic Koniaków lace shows how business and commerce are today the primary means of transmitting local cultural traditions. In fact, men and women such as Jerzy and Halina Wysocka have been successful primarily because of their ability to embrace the market as a new sphere for entrepreneurial activities. Their success, however, has come at the expense of the previously intimate relationship between state-sponsored ethnography, commerce, and authority. The consternation of Danuta Kucharska and other elderly, well-established lace makers was probably much less a question of age, religious conviction, or sexual mores, but the protest of a group of craftswomen who see their social and artistic authority slipping away together with the association of lace making with a national folk heritage and the state with the role as its guardian.

Today, several years after stringi first appeared in the galleries and websites selling lace from Koniaków, most lace makers and traders have few misgivings about crocheting thongs and recall the media hype, gossip, and conflicts with rolled eyes and amused smiles. "Where is the shame if people want to buy it?" one lace maker reasoned. With stringi and bras still bestsellers, lace makers have now expanded into making thongs for men that have proven extraordinarily popular. Unlike women's G-strings, thongs for men can still make some lace makers blush, while others are downright unapologetic: "Yes, I make stringi. Women's, men's, all sizes … Have you seen men's G-strings? Well, they are great, because you really need to decorate men's private parts!"

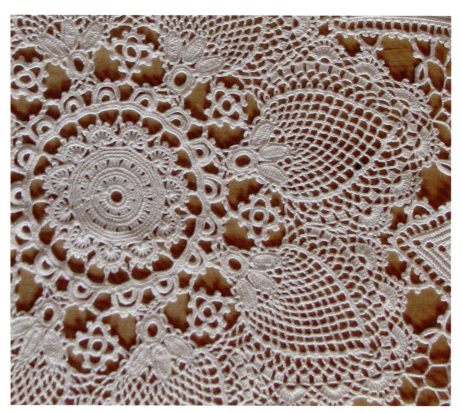

8.5 Fine, traditional Koniaków lace tablecloth worked in silk (detail), 2009. Designer: Beata Legierska. © *Nicolette Makovicky*

8.6 A young man inspects the designs of his mother, Ana Gemera. They sell lace and refreshments from a small stall outside their home near the summit of the Ochodzita Mountain. © *Nicolette Makovicky*

Across Poland, Koniaków has become synonymous with this form of quirky 'folk lingerie.' Since stringi first appeared in 2003, the Polish and international media have been quick to exploit the public's romance with the vernacular and the conception of the rural margins as spaces of tradition and religious conservatism. These ideas were projected onto the figure of Danuta Kucharska, the elderly representative of the establishment, while Halina Wysocka and her business were celebrated as the harbinger of change to the small community. Yet, while the press reported the story of the fracturing of a traditional community of craft practitioners under the pressures of a new post-socialist modernity, I think it can be better understood as the latest reinvention of an industry dependent on the customs and tastes of clients from outside the village. As a challenge to not only older forms of lace but also a defunct commercial structure, the success of the stringi as a product and a catalyst for the creation of new businesses seems part of a longer historical cycle of periodic reinvention of the craft. The history of local cottage industry is one of continual design innovation and the celebration of the insight and entrepreneurial spirit of named individuals such as Ana Rucka and Maria Gwarkowa, who figure in the popular imagination as single-minded pioneers. Within these celebratory narratives, cultural innovation is inextricably linked to commercial innovation: Design change is directly related to changes in the way lace has been sold and to whom. When Halina Wysocka and Jerzy speak about their choices to sponsor and market the stringi as authentic Koniaków lace, then their narratives and justifications are modeled on this local legend bringing together craft, creativity, and entrepreneurship.

References

Adamson, G. (2007), *Thinking Through Craft*, Oxford & London: Berg Publishers and the Victoria and Albert Museum.

Adamson, G. (2013), *The Invention of Craft*, Oxford & London: Bloomsbury.

Alexander, C. (1964), *Notes on the Synthesis of Form*, Cambridge: Harvard University Press.

Alfoldy, S., ed. (2007), *NeoCraft: Modernity and the Crafts*, Halifax: The Press of the Nova Scotia College of Art and Design.

Bauman, Z. (2005), *Work, Consumerism and the New Poor*, Maidenhead: Open University Press.

Crowley, D. (1992), *National Style and Nation State. Design in Poland from the Vernacular Revival to the International Style*, Manchester: Manchester University Press.

Crowley, D. (1994), "Building the World Anew: Design in Stalinist and Post-Stalinist Poland," *Journal of Design History*, 7 (3): 187–203.

Crowley, D. (1998), "Stalinism and Modernist Craft in Poland," *Journal of Design History*, 11 (1): 71–83.

Crowley, D. (2001), "Finding Poland in the Margins: The Case of the Zakopane Style," *Journal of Design History*, 14 (2): 105–16.

Dabrowski, P. (2008), "Constructing a Polish Landscape: The Example of the Carpathian Frontier," *Austrian History Yearbook*, 39: 45–65.

Gell, A. (1992), "The Technology of Enchantment and the Enchantment of Technology," in J. Coote and A. Shelton (eds.), *Anthropology, Art and Aesthetics*, 40–66, Oxford: Oxford University Press.

Gell, A. (1998), *Art and Agency. An Anthropological Theory*, Oxford: Oxford University Press.

Grygar, J., Hodrová, L. and Kocárková, E. (2004), "Konakowska Krajka TM. Vyjednavin. tradice a lidovosti umeni ve Slezskych Beskydech," in L. Hodrov and E. Kocarkov (eds.), *III. Antropologické symposium*, 56–76, Plzen: Aleš Cenek.

Heskett, J. (1980), *Industrial Design*, London: Thames and Hudson.

Hung, S. and Magliaro, J., eds. (2006), *By Hand: The Use of Craft in Contemporary Art*, Princeton: Princeton Architectural Press.

Jones, J. C. (1992), *Design Methods*, Chichester: John Wiley & Sons.

Kaneff, D. (2004), *Who Owns the Past? The Politics of Time in a "Model" Bulgarian Village*, Oxford: Berghahn Books.

Keeve, V. (2006), "Tangas: Heilige Höschen," *Stern* (April 13). Available online: http://www.stern.de/lifestyle/mode/tangas-heilige-hoeschen-3495178.html (accessed January 18, 2017).

Kinchin, J. (2004), "Hungary: Shaping a National Consciousness," in W. Kaplan (ed.), *The Arts and Crafts in Europe and America*, 142–77, London: Thames and Hudson.

Kocárková, E. (2005), "Hanysy do chałpy!' a jine reprezentace mista v beskydskym Trojvsi," MA thesis, Prague: Charles University.

Lawson, B. (1997), *How Designers Think: The Design Process Demystified*, Oxford: Architectural Press.

Makovicky, N. (2009), "'Traditional—with Contemporary Form': Craft and Discourses of Modernity in Slovakia Today," *The Journal of Modern Craft*, 2 (1): 43–58.

Manouelian, E. (2000), "Invented Traditions: Primitivist Narrative and Design in the Polish Fin de Siècle," in *Slavic Review*, 59 (3): 391–405.

Minahan, S. and Cox, J. W. (2007), "Stitch 'n Bitch," *Journal of Material Culture*, 12 (1): 5–21.

Myzelev, A. (2009), "Whip Your Hobby into Shape: Knitting, Feminism and Construction of Gender," *Textile*, 7 (2): 148–63.

Parkins, W. (2004), "Celebrity Knitting and the Temporality of Postmodernity," *Fashion Theory*, 8 (4): 425–41.

Pentney, A. (2008), "Feminism, Activism, and Knitting: Are the Fibre Arts a Viable Mode for Feminist Political Action?" *Thirdspace*, 8 (1). Available online: http://journals.sfu.ca/thirdspace/index.php/journal/article/view/pentney (accessed September 23, 2015).

Poloczkowa, B. (1968), "Koronki Koniakowskie," *Polska Sztuka Ludowa*, 22: 209–40.

Risatti, H. (2007), *A Theory of Craft: Function and Aesthetic Expression*, Chapel Hill: University of North Carolina Press.

Sennett, R. (2007), *The Culture of the New Capitalism*, New Haven: Yale University Press.

Sennett, R. (2008), *The Craftsman*, New Haven: Yale University Press.

Smith, A. (1991), *National Identity*, Harmondsworth: Penguin.

Stoller, D. (2003), *Stitch'n Bitch: The Knitters Handbook*, New York: Workman Publishing.

Surmiak-Domanska, K. (2003), "Hanba z trzydziestu kwiatkow," *Wysokie Obcasy*, 25 (10). Available online: www.wysokieobcasy.pl/wysokie-obcasy/1,53662,1732959.html (accessed September 23, 2015).

Szczerski, A. (2005), "Central Europe," in K. Livingstone and L. Parry (eds.), *International Arts and Crafts*, 55–76, London: V&A Publications.

Taylor, L. (1990), "News from Elsewhere," *Journal of Design History*, 3 (1): 59–62.

9 Functioning Forms/ Anti-Design

Vladimir Arkhipov

Design was conceived of as a revolutionary way of transforming life. These days, design has become the exact opposite: a fetish of modern consumer society. Design's only contemporary purpose is to create new things out of nothing. For the artist, however, design equals death. The artist's true mission is to create a substantively new vision.

My initial education was in engineering. After working for a few years at an aviation research institute, I began to explore other fields: medicine and visual art. I did not become a doctor but did take up sculpture after attending private classes and visiting various art studios. Then I saw Günther Uecker's 1987 Moscow exhibition. His works completely transformed my understanding of sculpture, plastic arts, and the object itself, and they inspired me to reconsider form. Up to 1993, I made objects from ordinary, everyday things. My aim was to reconcile the utilitarian and the exalted, while taking into account the experiences of the Russian avant-garde, Moscow Conceptualism, Dada, and Pop Art. By 1993, the social consequences of the transition from the USSR to rampant capitalism had become clear: the Soviet health care and pension systems, social welfare systems, and social safety net had been destroyed and had not been restored. For the first time, there were millionaires, and there were beggars. My audience's social and material stratification seemed to me a personal tragedy: They worked hard, had nothing to eat, and had no interest whatsoever in art. They stopped attending my exhibitions. I could no longer pursue my work as I had before, and I ultimately began considering the social dimensions of art.

Meanwhile, in 1994, I participated in an international exhibition in Munich and for the first time had the opportunity to see the works of young Western artists firsthand. It made me realize how untenable and baseless many artworks, mine included, are. Accompanied by a sense of confusion and despair, my search for a new orientation suddenly led me to the idea of the self-made, functional object (which is not to be confused with handcrafted and do-it-yourself objects).

Though I have been engaged in this project for fifteen years, my interest in it has not diminished. For many years, I have been asking people the question: "Why did you make this thing? What for?" While I still hope to learn their creative secrets, people answer with platitudes and give no substantive formulas. I hope they know it deep down (but do not reveal it, because they want me to draw my own conclusions). People solve concrete, everyday problems with their self-made objects and see no use for them beyond everyday life. The artist's business is reflection.

Long before becoming an artist, I was plagued by questions: "Why do collective farmers get up at five in the morning and work the whole day, but still have no running water, only outhouses, and earthen floors in their homes?" That was my childhood in the USSR. At that time, in the 1970s, I had no answers. But these questions returned much later, in 1994, when I was looking for a way out of my own creative deadlock. They resonated with a further painful question: "What is to be done?" Oddly—and wonderfully—the answer to these questions came to me one day as I was putting away winter clothes at a friend's summer home. A hook someone had made from a toothbrush suddenly caught my eye. Never before had someone's creativity sparked such a cathartic experience in me. The past and the present, tradition and innovation, the individual and the universal: This self-made hook contained it all. As I later realized, I was amazed by the unshakable honesty of this subject, by its utter aesthetic perfection, void of all reflection. It was the essence of original creativity, which has nearly ceased to exist in modern art and design.

In the past, design was conceived of as a revolutionary way of transforming life (for example, Bauhaus in the 1920s). Its main advantages were availability, broad appeal, and the potential for rapid improvement. These days, design has become the exact opposite: a fetish of modern consumer society. Design's only contemporary purpose is to create new things out of nothing. For the artist, however, design equals death. The artist's true mission is to create a substantively new vision. Truly outstanding design is design that is commensurate with substance. But, as a rule, there is a reciprocal exchange: The designer does not replicate the form directly from life, but adopts and revises it, draws associative parallels according to an applied problem. It is always possible to make a profit on the declining importance of some phenomenon. Devaluation is *en vogue* nowadays. But not every idea can be exalted. Journalists and critics consistently read my attempts to present new phenomena in art as 'national design' or 'folk art,' and 'my' creators are classified—with a certain self-indulgent sense of superiority—as handymen and 'do-it-yourselfers.' Neither is correct. My work is certainly not folk art, for I do not capture things, which have already been ascribed aesthetic value by their creators. Nor is my work national design, as none of 'my' creators aspire to its distribution. These are among my selection criteria for objects (more about them follows). We are dealing here with a special form of creativity: commodity folklore. Or, more precisely, post-folklore, since it regards neither national tradition nor inherited knowledge. Every thing is made in a certain place, at a certain time, and is the product of a unique, coincident set of circumstances.

Some factors that influence self-made objects are: the thing's level of necessity; the creator's professional skills, educational level, cultural fluency, and income; existence and availability of substitutes; place of residence (urban/rural); climate; the level of involvement of the creator's country of residence in the global economy; etc.

From the outset, self-made utilitarian things already exist (at least to me); that is, someone has already made them. Unlike regular things, they have not been created for sale, and there are no exact reproductions. If we understand design as a tool to attract customers' attention, as a consumption stimulant, then self-made everyday things are, by definition, anti-design: They repel the attention of ordinary people. The creators of such things do not try to display or sell them. In other words, their things serve a purpose only for them. In this sense, they are cultic objects. They are ideal: intended specifically for the person who created them. Others like them do not exist!

The links between people and things are closely related: A thing's beauty or functional perfection plays no role whatsoever. The person uses the thing as it is. Designers find such relations unacceptable. Certainly, compared to all surrounding things, the number of self-made objects is extremely small. But quantity is not the decisive factor here. The important fact is the act of creation and its result: the form devoid of any aesthetic intent. Such aesthetically pure and spontaneous form is desirable for the sophisticated viewer.

People co-create their visual environment and (even if they do not realize it) their aesthetic environment. If all the world's sculptors and designers were to cease to exist tomorrow, the creation of new forms would not decline. The creator of a landscape has a name: God. The forms that interest me bear their creators' names. Any professional artist is an artificial source of forms. My sources, by contrast, are natural: I can question them, record interviews with them, and take their photographs. Their ideas of 'chairs' were born before the 'chairs' themselves. Are we really living in the Neo-Platonic age? According to Aristotle, art is the imitation of reality. But what is the creation of reality? And how does creativity differ from art?

Our world depends on the continuous production of visual images. There are even people designated with their creation: artists and designers. They know well the task with which they are charged. They are sophisticated; they employ professional sleight of hand to impress us with perfection of execution, with technical and technological dexterity. But truth is not attained through cunning. Where is there room for a miracle? Where is the way out?

For me, the answers to these questions lie in these self-made items. Their creators have, wonderfully, created unique forms without striving to solve aesthetic problems. As an artist, it is my charge only to display them faithfully, not to spoil them. Our responsibilities are different: While the creators are responsible for aesthetic purity (though they know nothing of it), I search, select, and present their masterpieces. I do not appropriate their authorship (creators' first and last names are often presented alongside their portraits in exhibitions), and I attempt to display the items as organically as possible, without any changes. It is therefore possible to take an exhibited spade and dig up the ground with it after an exhibition. It is equally possible to hang that same spade on a wall (like an insured museum piece, its full value listed in the catalog and on the website). The creator-owner decides on a course of action. As a result, an amazing transformation takes place: Commonplace self-made items become art objects and then revert back to commonplace self-made items. The resulting chain, one I have conceived, pleases my artist's vanity. In reality, I consider my main achievement the triumph over my own vanity: In the works' signatures, my name is listed last. I view this project's potential as an independent methodology for identifying and representing national self-made items as visual objects.

The methodology described here can just as easily function independently of my participation. To this end, I will attempt to describe the selection criteria for objects:

- The preexisting collection must be taken into account during the selection (exhibiting, etc.) of further self-made objects. A self-made item similar to one already included in the collection is less interesting.
- The more a particular self-made object differs from articles sold in building superstores or on the used goods market, the more interesting the item is.
- Technical perfection, convenience of use, and quality of manufacturing are irrelevant.
- The self-made item should be functional and made without the utilization of templates, protractors, etc.
- If the item has been ordered, sold, or bought, it is of no interest, since it has undergone a Marxian process of alienation (money-goods-money) and thus lost its individuality and aura.
- The self-made thing should have a creator or a person (a family member, friend, or witness) who can attest to the item's origins.
- Objects whose creators are spiteful and aggressive will not be accepted.
- The less decorative embellishment added to an item, the greater its interest.
- Aside from the previous points, the aesthetic range of things is limitless.

The question is: "How long can this process of searching for and presenting objects go on?" Technically speaking, the process is infinite. In reality, however, this methodology ceases to function without delight, surprise, trembling, and admiration before another's creation. As new finds arouse these feelings in me, I will continue to search and display others' treasures.

Self-made objects are children of paradox: the free spirit of creativity crossed with a concrete need yields such fruits. Why do I find them so attractive? Because modern artists are slaves to strategy. They dream only of sacrificing themselves to pure creativity without ever leaving the artistic realm. But you can't have your cake and eat it too: the act of creation does not demand valuation; the creative act alone is itself enough. Art, however, does not exist without a determination of value (value of a work of art). The desire to strike a balance, to combine both, is normal and justified. But it requires a willingness to relinquish total control over the artistic product and allow the unpredictable to occur (the history of art houses and similar examples). My art links the unpredictable, an element of adventurism, with my confidence that self-made items can be found everywhere (in every country). I just never know exactly what I will find. Each item is connected with a concrete person, and the creator is not always easy to identify. I need his direct comments without any mass media intervention. I never know how many people I will interview or how our conversations will unfold. It is important that our dialogue is informal and that my interview subjects are not merely extras or bodies—otherwise, we will not find the objects' creators. My project requires the participation of many people. The result is a collective work of art: I saw an item; a second person translated; a third helped determine the address; a fourth remembered something; a fifth gave a phone number; a sixth said the creator is on holiday; a seventh offered me a glass of wine, and while drinking it, a new and interesting item caught my eye; and so on. But not every self-made object I find makes it onto my site, into the book or exposition. One of the selection criteria is also ethical: I will not accept an item from an aggressive creator. If a person is closed and unwilling to communicate, I do not try to force them into conversation. It is his or her choice, and I do not wish to cause negative emotions. I usually tell people what I am searching for and why, and if the person is open, everything goes well (two unemployed creators even managed to find work, thanks to this project).

Finally, here are some words about the phenomenon of self-making—its geographical, historical, and social features—as part of material culture:

- Among the first things Adam and Eve did upon their banishment from Paradise was to make a tool for food procurement.
- Rich and poor alike can create self-made items, but the poor more often transform the object world around them with their own hands.
- We have neither quantitative nor qualitative knowledge about this phenomenon. My finds always result casually from my indirect research method. We do not possess any scientific data.
- While self-made things from the Soviet era certainly have a 'Soviet' specificity (even nails and screws were different), it is generally impossible to guess the national origin of a self-made item: It could be Italian, German, or Spanish.
- Does the value of this phenomenon transcend the aesthetic?
- I have not yet revealed my search method, but it is not complicated.

The purpose of my searches is not to collect or possess objects, but to satisfy my interest in life's variety through informal dialogue, interaction with peers, and the revelation of new artistic principles, which are not contingent on commerce. The collection, electronic database, and website are related in and of themselves. I value an object not for its design or exhibition value but for the mere fact of its existence. The most compelling thing for me is the act of spontaneous creation of form.

What is my work all about when I show things made by other people? It entails finding things, entering into a dialogue with them and writing an interview with the authors, "to direct the soffits" to these masterpieces. Evidently, of the essence is always my strong artistic impression of what I just saw and my desire to share it with the viewer. The results of my research were always random—"I go who knows where and look for who knows what." But they are logical: Instead of the paradigm "I am an artist," the new paradigm should be "He is an artist." There are endless resources for the development of art when the artist doesn't see the artist in himself but in another who is far away from art. That is the future of art! That is why I show different things for which simple reflection is not enough to make them works of art. It is not the author's but the spectator's perspective, which makes these objects worthy of any museum: Authors simply do not know that every person, as Joseph Beuys said, is an artist.

Fifteen years have passed since I found my first self-made object. For a number of years, I had been searching for and collecting objects in Russia. At some point, the objects began seeking me out: People who liked my idea began calling me to tell me about objects they had seen. Ultimately, the geography of my searches spread beyond the borders of Russia: England, Ireland, Albania, Austria, Germany, Italy, Spain, Brazil, Australia, the United Arab Emirates, France, and Switzerland have all presented their self-made treasures to me. So I have collected a huge amount of material, which I would like to share with the entire world. I would also like to give people the chance to submit and display their masterpieces. In 2008, I created an independent information resource—an online version of my project—to which I uploaded information about the self-made objects: audio stories, narrative tales in original languages, photographs of participants, photographs of their objects.[1] But for some reason, designers have not erected a monument to me, regardless of the fact that I am able to extract free "ore" for them that is enriched by flexible, dynamic, and structural ideas.

The data preparation for the online museum is progressing slowly: About two thousand items from different countries are currently being processed. Since the online museum's inception, an interesting fact has emerged: The creators of self-made objects are so authentic that they do not hesitate to make public their homemade objects and photos. In contrast, people who have submitted photos of things with an already estimated aesthetic value have deprived us of our pioneering pleasure. Hence, their things are less interesting for us. Aside from the objects of known creative provenance, there is a category 'creator wanted,' in which anonymous things are presented as well. In addition to a complete listing of all objects, the online museum also has a search function, which allows visitors to find an object by its function, creator's name, year of creation, or country of origin.

---

1. Available at www.folkforms.ru. No web technologies are in place and the site needs to be redone, of course, but right now I am unable/lacking the financial support.

Vladimir Antipov: Shovel from the Road Signs, Moscow, Russia, 1998

In June 1998, I worked as a street sweeper on Kutusowskij Prospect. What happened? There was an infamous storm in Moscow. I don't remember if I've ever experienced anything like it; so many trees had been toppled and roofs were destroyed. And when the street cleaners had to do the cleanup, it was simply horrible. We worked nine to ten hours, and we had to load the truck with all these branches, beams, iron pieces, everything that was falling down from the rooftops. It was something absolutely unbelievable. We constantly loaded the trucks, cut the trees, cleared the spill—and then we got no money for it. We worked like idiots for two months, and we got only a hundred Rubels—but that is another story.

It's incredible how much we had to evacuate. So, I had the stuff thrown into the car and all of a sudden I had this traffic sign in my hand. I almost threw it aside, but it was so simple that it was kind of funny—I thought it would make a good shovel for the snow in winter. Two corners I did away with, sawn or broken off, and bent the third. I drilled a hole so a handle could be attached.

And look: It's become a shovel—and that is a picture: a workman. The picture did not really matter, but later, in winter, when I had to clear snow, I learned to appreciate it. I was bored and started holding the blade upright. Some drivers slowed down, others were enraged. Twice I survived by a miracle. The bastards! And with this blade, I cleared the snow in winter '98 and early '99 (see Figure 9.1).

Vasilii Arkhipov's Television Antenna, Kolomna, Russia, Around 1993

They put a re-transmitter on the hotel and then there were televisions that could receive the decimeter waveband. The antenna was a collective one, but it did not have a decimeter waveband on the master antenna. They didn't bother with one. Only afterwards did they bother to put one on it. In the magazine *Radio*, the dimensions were published, everything came from this, like the diagrams of the decimeter waves. We prepared this antenna according to these dimensions. But you know, the vibrators, or resonators, are everything. We made them from forks so that the reception would be better. We then split them and made them like paintbrushes, these copper vibrator/resonators. A fork is like a brush, I mean it splits like hairs on a paintbrush. So we took the dimensions from there. In my opinion, it all worked out very well. So we started to do it all quickly, connecting them onto the master antenna. Then we connected a mixer to the collective antenna and, of course, the decimeter antenna received the signal better than through amplifiers. And then everyone got rid of their amplifiers. The effect was noticeable from the very beginning. Everyone wanted to watch a particular program from St. Petersburg. My mother had the forks in her cupboard . . . Ha, ha, ha! I didn't buy them. My mother bought them when everything was collapsing around us. There wasn't anything else but forks to buy in the shops then. Although we ate with them, they weren't very good forks, in the culinary sense—but they went well with that antenna (see Figure 9.2).

9.1 Vladimir Antipov's shovel, Moscow, Russia, 1998. © *Vladimir Arkhipov*

Albina Leonidovna Falko: Children's Steering Wheel, Perm, 1978 (as told by her son, Mikhail Turbowski)

When I started working at Swerdlov in 1988, I made these parts. This is part of the engine of the TU-134. This piece is said to have had a defect. When I was a child, I had a sofa that could be unfolded, and in-between there was a stage you could climb on. And if you put aside a sofa cushion

9.2 Vasilii Arkhipov's television antenna, Kolomna, Russia, about 1993. © *Vladimir Arkhipov*

a column formed between the hinges. And when you shoved a stick into it, a child could use it as a steering wheel. In the 1980s, a steering wheel was a good alternative for home driving games. My son now plays with a real steering wheel from an old Lada car. But I was very happy with a home-made steering wheel. My mother made it for me; I believe it was the year 1977. It was made by my mother—how she dragged the pieces away from a munitions factory is a mystery to me, but what a blessing it was for me! There were so many interesting metal parts, I could play for hours with it and build with it (see Figure 9.3).

9.3 Albina Leonidovna Falko's children's steering wheel, Perm, 1978. ©
Vladimir Arkhipov

Alexei Tikhonov: Provisional Privy from a Stool, Ryazan Region, Russia, 1990 (as told by his nephew, Vladimir)

My grandmother lived in a village near Ryazan. In the summer, many relatives came to visit her on vacation. She lived alone in the village—her husband had died shortly after the war as a result of war wounds. You could see immediately that the house missed having a man around. The toilets in the village are mostly outside, and it's cold. In winter, going to the toilet is quite a problem—nobody feels like it. And one inevitably looks for possible solutions on how to relieve oneself without going outside. At the end of the 1980s, a relative from Tula came to visit grandmother for several summers. They called him uncle Lescha. He was already retired. Once he brought a multilayered veneer toilet seat with him. He said he had renovated his apartment and wanted to help improve grandmother's life. First, we didn't understand why he brought this seat, but soon afterwards he made this remarkable construction. What had he done? At the time, grandmother's daughter, my aunt, brought with her four stools; in the village shop, they didn't sell stools. This uncle Lescha took one of the stools and disappeared into the barn to work on it. After a couple of days, he showed us this construction. He attached the toilet seat to the legs of the stool with studs. Rubber cushions help the seat remain in a horizontal position. You can open the seat easily and put a bucket beneath (see Figure 9.4). It's not necessary to go out in winter—there is a comfortable toilet at home! He made it around 1989 or 1990. And grandmother used this 'stool' until her death in 1995.

Sven Hünemörder: Balalayka, Altai region, Russia, 2003

I was with my wife on our wedding trip at her home in Siberia, visiting my parents-in-law, and I didn't have a guitar with me. My wife, at the same time, was shooting a movie, and I was responsible for the music. I couldn't take my guitar with me in the luggage, and I knew that this wasn't going to be so nice. I locked myself in the toilet, a kind of wooden closet in the barn, and then my parents-in-law knocked on the door and called: "What is with you? Why don't you come out?" I thought to myself, maybe I find some things to fix together. In the barn, I found a genuine tin can, real Russian made, and a part of an old cassette recorder. I made holes in the can with a screwdriver, and in the evening, I had this idea for a little bit of music . . .

9.4 Alexei Tikhonow's 'close-stool,' the Ryazan region, Russia, 1990. © *Vladimir Arkhipov*

At the premiere of the movie, my wife should say some words about the scene, but instead I got up and played on this guitar. I had won a bet in the only music pub of Tashdagol. Shenia bet if I was able to play "Hotel California" on it. It's tuned like a guitar—or balalayka, as we call it—with four strings, but one that you play differently (see Figure 9.5).

Vladimir Arkhipov: Cases with a Homemade Handle, Bordeaux, France, 2009

At Bordeaux airport, when I got my suitcase back, the pusher grip was broken (see Figure 9.6). At the airport, I wrote a letter to Air France with a request to reimburse me for the damage. The employees at the baggage service said that I stood little chance of obtaining compensation or a replacement bag. The museum staff, who called there on my behalf, said I would have to wait for two weeks. Then I went with an interpreter to the headquarters of Air France in Bordeaux. There they listened to us sympathetically and gave the address and telephone number of the company. It

9.5 Sven Hünemörder's balalayka, Russia, Altai region, 2003. © *Vladimir Arkhipov*

turns out that this company is a business, where there are decisions about what you can do in each specific case. One of the Air France representatives simply recommended not to buy cases with handles in the future. . .

Anyone who has purchased a suitcase on wheels with a push handle can hardly imagine how they would transport their luggage without wheels. How should I now carry twenty kilograms? In the courtyard of the house where I lived, there was an abandoned factory with iron bars on the windows. The grids were old and some poles were broken. I removed one of them and made it into an oval shape. I tied the ends with tape. I attached the handle onto the suitcase with rope. When the rope is wrapped around a wooden stick and unraveled, the "push handle" operates in three positions: connected, removed, fixed.

References

Akhmerova, N., ed. (2011), *Vladimir Arkhipov—Functioning Forms: Notes on the Swiss Collection of Vladimir Arkhipov*, Zurich: Textem-Verlag.

Arkhipov, V. (2003), *Born out of Necessity: 105 Thingumajigs, and Their Creators' Voices, from the Collection of Vladimir Arkhipov*, M. Typolygon.

Arkhipov, V. (2006), *Home-Made: Contemporary Russian Folk Artifacts*, London: Fuel Publishing.

Arkhipov, V. (2007), Design del popolo: 220 inventori della Russia post-sovietica, Milan: ISBN Edizioni.

Arkhipov, V. (2012), *Home-Made Europe. Contemporary Folk Artifacts*, second edition, London: Fuel Publishing.

Knack, H., ed. (2003), NOTWEHR. Russische Alltagshilfen aus der Sammlung Vladimir Arkhipov, Krems: Factory—Kunsthalle Krems.

Sofronov, V., V. Misiano, H. Stegmayer and I. Truebswetter (2004), *Vladimir Arkhipov: Folk Sculpture: Archäologie der russischen Alltagskultur*, Rosenheim: Kunstverein Rosenheim.

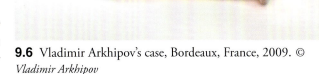

9.6 Vladimir Arkhipov's case, Bordeaux, France, 2009. © *Vladimir Arkhipov*

10 Coloring Cars: Customizing Motor Vehicles in the East of the Australian Western Desert
Diana Young

Things, including consumer goods, are used by Aṉangu and by other Western Australian Desert peoples to objectify various kinds of connections. Color is a way of exhibiting the liveliness in something, and Western Desert peoples regard cars, with their engines and batteries, as being somehow alive, as having agency.

At the Ernabella store, I fell into conversation with a man in the checkout queue about his car. Earlier in the year, he and his wife T. had been driving a metallic gold sedan, a Ford Falcon. Before that, he had driven a white ute.[1] I had not seen this latter vehicle cruising about in a while. Today, he is driving a vehicle with a white roof, a white bonnet, and one white door. The front panel containing the headlights is orange, a similar tone to the gold that makes up the remainder of the vehicle's paneling. It looks rather flash, I tell him. He says that he "nearly split the ute in half" in a crash, hence this new car; he has combined the gold Falcon and the white ute.

This chapter concerns the practice of customizing cars by Aṉangu[2] (Pitjantjatjara and Yankunytjatjara people) living in the Western Desert—an area that is called "remote" because it is far removed from the southern and eastern seaboard centers of population in Australia and lacks a

---

1. "Ute" is an abbreviation for utility vehicle, meaning a cab with an open tray behind.
2. Aṉangu means "person" and has become the way this group of people prefer to refer to themselves.

comparable infrastructure—who, since the early 1960s, have become avid car owners.[3] The manner in which owners modify their vehicles is culturally coherent; its visually arresting feature is the assemblage of contrasting colors on the car's exterior.

Much of this customization could be seen as born of necessity. Traveling over potholed dirt roads or across the bush in pursuit of game has dire consequences for the integrity of vehicles. Tires puncture and shred, batteries become loosened or flat, engines overheat. Additionally, there are few petrol stations, and cars frequently run out of fuel. There is also direct human agency in the dilapidations; people sit on or children might jump on the car bodywork, denting the panels and rendering doors or bonnet incapable of closing and in need of replacement.

In earlier 'first contact' times, metal was one of the things that traveled ahead of the colonists themselves; retrieved by Aboriginal people from items left by the settlers, it was made into axes and traded. In the 1870s, a telegraph line was built to connect Adelaide with Darwin. The material components of this European technical achievement—the wooden poles, ceramic transformers,

---

3. It was not until 1961 that a Pitjantjatjara person owned a motor vehicle, purchased through water drilling contracts (Dunlop 1962; Edwards 1994: 148).

10.1 Car on a homeland. © *Diana Young*

10.2 Blue and white car, Ernabella. © *Diana Young*

and iron footplates—were eagerly dismembered by Aboriginal people for their own creative and technical purposes: making axes and spear heads (Jones 2007: 116–17). A hundred or more years on, later generations of Aboriginal people still value shop-bought metal axes for chopping wood and carving, but they treat the materiality of the metal car in another way.

In the comparatively dry desert, metal lasts for decades, longer than almost any other material; although an individual car may seem to have a short life, its parts, especially the bodywork, survive for many years, viable for recycling. A car that 'dies' when it ceases to work in some irretrievable way is moved off the road and left there or towed back to the owner's homeland, where there may be many other car carcasses. Or it may finish up with other dead vehicles in the community car dump (see Young 2001). Such dumps contain a huge volume of vehicles. Cars abandoned by the roadside might become signposts, but if their end was catastrophic in some way, usually involving a fatality, the car might be burnt. All other dead cars are simply reused by Anangu to create hybrid, customized vehicles, as the man I talked to in the store described. It is the color of cars that makes them expressive vehicles. Respraying a whole car in a bright color such as red, yellow, or green is popular. A community car dump that I saw in 1997 contained many pink, purple, and orange cars. Brightly colored cars are young men's cars, designed to attract girls. Older men, who may be seeking attention for amorous or political ends, may indulge in such cars. These resprayed vehicles provide desirable spare parts for further 'alive' cars.

Access to Cars

Anangu came to ration depots, railway sidings, and missions in the period between about 1930 and 1970, leaving their life as hunter gatherers for 'institutionalized villages' (Peterson 2000: 206) that have since become known as 'communities.' Ernabella Mission, established in 1937 by the Presbyterian Board of Missions, was an enlightened regime among such villages, where Anangu were encouraged to return to their own country for periods of the year and did so using various imported beasts of burden—donkeys, horses, and camels (Hamilton 1987). The period between 1940 and 1970 was one where Western Desert people used animals as a means of transport for the first time before car ownership became a real possibility for many. Cars have enabled Aboriginal people to hunt over far greater distances, but it is the expansion in sociality that has been the main hallmark of the arrival of cars.

Cars have made new events possible and have vastly expanded the reach of existing ones, such as religious ceremonies, both Christian services and various kinds of traditional ritual derived from the Dreaming. There are Aboriginal football competitions between neighboring settlements and the sports carnivals in Alice Springs—the metropolitan hub of central Australia—and in the Warlpiri Aboriginal settlements to the north, which were only possible because of access by car. Sports carnivals are events where many culturally and linguistically diverse desert peoples congregate, traveling hundreds of kilometers to participate. There can be chauvinistic competition between communities; team football colors are painted on the petrol pumps at community fuel stations and sometimes on cars. But any journey or event is rarely for a single reason. Boys' initiation ceremonies, generated in part through social interaction at sports carnivals, now have a vastly increased social and geographical reach because of motor vehicles (cf. Peterson 2000). Local football matches are also a 'front' for other kinds of single gender ceremonies (2000: 211; Young 2001).

Cars are indispensable in the funeral culture that has swept the Western Desert since the turn of the twenty-first century. There is no longer a passenger air service from communities on the Anangu Pitjantjatjara Yankunytjatjara Lands, some 450 kilometers from the nearest town of Alice Springs, though recently a "bush bus" service has been instated. In short, a private motor vehicle gives one autonomy and power. It enables a person to extend their social network across desert cultures, where people remain committed to defining themselves through networks of relationships with others while simultaneously valuing their individual autonomy (Myers 1986; Peterson 1998). However, the acquisition of motor vehicles has not come without considerable human costs. Many people have died in terrible car crashes, and motoring offences on public roads have contributed to the imprisonment of young men.

Colorful Goods

When the Anangu arrived in such settlements, not only were the goods that they came across novel, many were also wonderfully brightly colored. A chromatic revolution took place in the post-World War II industrialized world, where colored plastic wares, laminates, synthetic dyes, and fabrics became available. For many Australians, as for Americans and Europeans, this injection of chroma was most apparent and desirable in interiors. A "fresh, completely different range of colors and designs" was available in plastic laminates to give home decoration "enchanting variety" declared the *Ideal Home* magazine in 1959 (quoted in Shove et al. 2007: 108).

Aboriginal people who came to missions, towns, and cattle stations during the mid-twentieth century from a life as hunter-gatherers in the bush were catapulted into a world, even in remote outback Australia, replete with novel goods of such enchanting variety. While the general population of Australia desired chromatic commodities as household *accoutrements*, the traditional bough shelter at the Ernabella Mission—where Aboriginal people remained until 1971—was roofed with spinifex grass, tarpaulins, or sheets of iron. Storage was limited. Anangu cooked on an open timber fire and sat, as mostly they still do, on the ground, the land, the 'country' that holds the energy and spirit of the Ancestors who created it.

It was portable colored things pertaining to their bodies that Anangu first desired among the settlers' novelties: cloth, wool yarn, dyes, and paints (Young 2010). Now that color has become 'visual junk' in the environment, as American sculptor Donald Judd wrote, it is arduous for metropolitan dwellers to see color as anything more than arbitrary and superficial (Judd 1994). It is hard to imagine the captivation exerted by colored things that, for Aboriginal people, imitated and even amplified the appearance of the land at its most fecund.

For Anangu, the land is where the power of the Creation Ancestors lies. These beings created the features of the earth and sky through their activities during what has come to be glossed in English as the "Dreaming." They then went into the earth (or sometimes up into the sky), where they remain to this day. The Creation Ancestors took many forms—animal, bird, human—and often changed form as they traveled and became embroiled with others.

Ancestral power becomes tangible to present day humans in a number of ways. One of these is the capacity of a body—human, animal, bird, plant, or country—to change the quality of its surface. The surface of the land is transformed after rain, the red sandy earth becomes green with new leaves, followed by a burst of perhaps yellow, purple, or pink from flowers and a further change as all the plants fall to seed. Edible fruits and seeds transform their skins through color changes, which the women understand as a rhythmic and predictable sequence, a form of knowledge. For Aboriginal people, the novel colored settler things provided a kind of "technology of enchantment" (Gell 1992); they provided a means of materializing and developing ideas and connections about the presence of the Creation Ancestors, which hitherto had been confined to evanescent effects across the landscape or painstakingly produced during ritual. Anangu appropriated colored materials for multivalent purposes, for enchanting one another. Only in the realm of artworks for sale to the market have they deliberately employed color to enchant the buyer, the 'other,' the non-Aboriginal person (Young 2010).

Coloring Cars

Attending social events in style, appropriately attired both in terms of clothing and car, today involves color. Yet, the growing body of ethnographic writing on the effects of cars on Aboriginal people in remote Australia remains, with a few exceptions, firmly unengaged with the materiality of vehicles and their design (Hamilton 1987; Myers 1988; Peterson 2000; Stotz 2001; Redmond 2006). The land, country, remains a constant, something that living humans must care for, keep, while store bought commodities can be left in the dirt or broken with impunity and rapidity—a toy, perhaps, or a spanner used to tighten wheel nuts, or a car. Anangu treat things, by outsider's standards, carelessly.

Commentators of Aboriginal people's lives interpret these things, including Western industrially produced commodities, as disposable in the service of relatedness. That is, if someone who claims kinship or friendship with you asks for something—a share of food, money, the shirt on your back, petrol, to borrow a car—you must give it to them. To do otherwise would be to deny their relationship with you. This has been dubbed "demand sharing" (Peterson 1993). Owning a car, especially a four-wheel drive with its capacity to go anywhere, elicits constant demands from others (Stotz 2001; Austin-Broos 2006; 2009). A solution to dissipating tensions generated by shared assets, a car being a good example, is to dispose of them (Myers 1988).

This treatment of goods has led to the confirmation of the idea that industrially produced 'Western' things are unimportant for desert people in comparison with human relationships. Such a view also locks neatly with prevailing Western notions that regard materiality as an unwarranted emphasis on things at the expense of an emphasis on persons (Miller 2006). In romantic popular discourse, Aboriginal people are often regarded as so spiritually aware that they do not care about the material world. Yet, many Australian Aboriginal people lead lives of great poverty and need more consumption, not less. Spirituality is not necessarily opposed to materiality for them.

Anangu generally show little interest in keeping the monetary value of a commodity. It follows that they are uninterested in emptying out the material particularity of a vehicle to maintain its market value in the way of settler Australian or American culture, where the aim is to erase all traces of people and their activities from an object to maintain its potential as a commodity (Spyer 1997; Young 2004). Rather, Anangu aim to accumulate these traces as signs of accumulated social relatedness without concern for monetary depreciation (Austin-Broos 2006).

There is a deliberate concerted effort by Anangu to change the appearance of a car along with an acceptance that the course of its social life will change the vehicle, too. As they are used and customized, cars acquire a handmade appearance, the antithesis of machine made sleekness. Patterned fabric screens without window glass and bodywork panels are sometimes hand painted; an even covering of packaging and other detritus festoons the interior. All this is simply considered part of the car. The durability of things is not the point here. Things flare into view, have their moment in time, anchored to a particular place, journey, or event, but when these are finished, the object is discarded onto the ground.

In his furniture, Dutch designer Martin Baas explores why dust is not considered part of things: Why polish it off? Similarly, architects such as R and Scie use anti-Modernist materials on their buildings, which are designed to attract dust and algae (Kaji-O'Grady 2010). These approaches allude to a certain attitude to 'nature' and perhaps time and mortality. Anangu, though, enjoy a car that appears used because it shows that the vehicle is fully socialized (Stotz 2001; Austin-Broos 2006, 2009). But one of the most common car colors is the color of the dust of central Australia, metallic gold, copper, or beige that already looks as though it has traveled far on the reddish dirt roads.

Processual Color

There is a Pitjantjatjara/Yankunytjatjara word, *walka*, which translates as "meaningful mark making" or "design," and Anangu search for this everywhere: on the skin of a lizard, on clothing, on cars. There is no distinction between natural and man-made materials in this regard. Any contrast, even if only 'go faster' stripes or trim, is admired by people more than one plain color. The greater the contrast, the more "flash" the car is deemed by people. For instance, my companion pronounced a white car with gray stripes that I admired as being only a "little bit flash" because of the *walka*, the design did not have enough contrast.

Things achieve the epitome of effectiveness and "flashness" through bright coloration or compositions of contrasting colors. Just as bush fruits pass through known stages of appearance, which is represented in paintings by women artists as different stages of coloration in their skins, car owners create sequences of transformation in a car's bodywork (Young 2010). This they can achieve by reusing paneling from scrapped vehicles or by applying paint to the car's existing panel work. Any one vehicle may undergo several transformations of its bodywork before it is left in a car dump and in turn reused.

For instance, Maria and her husband Junior had a rapid succession of cars between March and November 1997. Each one was speedily modified. In May 1997, they were driving a parrot green Ford sedan with one white door. By July, the car had acquired a new yellow bonnet. In mid-August, this car was parked neatly at the back of their homeland in the death row for cars and Junior was poring over the bonnet of a blue car with a white roof. By October, this car was also dead. They had a white sedan for a few weeks then swapped it with another family member for a metallic blue car.

An anthropologist working with Arrernte Aboriginal people at Hermannsburg, who have a different, earlier history of missionization than the Anangu, has argued that nowadays

10.3 Blue Toyota 4WD on a homeland. © *Diana Young*

objectification[4] is through kinship for them and no longer, as it was in the past, through country (Austin-Broos 2006). Around Ernabella, people do continue to define their relationships with one another through their ties to land, although these may now take different forms. The village where one lives may take precedent for many younger people when it comes to defining the country where they consider they belong. The Ancestral Dreaming Track nearest to the settlement will become their primary identification, depending on their gender. For old people, their attachment to the place where they were conceived, born, or grew up defines their connection to specific Ancestral Beings. Things, including consumer goods, are used by Anangu and by other Western Desert peoples to objectify these various kinds of connections, and the colors of those things materialize many nuances. Color is a way of exhibiting the liveliness in something, and Western Desert peoples do regard cars with their engines and batteries as somehow alive, as having agency (Stotz 2001). There is scope for signaling relatedness as well as individuality. The colors of cars can express the objectification of oneself in relation to community, country, and to kin. There is even scope for individual self-expression but within culturally recognized rules.

---

4. For instance an advertisement in a 2010 Australian women's magazine for Nissan Micra shows different colored cars—"11 funky colors"—as rings on a young woman's fingers. The ad offers a means of objectifying oneself through personal choice of a colored car. See Miller in this volume.

The envelope that is the car body is like clothing enfolding those inside; changing its outward demeanor sends signals to others in the world outside as it travels or while it is parked. There is an identification of the owner with the vehicle, a man with his yellow Toyota, for example (Cane 2002: 216). The identification of man and car is reciprocal. The constancy of identification as color—"that red one" or "that yellow one"—will continue even when the car is visibly transformed, acquiring paneling that doesn't match the original in color. Anangu assume a capacity for processual change in a car just as they do in bush foods, the landscape, or the human body. One can name a substance for what it will become after transformation— "white" ash, for example, from brownish tree bark. There is an idea of constancy that accommodates change.

The car's colors can be a general statement about beliefs and practices or articulate an identification with a specific place. The most frequently created color combination of blue and white (usually a blue vehicle originally with white replacement panels) is a declaration of Christian beliefs. Christianity is also anchored in ideas about land and sky and the whereabouts of both Jesus and the devil for Anangu. The fire Dreaming that wends its way across huge tracts of the Western Desert is identified with red and yellow, and this combination of panel colors is sometimes created in cars, too.

10.4 Red and white car. © *Diana Young*

As already mentioned, there are also football-team-colored cars, sometimes tricolored to match the football kit. A local Aboriginal community football team wears black and white, also colors used by Anangu in certain religious ceremonies. However, it is an unusual color customization in cars. In 1998, a customized Chevrolet, driven by young men, cream with a black bonnet and roof and an (initially) pristine chrome bumper, cruised between Ernabella and an easterly homeland. The car lasted for some months before finishing up in the car dump at another small community.

An elderly senior man, who was acknowledged as the "boss" of a homeland with a powerful sacred site, drove an old Toyota (a four-wheel drive vehicle) with a carefully hand-painted, contrasting colored roof. These colors are associated with Ancestral activities at his homeland. Another old Toyota, classed as Anangu from a neighboring community, was navy blue with a replacement orange bonnet from another car and matching orange bumper panel. It also had a hand-painted panel and roof of orange house paint on top of the original blue to give a regular contrasting variegated effect across the whole vehicle.

Driving is a way of keeping oneself in touch with the country without the labor of walking it. The car is not only socialized through its relationships with people but also through the country it crosses. There is reciprocity between the car, its occupants, and the land it travels through (Young 2001). Anangu consider the landscape as always being in a state of becoming, and a car is a processual thing, too. It is modified by its journeys and by its occupants, and at the same time it alters the country that it crosses with its tracks. This is where color offers a multitude of possibilities, and the customization of vehicles is by both humans and landscape. This design work by Aboriginal Western Desert dwellers is directed outward at others, at objectifying networks of relationships as well as an individual's prestige within them. Both cars and colors were novel to Aboriginal people. Assimilating motor vehicles into an aesthetic of mobility that is reciprocal with their actual mobility by means of colored materials is ingenious. It is a process that endows cars with humanity. Cars accumulate social capital as they circulate and become crusted with rubbish and acquire different color body panels. In short, the more variegated the vehicle's body panels, the more highly socialized yet individualized it has become. In what I have dubbed here 'customizing,' Aboriginal people are redesigning goods, not merely circulating them. Aboriginal appropriation of a non-Aboriginal thing is completed through its progressive redesign—something only revealed through rich ethnographic engagement with the user. Though the brand of a car is important, especially for four-wheel drive vehicles (Stotz 2001; Redmond 2006), the visibly socialized car and all its nuances prevail, rendering the idea of keeping such traces at bay in a product obsolete.

Addendum: A Work in Progress

In the intervening years since the first edition of this volume, the Global Financial Crisis has had an effect on cars in the Indigenous freehold lands of the far north-west of South Australia. The number of tourists visiting the Uluṟu-Kata Tjuṯa National Park halved in number from pre-2008 to the years following. The gate entry fee to the National Park is partly distributed to those Indigenous people who can claim Traditional Ownership of that country. This annual distribution, an injection of cash used for car purchases, was anticipated for months in advance of its arrival date by the recipients. The dwindling of tourist numbers and gate monies has lessened the rate of car acquisitions among Anangu and hence the number of cars in circulation. With various government rules imposed, such as changes in "work for the dole," people are financially worse off. The Global Financial Crisis also impacted on the sale of Indigenous art with substantial price falls so that most artists receive less in earnings. Overall, due to these combined factors, there are fewer cars being acquired.

There seems to be less driving about too. There are fewer cars on the road during the week, fewer trips out bush for hunting, except at weekends, because time and work are now more and more accounted for in a governmental bureaucratic sense. Petrol money, let alone car repair funds, can be hard to find. Most houses in the community have at least four dead cars and two live ones arrayed outside and inside the yard fences. Following some fatal car crashes there are even fewer homeland residents. Homelands still carry their cargo of disused cars dating back some decades, an archaeology of car designs and customizations, but these are off limits to anyone but the families who have rights to that place.

The dead cars that were all over the land in the 1990s were almost all cleared away under some enterprise scheme in the 2000s, meant to generate jobs and income for Indigenous people. A new layer of abandoned cars is however starting to accrue providing more spare parts for customization.

The cars people drive now are the second-hand cars that were new in the 1990s and early 2000s with their global 'commodity' colors: white, silver, dark blue, or black. These colors for car bodies are easily retouched (especially white) and exemplify the trend for cars that are easily sold on, cars that are not individualized in ways that impede their smooth sale and life as commodities (Young 2004). Anangu are not interested in this and anyway cars are mainly in the last stages of their viability as moving machines once they arrive on the red dirt. The cultural aesthetic of combining car parts to create contrast and visual complexity has continued. In 2015, there were several cars that incorporated black body panels in previously white cars. Black and white is connected with death and an expression of mourning a family member. These are also the colors of various football teams.

There were some men's cars, brightly colored "flash" cars, driven by men wanting to make an impression, wanting to expand themselves in space politically or sexually. Cars can be resprayed in Alice Springs, where increasing numbers of people spend their time. In 2015, the community I visited boasted two noticeable men's cars: a bright green metallic sporty car with two black stripes on its bonnet and a bright orangey gold metallic car. The latter color conveys a similar impression to the luminous orange of the nearby rocky ranges in a good sunset. These colors are evoking elements of the landscape's spiritual vitality that in turn indexes its containment of Ancestral power.

The vitality of the Ancestors is expressed in the transformative ability of the land with its brilliant green growth after rain.

The antithesis of these flash men's cars are the anonymous ones—mostly dark blue and silver with no modifications and they are far commoner and hard to see in the landscape bringing to mind the way old men wear dust colored clothing and are seemingly at one with the land. The old men who maintained four-wheel-drive Toyotas in modified colors, that I wrote about in this chapter, are dead (along with their cars) but a new generation of young men toil in the yards of their relative's houses fixing up car engines and bodywork. Customized cars as bodies that connect strongly with the spiritually imbued earth are a profound expression of an ontological state, of the continuing pride that most Anangu have for their country and their belonging to its beauty and vitality. Cars express the relation of people to the land and to kin and perfectly encapsulate the shifting nature of these relationships. Cars, too, are always unfinished—a work in progress.

References

Austin-Broos, D. (2006), "'Working for' and 'Working' among Western Arrente in Central Australia," *Oceania*, 76 (1): 1–15.

Austin-Broos, D. (2009), Arrente Present, *Arrente Past: Invasion, Violence and Imagination in Indigenous Central Australia*, Chicago: University of Chicago Press.

Cane, S. (2002), *Pila Ngura: The Spinifex People*, Washington: Freemantle Art Centre Press.

Edwards, W. H. (1994), Pitjantjatjara tjukurpa tjuta (= Pitjantjatjara Stories) (recorded and transcribed by Bill Edwards), Underdale, S. Austral.: University of South Australia.

Gell, A. (1992), "The Technology of Enchantment and the Enchantment of Technology," in J. Coote and A. Shelton (eds.), *Anthropology Art and Aesthetics*, 40–66, Oxford: Oxford University Press.

Hamilton, A. (1987), "Coming and Going: Aboriginal Mobility in North-West South Australia," in *Records of the South Australia Museum*, 20: 47–57.

Jones, P. (2007), *Ochre and Rust Artefacts and Encounters on Australian Frontiers*, Adelaide: Wakefield Press.

Judd, D. (1994), "Some Aspects of Color in General and Red and Black in Particular," *Art Forum*, 32 (10): 70–110.

Kaji-O'Grady, S. (2010), "A Wound to the Head for Undead Modernism," *Monument*, 95: 33–6.

Miller, D. (2006), "Consumption," in P. Spyer et al. (eds.), *The Handbook of Material Culture*: 341–54, London, Thousand Oaks & New Delhi: Sage Publications.

Myers, F. (1986), *Pintupi Country Pintupi Self. Sentiment, Place and Politics among Western Desert Aborigines*, Berkeley, Los Angeles & Oxford: University of California Press.

Myers, F. (1988), "Burning the Truck and Holding the Country: Property, Time and the Negotiation of Identity among Pintupi Aborigines," in T. Ingold, D. Riches and J. Woodburn (eds.), *Hunters and Gatherers 2; Property Power and Ideology*, 52–74, Oxford, New York & Hamburg: Berg.

Peterson, N. (1993), "Demand Sharing: Reciprocity and the Pressure for Generosity among Foragers," in *American Anthropologist*, 95 (4): 860–74.

Peterson, N. (1998), "Welfare, Colonialism and Citizenship: Politics, Economics and Agency," in N. Peterson and W. Sanders (eds.), *Citizenship and Indigenous Australians*: 101–17, Cambridge & Melbourne: Cambridge University Press.

Peterson, N. (2000), "An Expanding Aboriginal Domain and the Initiation Journey," in *Oceania*, 70 (3): 205–16.

Redmond, A. (2006), "Further on up the Road: Community Trucks and the Moving Settlement in Moving Anthropology," in T. Lea, E. Kowal and G. Cowlishaw (eds.), *Critical Indigenous Studies*: 95–114, Darwin: Charles Darwin University Press.

Shove, E., M. Watson, M. Hand, and J. Ingram (2007), *The Design of Everyday Life*, Oxford & New York: Berg.

Spyer, P. (1997), "Introduction in Border Fetishisms," in P. Spyer (ed.), *Material Objects in Unstable Spaces*, 1–11, New York & London: Routledge.

Stotz, G. (2001), "The Colonizing Vehicle," in D. Miller (ed.), *Car Cultures*, 223–44, Oxford & New York: Berg.

The Aborigines of Australia, 1962, film directed by I. Dunlop, Sydney: Commonwealth Film Unit (Screen Australia).

Young, D. (2001), "The Life and Death of Cars; Private Vehicles on the Pitjantjatjara Lands South Australia," in D. Miller (ed.), *Car Cultures*, 35–58, Oxford & New York: Berg.

Young, D. (2004), "The Material Value of Colour; The Estate Agent's Tale," *Home Cultures*, 1 (1): 5–22.

Young, D. (2010), "Clothing in the Western Desert," in Joanne Eicher (ed.), *The Encyclopaedia of World Dress and Fashion*, Oxford: Berg.

Young, D. (forthcoming), "Colours as Space-Time," in D. Young (ed.), *Re-Materialising Colour*, Wantage: Sean Kingston Publishing.

11 The Internet, the Parliament, and the Pub
Lane DeNicola

Internet-of-Things proponents and designers of the present moment often build rhetorically on a virtuous vision of a new egalitarianism derived from a restructured relationship between humans and the built environment. Undeniably that vision must be accounted for in anthropologists' analyses, but it must also be set in analytic relief with what empirically seems a wilder and woollier terrain, one just as filled with boors, blowhards, opportunists, and miscreants as any pub one might care to frequent.

I want to discuss a recent movement in the field of industrial design and what it might mean for anthropological approaches to object culture, but let me start with a quick story about my car keys. A little over a year ago as I write, changes in my personal circumstances meant that for the first time in roughly fifteen years I would be relying heavily on an automobile to commute to my full-time workplace. A silver lining to that change was that it afforded an opportunity to do something I'd wanted to do for some time: try out one of the new breed of fuel-efficient vehicles. In comparison with most Westerners, if I had to guess I'd say the purchase of a new-model vehicle is an uncommon occurrence for me, having happened only once before (1989) in nearly five decades of personal history. As a result I went into the process knowing there was a lot I didn't know. After some consideration I settled on a new all-electric model, which, while not exactly "inexpensive" for what is essentially a sub-compact, enjoyed a substantial tax incentive from the state in which I reside and averaged only about US$20 per month in "fuel" (electricity). Aside from the innovations at its core, the vehicle incorporated a number of amenities that struck me (as someone used to older, well-worn automobiles) as technologically exotic: seat warmers, tire-pressure sensors, a satellite radio, wireless connectivity with my smartphone, and so on. One of these "innovations" in particular—the ignition key—has proven an unexpected challenge to the way I've grown used to thinking about vehicles and driving.

To put it in less-than-technical terms, the car "knows" when the key is nearby.[1] On its own this wouldn't necessarily be that big of a change. My partner and I have owned a car or two with key fob "remotes" that allowed the owner to unlock the doors from a distance, and this key does work that way as well, but it's also importantly different. To unlock the door or the trunk you simply use the button on the door handle while you have the key "on your person." In bodily terms, you don't search your pockets or purse for your keys as you approach the car; as long as they're "on you somewhere" you can open the door. The same goes for "starting the car up." Rather than inserting a key into a lock-like switch that you then rotate to engage, you simply place your foot on the brake and push a power button while the key is "ready at hand." Naively this might seem an unqualified convenience, but my experience is mixed. Try as I might, I cannot completely let go of the niggling anxiety I feel at not being *sure* I have my keys "on my person" until I try to open the door. In abstract terms, it has transformed "authentication"—*I have the authority to enter this vehicle*—from a matter of material mechanism to one of ambient presence. To complicate matters, the car "knows" a number of other things as well: when the key is *inside* the vehicle versus *outside;* which door the key is closest to; and when an "adult-sized" person is sitting in a front seat.[2] This sensory capability allows the car, for example, to inhibit the unlocking of the door *opposite* the key-holder (possibly a security measure) and to inhibit the door locks when the keys are *inside* but no adult is in a front seat. The sales representative, clearly not that sure himself of all the implications of this arrangement, reeled off a rote but reasonable design rationale: it prevents you from accidentally locking yourself out.

As the mundanities of middle-class life in America go, this has effected a fairly potent reconfiguration of human-object relations. Appadurai (1988) noted long ago that "the powerful contemporary tendency is to regard the world of things as inert and mute, set in motion and animated, indeed knowable, only by persons and their words" (p. 4). Yet on several occasions I've elicited the help of my partner to conduct experiments, looking for clues that would help me to understand who or what "says" or "knows" what when (she possesses a *second* key which the vehicle can apparently distinguish from the first—the complexities multiply!). This may not be quite the sort of object "enunciations" Appadurai had in mind—*may* not be—but it's clear that my own normalized driving practices and posture toward automobiles must be massaged to suit.

---

1. A bit more technically: Since the invention of such systems in the mid-1990s, these have conventionally been referred to as "smart keys." When the "start" button or a button on a door handle or rear hatch is pressed, a transceiver on the car sends out a signal, interrogating any keys of the right type within about a meter. If a key returns a signal, and if this signal is an appropriate one (the key must be registered with the car in advance), the car will start, or the door on the appropriate side will unlock.

2. Automobiles are increasingly equipped with seat weight sensors to inhibit potentially deadly airbag deployment when children or infants are in the seat. However, the signals from these sensors may serve additional functions, such as those described here.

The Internet of Things

This vignette is intended to set the context for a discussion of what is being generically referred to these days as the "Internet of Things," a discursive confluence of industrial design and digital media, perhaps the latest instantiation of the technological manifest destiny that has long been proffered to us Moderns (the "Electric Age," the "Space Age," the "Green Revolution" and similar imaginaries). The reader will not be especially surprised if my intention is neither to laud nor apologize for this new technoromantic vision, but there are already very clear signs that it has gained broad purchase and, I think, begins the unfurling of a vast terrain for anthropological insight into object culture. My objective here, beyond attempting to articulate the relevance of this development for the study of design, is to point out that the concept of the colloquy of *things* is not new for anthropology, but its popularization within dominant industrialized societies may be.

It is not an especially bold guess that most people—by which I mean not just Western Moderns, but the majority of the earth's human population—would agree that consumer technologies such as mobile phones, social networking sites, and videogames are powerfully shaping our understanding of the world and interaction with each other. Since this array of "consumer-level" communications and media appliances is the most broadly familiar to the widest variety of people, to a degree it only makes sense that such technologies would figure most prominently within anthropological study. In most senses they are both clearly present and comparatively apprehensible, designed as they are to be used by "the average consumer." Organizing the Internet into tiers of mediation, we could reasonably refer to such technologies as the *human-human tier*, wherein the artifacts involved have "interaction and exchange between humans" as their primary end.

The portion of the Internet that this ignores, however, is growing at a stunning pace. Consider that an expanding variety of pedestrian activities leave electronic traces—not just formal "communications and entertainment" but commercial transactions, consumption, civil discourse, physical movement, and so on. From "Quick Response" codes and tiny radiofrequency ID tags to environmental sensors, data storage, cellular and Wi-Fi transceivers, and full-blown embedded computers, digital technology is now widely employed in many industrial sectors, connecting material objects to electronic databases, histories of production, and communities of use. In their early manifestations of course these technologies were stand-alone appliances (e.g., a GPS receiver), but their proliferation has been accelerated primarily as a result of being "piggy-backed" on originally unrelated devices—mobile phones, digital cameras, and so on. This has instilled "location awareness" and "data logging" as default properties of many objects and spaces. Illustrative examples include the unabated growth in the "smart homes" and "connected cars" sectors, where proponents hawk networked thermostats, door locks, security or dashboard cameras, onboard navigation systems, and integrated digital audio, all accessible (or exchanging data) via the Internet. One thing such cases have in common is that *a person* is still typically assumed to be "in the loop," controlling or consuming "data" with immediate functional utility. Let us call this the *human-object tier*. Certainly "the home" and "the automobile" are celebrities within the vast cosmos of artifacts, stand-ins for the universe we inhabit and core platforms for the expression of who we are. On that basis, one could argue that these are exceptional examples and not especially generalizable, yet even more pedestrian artifacts—sneakers with embedded geolocation receivers, for example (DeNicola 2012)—have been designed with the specific idea that the routes they record have immediate utility to a human engaged in a narrowly defined activity (e.g., jogging).

As conceived by its proponents, however, the Internet of Things (IoT) lies still further down the chain of mediation. For IoT designers, coming together through such venues as O'Reilly Media's "Solid" conference, the prospect of "revolutionary advances" goes beyond added convenience or customized "user experience" to the very core of our relationship with the built environment. Expand those sneakers' sensors to other modalities and increase their onboard memory many orders of magnitude. The utility of the "data" they collect might well be at some remove in space and time from its collection, but no matter. Data "stands in reserve," woven in with the value of the artifact as a whole. No longer is "data" the email, image, map, or music track ready for "end use," rather it is reams of sensing logs, status updates, authentication keys, and links to other objects. The essence of a pair of sneakers becomes intensified when they "know" or make legible the details of their history, the sociopolitical context of their own manufacture, their mean time between failures, the toxicity and biodegradability of their materials, the demographics of those most likely to purchase them, the labor or trade agreements under which they were made economically viable, and so on. This "data" we could refer to as *the human/object tier*, connoting a superposition of alternatives with a slash rather than the interface suggested by the hyphen. Here artifacts are designed to encapsulate and render themselves as a locus of human relations. One could argue that a knot is merely a configuration, not materially different from the rope in which it's tied, yet the distinction could not be more relevant to human action. Similarly, artifacts are best understood as crystallizations, bundles or configurations of human relations, and while this is hardly news for those who study object culture, the reification and popular sublimation of the idea via the field of industrial design certainly would be.

Critical anthropologists may first observe that—like its "revolutionary" antecedents—the most likely near-term ramifications for the design of the Internet of Things will be shaped by and for elites, with "externalized costs," environmental distress, social inequity, and similar unintended consequences passed on to majority populations. On the other hand, anthropologists of digital culture will also be aware that the perceived utilitarian importance of (for example) mobile phones within rural and developing world contexts appears to have grown at least as great in recent decades as it has for developed world cosmopolitans. Again, my specific point here is neither to critique nor to advocate, but rather to point out that a discursive movement has gained coherence and to suggest how anthropologists might make some sense of it. Before dismissing too quickly the revolutionary rhetoric deployed by IoT devotees, we can attempt a fuller account of how it operates. At an abstract level (and particularly among working technical designers) "digital" denotes the regime of logic and *discrete* (as opposed to *continuous*) mathematics, with "data" registered as quanta (bits) rather than smoothly varying quantities like temperatures or voltages. This is an abstraction whose material instantiation in silicon and microminiaturized electronics is marbled through a vast global network of material flows. At the level of popular discourse, however, the term "digital" connotes a relative historical frame—"physical" or "analog" media (e.g., paper) is the old and wasteful, "digital" is the new and efficient. "Digital" alludes to the "Information Revolution," accelerating innovations in consumer technologies and amateur media production and distribution. It references the democratization of communication, enhanced participation, and reinvigorated civic life—while at the same time raising the specters of alienation, sedentarized domestic life, pervasive pornography, and unchecked prejudices. It stands in for the privileging of network access over physical location, coding such qualities as mobility, translocality, and individualism as "virtuous." The "digital" precipitates norms of exact replication, concepts of "patterns" as property, and fluid and instantaneous exchange—as well as complexity, ephemerality, inscrutability. It capitalizes on the metaphors of numerology and esoteric traditions, paradoxically engendering both anonymity and surveillance. It also implies artificiality as opposed to organicism, but the obvious hybrid examples of genetics and bioinformatics lend it a chimeric quality. Arguably the synthesis represented by the digital yields a "new organicism," a reprise of the living/not-living Frankenstein's monster in the figure of the cyborg (Haraway 1991).

The Parliament of Things

Of course, the regular reinforcement of this qualitative division between "digital" and "physical" entails no small measure of work. In its essence, it bears a striking similarity to other grand dualisms, such as the one Latour (1993) famously articulated between society and nature. A foundational project of modernity, this reordering of the ineluctable interdependence of society on the one hand and the "natures" perceived by pre-moderns on the other became (he argued) unsustainable in the postmodern era. No longer, for example, could we leave intact the illusion that the sprawling infrastructures required to sustain contemporary societies were generally decoupled from environmental consequence. Neither were the "pure objects" modern science reputedly made of "nature"—races, microbes, genes—so unequivocally separable from their social milieu. Rather, these must be understood as *quasi-objects*, indivisible assemblages of both physical objects and enunciations, nature and culture, with scientists and other actors standing in as mediators or interlocutors, those who would speak on their behalf:

> *Let us again take up the two representations and the double doubt about the faithfulness of the representatives, and we shall have defined* the Parliament of Things. *In its confines, the continuity of the collective is reconfigured. There are no more naked truths, but there are no more naked citizens either. The mediators have the whole space to themselves. . . . Natures are present, but with their representatives, scientists who speak in their name. Societies are present, but with the objects that have been serving as their ballast from time immemorial . . . what does it matter, so long as they are all talking about the same thing, about a quasi-object*

they have all created, the object-discourse-nature-society whose new properties astound us and whose network extends from my refrigerator to the Antarctic by way of chemistry, law, the State, the economy, and satellites. The imbroglios and networks that had no place now have the whole place to themselves. They are the ones that have to be represented; it is around them that the Parliament of Things gathers henceforth. (p. 144, emphasis mine)

Consider this invocation of "parliament" (from the French *parlement*, "discussion") as a metaphor for a seemingly disparate network of human/non-human actors, one engaged in a vigorous, ongoing democratic process, one of self-ordering and reflection. It is almost as if—at the risk of relishing the homology a bit too much—the early progenitors of the Internet of Things got assigned *We Have Never Been Modern* in the 1990s while they were thinking up their industrial design capstone project. Artifacts in the Internet of Things are inscribed with their own material dependencies; they serve as "links" into the networks of individuals and communities that make use of them. They become "animated" to an extent and are accorded agency, interacting with humans and each other via a literal Network. "Socially responsible consumption" is enabled by the new transparency of industrial production and its effects. A certain optimism, endemic to technological revolutionaries (and perhaps only a bit peculiar for a critical philosopher/ anthropologist of science), is evident in the supposition that the exchanges over these networks could or would resemble parliamentary discourse.

This may be reasonable enough in the context of major issues in science with broad societal impact—the spread of disease, the risks of nuclear power, climate change, and so on. Arguably a critical mass of the actors involved will indeed be driven primarily by understanding, discussion, decision-making, and action on such matters. What of the people "on the ground" in this discourse? The parents trying to get their kids to wash their hands where water is a precious commodity? The consumers who aren't entirely sure how their power is generated or why they should care? The coal miners trying to ascribe meaning to all of this "vocational retraining" suddenly laid as an inevitable part of their futures? They too will have their representatives in this parliamentary space, but more to the point that space would presumably be recognizable as "parliamentary" via its *conventions and rules*—who may speak when and about what.

The Pub of Things?

Let us shift for a moment, then, away from context of "technoscience" writ large to that of the everyday objects that populate human lives. However compelling the resemblance, the parliamentary metaphor may prove an ill fit for the cultural researcher sussing out (for example) the way the meaning we attach to photographs changes when those photographs are transmitted automatically to a networked frame on our parents' wall, or certainly the anthropologist working with IoT designers at Intel, or trying to make sense of DIY design communities coming together via the Instructables website. A naive transplantation of the Parliament of Things into the context of the Internet of Things is interesting in its suggestion of the radical potential of "human-object relations rendered legible," but limitations become quickly apparent. Given the fact that, especially early on in this anticipated trajectory, anthropologists will be listening to how people *talk about* artifacts differently (or not), it's relevant to consider the types of stories that can be told, the characters or roles that "things" (in the enriched sense of the Internet of Things) can be allotted when they are transmuted into IoT "actors," connected to and affected via the Internet.

In one distillation, such objects can "watch" or "listen" (registering ambient temperature, say), they can "record" (maintain a history of that temperature over time), they can "signal" or "speak" (regularly updating you via TXT on the temperature) and they can "act" (shutting off a furnace). This palette of behavioral modes lends itself to a diverse set of anthropomorphisms, "characters" to be discursively mobilized by human user/occupants. A traditional set of car keys is a sort of "credential," comparatively "mute and inert," but a car that appears to be "aware" of the presence and identity of those keys makes them something else entirely. The aforementioned examples of smart home security devices lend themselves to a characterization as "guards" or "sentinels," vigilant and mostly silent except to signal irregularities. "Agents" and similar proxies, automatons empowered to act on your behalf, have been a prominent character type on auction and investment websites for some years, and the field of tele-robotics has brought that character type into the artifactual realm. Compromising audio and video recordings of celebrities and others are today a pop-culture genre, to the point that online clearinghouses do a thriving business helping to sort through such troves, casting smartphones, smart pens, teddy bear "nanny cams," and similarly inconspicuous artifacts not just as *the instruments* of spies, voyeurs, and paparazzi, but as enabling actors in their own right. Commercial constructions such as Apple's *Siri* and more recently Microsoft's *Cortana* are quite literal but archetypal examples of "the guide" or "concierge," elsewhere manifested as the guide, oracle, or personal secretary. Their role is to help human "visitors" or "tourists" navigate the wild proliferation of hybrid physical/digital things in this chaotic foreign space. The relationship is an interrogative one. We could likely expand this list, but the broader point is that there are limits to the speed with which humans' long-standing relations with the built-environment can change. Artifacts or spaces must "make sense" not just in idealized function but in practice, in the same way computers could be sensibly appropriated within the domestic sphere only via reference to the typewriter and the television. The ascription of "character" is a method commonly employed by designers for making that connection, if only for certain classes of products, and analysts of object culture will likely be able to capitalize on anthropology's cross-cultural fluency in storytelling and character when analyzing such artifacts.

So we have before us a scenario, a middle class society wherein the domestic sphere is ubiquitously networked and permeated with digital computing. In the home, each tick of the power meter or unlocking of a door contributes (so the narrative goes) to the potential of "the quantified self," each passage of automobiles on the highway becomes an opportunity for a mutually beneficial data exchange. Yet anthropologists would undoubtedly be surprised to learn that home security, traffic volume, and carbon emissions were the only (or even the most) common topics in this discourse. What of the advertiser eager to capitalize on our consumption practices? The chronic speeder looking to avoid tickets? The voyeur spying on his neighbors? In contrast with the discursive metaphor of the parliament, this checkered terrain arguably resembles the traditional public house or "pub" (coincidentally, a space trafficked by anthropologists at least as often as parliament houses). The pub as an idealized space is undeniably one of discourse and collective interaction, and without a doubt it has its own set of conventions and perhaps even a few rules about who may speak when and about what. However, intercourse there is typically less formalized and scheduled, less planned or "goal-oriented." Liaisons are more often serendipitous, and the topics may range widely from the trivial, coarse, and sensational to the nuanced, politically grand, or philosophically challenging. Fewer hearings and inquiries, more darts and pick-up lines.

The Pub of Things would foreground just these dimensions, rendering the myriad trivial exchanges of the IoT at the micro level as nonetheless relevant signs through which meaning-making even at the macro cultural level could be discerned. Might we draw in an altogether different literature, one that newly refracts the Internet of Things via critical social insights into the public sphere (Habermas 1989) and the "third space" of coffee houses, bars, and pubs (Watson 2002)? IoT proponents and designers of the present moment often build rhetorically on a virtuous vision of a new egalitarianism derived from a restructured relationship between humans and the built environment. Undeniably, that vision must be accounted for in anthropologists' analyses, but it must also be set in analytic relief with what empirically seems a wilder and woollier terrain, one just as filled with boors, blowhards, opportunists, and miscreants as any pub one might care to frequent.

References

Appadurai, A. (1988), *The Social Life of Things: Commodities in Cultural Perspective*, Cambridge & New York: Cambridge University Press.

DeNicola, L. (2012), "Geomedia: The Reassertion of Space within Digital Culture," in H. A. Horst and D. Miller (eds.), *Digital Anthropology*, London and New York: Berg.

Habermas, J. (1989), *The Structural Transformation of the Public Sphere*, Cambridge: The MIT Press.

Haraway, D. (1991), *Simians, Cyborgs, and Women: The Reinvention of Nature*, New York: Routledge.

Latour, B. (1993), *We Have Never Been Modern*, Cambridge: Harvard University Press.

Watson, D. (2002), "Home from Home: The Pub and Everyday Life" in T. Bennett and D. Watson (eds.), *Understanding Everyday Life*, Oxford: Blackwell/Open University.

12 Interior Decoration— Offline and Online

Daniel Miller

We can appreciate what people spend much of their time doing online, once we realize that online worlds—just as much as offline worlds—gift us an insight that is surely the foundation of any broad-minded design anthropology: the appreciation that interior design is not limited to professional expertise. It is actually a foundational attribute of merely being human.

Introduction

Mary, who lives next door to you, is a museum curator and designer specializing in interior decoration; indeed you could say she is something of an artist. Okay, perhaps her name is not Mary. Actually I have no idea what the name of your next-door neighbor is. But the point I am making is that I don't need to know their name. Whoever you are, and whatever the name of your next-door neighbor, I am going to persuade you that that person is actually a museum curator and interior designer and perhaps something of an artist.

For me to be able to make that claim it would have to follow that everyone who has a place to live in can be described in those terms. Finding an 'anyone' within an 'everyone' is not an easy task; which is why this paper is based on a rather peculiar experiment: an exercise designed to capture the idea that all people are equal in their capacity to exemplify this interior design and curating capacity. For this purpose, the first examples used in this paper come from a publication called *The Comfort of Things* (Miller 2008). The book is a description of the material culture of thirty households mostly from a single street (and its side streets) in South London. The thirty were selected from the one hundred that took part in this anthropological study. But I will then move from these offline worlds to the way people curate what they post online, since we can see that one of the key failures in understanding online life today is the failure to recognize first that this is a place in which we now live, and second the analogy with curation and interior decoration that could help us understand the content of much of what we post.

Householders as Museum Curators

What does it mean to suggest that we are all museum curators? Well, to curate is to feel responsible for, and look after the objects in your possession. To be a museum curator suggests that at least some of these objects will be chosen for public display, and these will illustrate some theme. Mostly, they are historical evidence for past events, but they may also be evidence for taste, or the work of an artist or some such conceptual framework. If households have selected from their possessions which objects to display, and given thought to how they will be organized and presented, then it is reasonable to see a normal householder as at least analogous to a museum or art gallery curator.

One of the reasons an object may be selected for display is that it has become inalienable (Weiner 1992). Something that perhaps once was a mere commodity that could have been owned by anyone. But over time possession itself has turned it into something that has deep resonance for that family, not just a display item, but perhaps even a potential heirloom. At this point, it is inalienable in the sense that no one would sell such a thing; its monetary value is just not the point. For the elderly, it is likely to be time that is the principle behind curation. This museum is in effect a *précis* of their past.

Such was the case with Dora. We carried out an inventory of all the objects found in her living room. On reflection, these turned out to be a résumé of her full life. One of the most poignant is the bright red piggy bank that today she still fills with twenty pence coins. When full it contains fifty pounds, which can be spent—a routine that reminds her of her origins in poverty. There is one photo of her as a little girl, living a life made hard from birth when her father was gassed in the trenches in World War I, and another photo of her as a Girl Guide. There is just one table inherited from her mother, and from the period when she first worked is her sewing machine, also a decorated box, and a valance from the Jewish family that ran the alteration shop where she was employed. There is a picture of the first wedding dress she made for herself, six decades ago, that sees its counterpoint in several examples of needlework from recent years.

Though she has the two engagement rings from her two marriages, few possessions—only the government condolence letter for her first husband's death—remain from the first marriage, which was mired in poverty. From the second marriage, which took her to Portugal and Spain, she has a table, a carpet, and an ornament from Portugal. She displays a photo of herself with her husband at a dinner party, another of one of his ancestors, and a decorated box from his family. Following his death she left most of their lavish belongings to his family, returning to England to unpack some of those things she had saved on her own account. Of these she treasured the stylish cutlery, egg cups, and silver cups from a high class London shop. With the thrift that is reflected in her piggy bank she would buy cutlery one at a time until she reached five, when the manager would give her the sixth for free. She has a certificate from the ambulance service she worked with during the war, and a photo of the luncheon room where she worked afterward for twenty-five years, ending with a certificate of freedom from the City of London where the luncheon room was sited. There is a picture from when she looked really good in the 1960s, a photo of a close friend, a letter from Mrs. Thatcher, and a picture from a holiday in France. There is no reason to imagine that Dora intended this résumé effect. It is rather the result of this "economy of relationships," such that each significant relationship, whether to persons or periods and events of her past, ultimately became reduced to just one or two objects, as other mementos make way for other relationships. Clearly the more relationships one has lived through, the more any one relationship has to be pruned back to one or two total mementos in the performance of economy.

Household curation is generally balanced between two principles. The first, exemplified by Dora, claims no aesthetic relationship between what is displayed since the logic is derived from their function as memorabilia. But most younger people will at least, to a degree, follow a competing principle of curation, the imposition of interior design. On this street there were some extreme examples of paramount design. The house that proclaims there is "no color but cream." The house whose doctrine is that objects must express dynamism, not make museums. So on the walls are not pictures, as in other houses, but clothes hung as decorations, which can be changed over time. Thirty pairs of jeans are carefully ordered according to the precise degree of wash, fade, and distressing. A similarly overt cosmology is evident when one walks into a Feng Shui house. It speaks to a life that insists no sentiment or other interest can disrupt the tyranny of calm order. Gifts from relatives—indeed all gifts—are carefully stowed away in unseen cupboards or given away. Here, light, the sound of fountains, rock and wood, are all where they should be, consistency resolving contradiction. This Feng Shui is just as important as an antidote to his wife's stressful work as a management consultant as it is to a householder's own work as an acupuncturist with an Eastern spiritual inflection.

Most people offer a compromise between these two conflicting principles of biography and design. Often, the core linkage is that biography is not usually directed to the person alone but is a material expression of the way identity comes from relationships. To preempt the second half of this paper, much of what we see can be de-coded once we realize that home decoration mainly reveals the individual as a 'social networking site.' Di, for example, like many others, wants to retain something of her parents' possessions as memories, but doesn't want these to undermine the autonomy she has carefully constructed for her own life. So when they move house she takes certain things, but keeps them today, not in the house, but in her garden shed. The shed is both near enough and far enough to exemplify the place in her life she wants her parents to inhabit. This matters because the most consistent relationship she has cultivated in her life is to the house itself. Starting from her hippy days, the house became the repository of ethnic paraphernalia that stands also for her liberal attitudes reflected today in her work with immigrant children. Even her husband at their divorce knew he could not ask for things from this, their once shared, house. The house is full of her emotional repertoire. It has places to cry in, to have great sex in. She can look at a wall of tickets to rock gigs she has been to. But it is also her logistical base, without children, the object of her practice of care. The house links the very particular schema of emotions and pragmatism that is Di's aesthetic form.

If Dora as a curator has objects that mark her identity as a social networking site at each stage in her life, the same principle can be applied to the spatial design of the interior. One Irish couple, who have retired from a life of owning pubs, recognize that the photographs and images on display are so numerous that they joke there is no need to paint since you cannot see the color of the walls behind. On careful inspection, it emerges that the relationships are grouped around themes. One cluster relates to their lives as publicans. There is another area that is effectively a Catholic shrine of religious images. Yet another is dedicated to the educational qualifications of relatives. But as well as kin, there is also a small area which preserves mementoes to deceased customers, some of whom, one comes to realize, ended their lives with no one else to remember them but the landlords of their favorite pub. Sports, weddings, Irish Republican heroes, childhood, and holidays all constitute additional genres of relationships that jostle for room within an economy constituted essentially by the size of space available for explicit memorialization.

One way to define anthropology as opposed to, for example, psychology or economics, is to recognize that while these other disciplines tend to focus upon people as individuals, anthropologists see people as social networking sites. Understanding the way this is revealed in the home interior takes us part way on the route to the shift from offline to online. The other is an appreciation that this curation can involve immateriality as well as materiality. The case of Malcolm conveniently makes this point.

Malcolm's work fluctuates between Australia and the United Kingdom, but what he understands as his permanent address is his email, and the nearest thing to home is his laptop. Both his friendships and his work are largely organized by email, a place he constantly orders, returns to, cares for, and where, in many respects, 'his head is.' But to understand the intensity of this relationship to his laptop, we need to read the anthropologist Fred Myers (1986). Because, Myers notes, that for many Aboriginal groups there is a tradition of avoiding the physical possessions of the deceased. Malcolm's mother was Australian Aboriginal and most of her possessions were indeed destroyed at her death. But he took from her a mission to locate and preserve the history of his family, including those members once taken away from their parents. As he sees it, too much Aboriginal history is viewed as lying in police records; he wants a proper archive he will deposit in an Australian State archive.

Malcolm has an antipathy to things. He has given most of his inherited or childhood objects away. In his devotion to immateriality he prefers anything digital. He is getting into digital photographs. He downloads music and immediately throws out the covers. Very unusual in this street study, he even gives away his books after he has read them. One could relate this to his mobility, one could relate it to his interest in the potential of new technologies, one could relate it to this Aboriginal inheritance. There is more. His father sold antiques but the result was that as soon as he started becoming attached to things in his childhood, they would be sold—another possible source of his detachment from things. Once again then, his personal habitus (Bourdieu 1977) is over-determined, meaning that people do things usually not from a single influence or cause, but from the reinforcement that comes from several different influences. Even Malcolm cannot decide how much his mobility is cause and effect. But the overall result, as he puts it, is "I think I've set myself up to be out of touch with objects and things, so there's probably something psychological behind that." He has a more ambiguous relation to less tangible things like documents, sorting both his mother's and his own things into neat box files. But his real identification is with digital forms. He constantly updates and sorts his emails, which becomes the updating of his social relationships. In going through them he recalls all those friends he owes emails to.

One could try and stretch the Aboriginal inheritance. The laptop as a kind of digital dream world that connects current relationships with those of the dead; a place he comes in and out of, as more real than merely real life. He retains this intense concern with lineage devoting much of his time to creating order out of kinship history. He seems obsessed that if he were to die, that thanks to constantly sorting his emails, he would leave a legacy that was archived and up-to-date, so no one would have to do the work he did recovering and ordering his ancestral lives. But for my purpose, what he typifies is first the multiple determination of his cosmology. Both father, mother, and his work come together as possible explanations. One could not claim to have predicted him, but given what we now know, this relationship to his laptop that at first seemed so bizarre, can certainly make sense. It is an aesthetic, a material cosmology. One can see how the horizontal dimensions of order—the various current influences—merge with the vertical of historical influences to produce this over-determination in his background.

Curating the Online World

Over the last few years most of my research has been concerned with the study of the Internet and social media. One of the problems faced by academics in this field is the way people dismiss online activity as trivial. If people spend time on de-tagging photos or in other ways organizing how they appear to others online this is seen as a displacement activity. Yet, once we see the analogy with our use of ornaments on the mantelpiece and posters on the wall we can see that this is just the same activity as interior decoration, only transposed to a different place. But first, we must acknowledge that this is in some ways where people live.

In 2012, I published a book with Mirca Madianou called *Migration and New Media* (Madianou and Miller 2012). This was a study of Filipino domestic workers in England who had left their own children behind in the Philippines. One of my closest informants was actually not a mother. She is a young woman who works in London partly as a cleaner, mostly as a carer for the elderly. She has been in London for two and a half years. During that time, except for those occasions when I have insisted that she comes out with me, she has never been to a film, or a pub, or practically any other form of London site or institution. All she ever does is work, return to her home where she sleeps in a bunk bed above another Filipina worker so that both can save as much money as possible. Much of her leisure time is spent in direct communication with her family, including social networking sites, which used to be dominated by the social network site Friendster and now more by Facebook. One could say that she works in London, also that she sleeps and eats in London, but in many respects she lives with her family not in the Philippines but really and truly on Facebook.

Once we recognize that online can be a living space then we can use ethnography to investigate more seriously the way people decorate and curate these spaces. Sometimes, the reason a person lives on Facebook may not be migration but a change in their own condition. In another book called *Tales From Facebook* (Miller 2011), I give a story taken from research in Trinidad about a man I call Dr. Karamath. A distinguished expert on human rights he had spent much of this life traveling as a Caribbean representative in many international forums. In his sixties, Dr. Karamath suffered from a serious injury such that from now on he will always be housebound in Trinidad. But then using Facebook, bit by bit, Dr. Karamath replicated exactly the kinds of networking relationships that he had fostered before his illness. He soon found that even for someone with as international and cosmopolitan experience as himself, who had met so many people in so many lands, Facebook could take this whole operation up a gear. He could now be in contact with yet more people in yet more countries, and far more effectively than had ever previously been the case. Before it had mattered that this friend was in Washington and that one in Toronto, and there were weary overnight flights and the cold alienating layovers in airports to negotiate. Not any more.

On Facebook he could be simultaneously in many countries. He developed new transnational friendships with people who have a similar interest in politics—but also share an affection for a specific art form: the posters and agitprop from the 1960s that dominate his home decoration and that of some of these friends. It was clear that, even though they had never met, thanks to their facility with a webcam, this little coterie of friends had a good knowledge also of the art works, prints, and paraphernalia of their respective homes. It seemed as though Facebook with its complementary cousins, Skype and webcam, had managed to somehow replicate the older circuit of cocktail parties in which each had in turn hosted the group. So the decorations of the home could still create an ambience that helped generate productive conversation and friendship.

For Dr. Karamath, a key to this linkage is webcam and the next stage in this research on Trinidad was a book concerned specifically with the impact of webcam (Miller and Sinanan 2014) including the way webcam has contributed to this sense that people can live together in an online space. One of the most remarkable conclusions was that webcam works much better when you treat it like a home than when you treat it as a communication device.

A Trinidadian studying in the United Kingdom and her long-term partner with whom she had lived for two years prior to the separation would have webcam on the entire time, even to the extent of watching each other while one or the other was sleeping. The importance of such 'always-on' media is that they actually obviate the need to directly communicate. As she noted, "But what was nice about it was that it wasn't demanding, so it wasn't like we had to be in contact with each other."

'Always-on' webcam meant a return to the co-presence of a shared home, where mostly they would have been getting on with their own work, knowing they might have a conversation when cooking or eating. In fact, the same individual makes quite sure never to establish a Skype correspondence with her mother precisely because she feels terrified at the idea of an equivalent demand for co-presence. In such cases, the same ambience that is created through the shared co-presence in the curated spaces of the kitchen or the TV room is now shared equally online, but often alongside online spaces such as Facebook.

Most recently, I have worked within a team of nine anthropologists who simultaneously carried out fifteenth months of ethnography in nine locations of which two were in China and others in Brazil, Chile, India, Italy, Trinidad, and Turkey (Costa et al. 2016). Again, we can find examples of where it is the interior design of online contexts that show us where people live today. One of the projects represents what may have been the largest migration in human history. Over 200 million Chinese people moved from rural areas to work in factories. Xin Yuan Wang (2016) lived for fifteen months in one of these factory towns. She feels that she studied two migrations; one was from the village to the factory, but the other was simultaneously from their non-working life being mainly spent offline to their non-working life today being mainly spent online, since they spend much more time on Chinese social networks than mixing with other factory workers. Both of these migrations were intended to bring them closer to the modern life of China, symbolized by places such as Shanghai. But she argues that in many ways it is the migration to living online rather than the migration to living in the factory that has done more to fulfill their aspirations. Online they curate their QQ sites (QQ is the main Chinese social media platform) with images of the weddings and consumer goods they strive for, and through the organization and curation of these images at least in some sense feel they possess them.

But actually we do not have to just consider the condition of migration or mobility. My own ethnographic research project (Miller 2016) took place in some villages north of London. As part of this research, I came to realize that the practice of interior decoration has recently become the primary mode by which children socialize. The impulse to do this has been evident for decades as the first time teenagers achieve spatial autonomy we saw a riot of bedroom decoration. But quite early on Horst (2009, 2012) recognized the link between this and their online activity. On the one hand, they lived in teenage bedrooms where adults were not welcome, and which were heavily decorated as teenage bedrooms in styles their parents often did not like. At exactly the same time, they decorated their MySpace profiles in colors but also music and digital decorations. Horst noticed that often the colors they used for their bedroom continued into the colors they used for their MySpace profile. And remember, the bedroom was just as cut off from adults as the online. In short, offline and online are parts of the same continuous life just as a smartphone in your pocket ensures you can remain connected with this online world.

So the imperative toward interior decoration was already evident. But thanks to the ability to craft interior decorations online this can start to develop even earlier. In my ethnography, I found that the dominant platform for the younger age was now Minecraft and that many of those playing were under ten years old. The basis for playing Minecraft is often building oneself a home. Indeed, if you visit a platform such as Pinterest you can find sections devoted to the decoration of home interiors called "interior design."[1] Parents are now extremely confused as to what is going on here. They see a bunch of children in their living room, none of whom are talking to each other as all are absorbed online, but online they are bonding through Minecraft building homes and interiors. So is this good socializing between children meeting face to face, or as in Sherry Turkle's (2011) phrase, are they "alone together," being antisocial? Is this good working with their hands? Is it, as one parent put it, "the new Lego?" Or a sign that children no longer build things by hand? But then it is doubtful the parent did much of her own DIY in the act of interior decoration.

Finally what does this tell us about the relationship between anthropology and design? One of the initial tasks of anthropology was the exploration of worlds that were unfamiliar. The idea was that through empathetic engagement with peoples, often in those days tribal peoples, we would bring back an account which humanized those others and showed how from their point of view their cultural practices were merely life experienced as normal and as mundane as we experience our own. Today, the alien and exotic world that people are struggling to understand is often online. But in this chapter I have argued that an approach from *Design Anthropology* can accomplish this same task of reducing the different to the ordinary and mundane. The point has been to show that we can appreciate what people spend much of their time doing online, once we realize that online worlds—just as much as offline worlds—gift us an insight that is surely the foundation of any broad-minded design anthropology: the appreciation that interior design is not limited to professional expertise. It is actually a foundational attribute of merely being human.

The key technology we used to inhabit the world around us in the past, and that we will use to inhabit this new online world, is the technology of interior decoration, that which makes an abstract space into a personal or family space. We make ourselves AT home through making ourselves A home. So, as argued in our *Theory of Attainment* (Miller and Sinanan 2014: 4–20), the shift of our skills as interior decorators from offline to online does not make us less human or post-human. The point of this chapter is to show that interior decoration is one of those crafts that makes us all ordinarily human, irrespective of where this takes place.

---

1. https://www.pinterest.com/danielmeg/minecraft-interior-design/

References

Bourdieu, P. (1977), *Outline of a Theory of Practice*, Cambridge: Cambridge University Press.

Costa, E. Haynes, N. McDonald, T. Miller, D. Nicolescu, R. Sinanan, J. Spyer, J. Venkatraman, S. and X. Wang (2016), *How the World Changed Social Media*, London: UCL Press.

Horst, H. (2009), "Aesthetics of the Self: Digital Mediations," in D. Miller (ed.), *Anthropology and the Individual*, 99–113, Oxford: Berg.

Horst, H. (2012), "New Media Technologies in Everyday Life," in H. Horst and D. Miller (eds.), *Digital Anthropology*, 61–79, London: Berg.

Madianou, M. and D. Miller (2012), *Migration and New Media*, London: Routledge.

Miller, D. (2008), *The Comfort of Things*, Cambridge: Polity.

Miller, D. (2011), *Tales From Facebook*, Cambridge: Polity.

Miller, D. (2016), *Social Media in an English Village*, London: UCL Press.

Miller, D. and J. Sinanan (2014), *Webcam*, Cambridge: Polity Press.

Myers, F. (1986), *Pintupi Country, Pintupi Self*, Washington, DC: Smithsonian Institute Press.

Turkle, S. (2011), *Alone Together*, New York: Basic Books.

Wang, X. (2016), *Social Media in Industrial China*, London: UCL Press.

Weiner, A. (1992), *Inalienable Possessions,* Berkeley: University of California Press.

13 Designing Financial Literacy in Haiti

Erin B. Taylor and Heather A. Horst

Our main lesson learned is how difficult it is to educate customers. When we launched the service we assumed it would be something like selling a mobile phone, where you stick a mobile phone into someone's hand and almost anyone can start using it quite quickly because it's very easy to understand. With a mobile banking service or a mobile money service it's not quite that easy.

—Maarten Boute, former CEO of Digicel, Haiti, 2012[1]

Introduction

Mobile money services have grown exponentially over the past decade and are now available in over sixty-four countries, primarily in Africa, Asia, and Latin America.[2] Promoted as a promising way to bring a range of financial services to poor individuals and households by "riding the rails" of existing telecommunications and financial infrastructures (Mas and Morawczynski 2009; Maurer, Nelms and Rea 2013; Maurer 2015), users of mobile money services can store and send money, pay merchants, and even take out insurance and loans. Alongside relying upon telecommunications infrastructures, mobile money services also hinge upon users' familiarity with text messaging

---

1. Quoted in "Mobile Money Plan Stumbles at Start in Haiti," *The Daily Caller*, October 6, 2012, http://dailycaller.com/2012/06/10/mobile-money-plan-stumbles-at-start-in-haiti/.

2. GSMA Mobile Money Tracker, 23 December 2015, http://www.gsma.com/mobilefordevelopment/programmes/mobile-money/insights/tracker

(SMS) on a mobile phone handset that is used to manage credit and textual information. Given the growth in mobile phone subscriptions globally (Ling and Horst 2011; World Bank 2015), the widespread ability to use and navigate a mobile handset would seem to provide a logical design solution to the challenges of financial inclusion (Donovan 2012). This has certainly been the case with M-PESA, Kenya's first mobile money service, which now boasts a customer base exceeding 15 million users out of a population of 45 million people (Singh 2013; *The Economist* 2013). However, as Boute points out, extending everyday use of mobile phones to mobile money services is not so simple in practice. Providing greater access to financial services for the poor has therefore been uneven, despite a general enthusiasm across industry, government, and development sectors (Flores-Roux and Mariscal 2010; Mas and Radcliffe 2010).

In this chapter we examine how the usability of mobile money services is intertwined with issues of literacy as one of a series of challenges that mobile money service providers face in promoting their adoption. Drawing upon a case study of Digicel's and Voilà's mobile money services in Haiti between the years 2010 and 2012, we focus upon the materials used to disseminate and teach mobile money product literacy (e.g., advertisements, brochures, cartoons), demonstrating how different kinds of literacies converge as people attempt to use a mobile handset to make money transactions. To illustrate this process of mobile literacy, we begin by giving an overview of literacy-related issues in mobile money design and the limitations of concentrating on literacy as a barrier. Second, we provide a brief history of mobile money in Haiti. We then explore how promotional literature has harnessed familiar genres to educate users about mobile money, and we discuss the attendant role of social learning in increasing product literacy in Haiti to demonstrate different kinds of learning needs and their limitations. We conclude by arguing that mobile money design should take into account different kinds of literacies, but also think beyond them to how consumers engage with products on an on-going basis in different social contexts.

Designing Mobile Money

Mobile phones are especially promising "platforms" for additional services, particularly ones aimed at poor populations since their use is so widespread globally. Whether using computers or tablets to enhance education, or mobile phone handsets to communicate market prices, users' experiences center around a device. To be used successfully, the hardware and software need to be appropriately designed, and its user must possess adequate working knowledge of the device's features. They are often likely to need both technical and textual literacy, and—in the case of financial services or purchases—financial literacy.

The foundational literature on mobile phone use tends to support the use of mobile phones as development tools, since skills in using mobile phones tend to be high across the board. This includes texting, one of the most common practices in mobile phone use, despite the fact that it depends upon users being textually literate. Use of texts is particularly strong among youth and in the global south where the cost of communication via SMS is often cheaper than calls (Ling and Horst 2011; Slater 2014). Pertierra, for example, notes the widespread practice of texting and SMS in the Philippines, which supersedes texting in more industrialized contexts (Pertierra 2006, 2007). In her article on language and texting practices in multilingual Senegal, Lexander (2011) suggests that among low-income mobile phone users text messaging is common and, among youth, enables code switching between different languages depending upon context, the nature of the relationship, and other factors.

Despite these seminal examples, however, SMS and other mobile phone-related literacies are not ubiquitous. And yet, the assumption that customers already know how to read, write, use money, and even use a mobile phone, frames product design. As a result, learning considerations often focus upon teaching customers about the product. Usability issues arising from assumptions of product familiarity and literacy have long been known to affect the success of ICT4D[3] initiatives (Medhi, Sagar and Toyama 2006; Donner et al. 2008; Ho, Smyth, and Kam 2009; GSMA 2015a, 2015b). With respect to mobile money, consumers face at least two broad barriers. First, as social science and behavioral economic research has thoroughly documented, issues of familiarity, trust, and "loss aversion" can inhibit the uptake of new products (Brown, Zelenska, and Mobarak 2013; Yao, Liu, and Yuan 2013; Osei-Assibey 2015). Second, using a mobile phone to make financial transactions requires at least four different kinds of literacy: textual, numerical, technological, and product literacy. At the commercial level, there is also the problem of "scaling" mobile money, sometimes referred to as the "chicken and egg problem" in which customers will not use mobile money if the agent network is not extensive, while businesses will not sign up to be agents unless they have a large customer base (Mas and Radcliffe 2010).

Despite a great deal of enthusiasm, then, relatively few mobile money services have managed to attract large numbers of regular users. One major exception is M-PESA, whose success is often attributed to the fact that there were preexisting needs, infrastructures, and experiences of using mobile handsets to make financial transactions. Indeed, before M-PESA was developed, Kenyans were using airtime as substitute money, sending it to each other across the country. M-PESA simply formalized a service that Kenyans were providing themselves. Hence, problems with product knowledge and scaling were never a serious issue, since the first, informal version of the network developed spontaneously through people inventing ways to fulfill their own financial transaction needs.

Literacy can be a useful concept to apply in contexts where skills in reading, writing, and using Information and Communications Technologies (ICTs) are below global standards. Mobile money as a development tool is targeted at the poor or very poor in developing countries, and these groups tend to have the lowest textual and numerical literacy levels (Singh 2013; Maurer 2015). Literacy is important for mobile money, since it relies on users navigating an interface and interpreting text menus, text messages, and in some cases, entering strings of numbers to make transactions (Losh 2015).

---

3. ICT4D stands for Information and Communications Technologies for Development.

However, not all user experiences can be reduced to the concept of "literacy." Since technology is always changing, we are always learning; hence we are always, to some extent, illiterate. This reinforces a need for an emphasis on continual learning. As Boute pointed out with respect to Haiti, the issue was not the design of the mobile phone per se (since people already knew how to use them), but the failure of mobile phone providers to adequately explain this new feature. In what follows we outline the major literacy and learning issues and the ways in which Mobile Money Operators (MMOs) have attempted to counter them through "entertainment-education."

Mobile Money in Haiti

On June 10, 2010, six months after a catastrophic earthquake that leveled much of Port-au-Prince, the Bill and Melinda Gates Foundation and the USAID-funded Haiti Integrated Finance for Value Chains and Enterprises (HIFIVE) announced the launch of the Haiti Mobile Money Initiative (HMMI) to stimulate the development of mobile banking services in Haiti (HIFIVE 2010). The HMMI offered US$10 million in prizes and US$5 million in technical assistance for companies to develop and expand mobile banking services across the country.

Mobile money was initially conceived of as a way for NGOs to move money in Haiti, given that widespread damage to financial, communications, and transport infrastructure had crippled Haiti's underdeveloped financial system. In the longer term, however, it was also a potential solution to Haiti's inadequate financial infrastructure and a way of speeding up the circulation of cash, saving time and money. Banking infrastructure is scarce, and approximately 66 percent of bank branches are located in Port-au-Prince (Goss 2011; Taylor, Baptiste, and Horst 2011). Accessing bank branches can be difficult, and using them can be time consuming. Besides being badly distributed, bank branches are inefficient. Lines are long, with people often waiting hours to make a transaction. Microcredit institutions such as Fonkoze cover a larger portion of the country, and formal remittance services such as Western Union and Caribe Express are also better distributed. But remittance services such as Western Union can be very expensive to use, especially when people wish to spend small amounts of cash.

This leaves a gap in the market for transfers and merchant payments that have generally been filled by informal services. Mobile money is an attempt to bridge this gap. It is a way for people without bank accounts or Internet to access basic banking facilities through their mobile phones. They can deposit money, store it on their SIM cards, pay for airtime, and transfer money to other people. Unlike its banking system, Haiti's mobile telecommunications infrastructure is well developed, and mobile penetration is growing rapidly. Mobile money enables a wide distribution of service points, flexibility in how it is used by customers, and operates with preexisting technology. This means that the service has the capacity to expand far more rapidly than banks, which depend upon cumbersome infrastructure.

In the six months leading up to the launch of mobile money in Haiti, our team conducted research in three sites to get a sense of the need and desire for mobile money among individual

Haitians (Baptiste, Horst, and Taylor 2010). Generally speaking we found that people were enthusiastic about the idea of using their phones to make transactions. Our interviewees particularly cited the time and cost of sending money and security issues concerning carrying money as reasons why mobile money might be preferable. In Haiti, it is a common and low-cost way to send money around the country via public transport. They either travel themselves, send the money to a friend or relative who is traveling, or entrust the cash to a truck driver or boat captain. In one remittance route that we identified in the south of Haiti, boats travel along this route twice a week on market days, carrying goods, passengers, and money from the Dominican border to the town of Marigot. The boat journey takes around seven hours. Security is also an issue, as people carrying cash run the risk of being robbed. Moreover, beyond security issues, Haitians tend toward a cultural aesthetics of concealment, which makes the ability to hide money valuable in a symbolic as well as a practical sense (Taylor and Horst 2014).

As 2010 drew to a close, there were two publicly available mobile money services in Haiti: Digicel's TchoTcho Mobile and Voilá's T-Cash (see Figures 13.1 and 13.2). The two services were very similar in what they offered and in their pricing structures. They permitted customers

13.1 A Digicel mobile money outlet in downtown Port-au-Prince. © *Erin B. Taylor*

13.2 T-Cash's logo, Se lajan kontan!, aims to convince customers that mobile money is just as good as cash. © *Erin B. Taylor*

(both Haitians and foreigners, including the many NGO employees working in Haiti) to deposit, withdraw, and transfer money using SMS-based menus (Taylor 2015). TchoTcho Mobile's and T-Cash's mini-wallets held up to 4,000 gourdes (US$92.27) (raised from an initial size of 2,500 gourdes). To register for TchoTcho Mobile, all customers needed to do was dial *202# on their mobile phone and choose the registration option. For T-Cash, customers needed to call a registration number and speak with an operator. With either service, in order to open an account with a full wallet, which held up to 10,000 gourdes (US$250), customers needed to present identification at an official mobile money agent (called an *Agent Authorisé*). Customers deposited money in their mobile money accounts by taking their cash and their mobile handset to a mobile money agent (Taylor, Baptiste, and Horst 2011). This could be any legally registered business, such as a grocery store, a restaurant, a clothing store, or a cybercafé. Mobile money agents are normally small to medium-sized enterprises (SMEs), with Digicel stores and the microcredit institution Fonkoze also operating as agents (see Figures 13.3 and 13.4).

13.3 Branding in a Digicel office in Port-au-Prince, with advertisements in both French and Haitian Creole. © *Erin B. Taylor*

To become a mobile money agent, businesses undergo training and receive a phone with a special SIM card that they use to conduct cash-in and cash-out transactions. Larger businesses that have computers and a reliable Internet connection can use software instead. Agents use a mobile handset with a special SIM card, or a computer with Internet access, to register the customer's deposit. The customer then receives a text message indicating that the deposit was successful and stating their new balance. Afterwards, the customer can transfer that money to anyone else with a mobile money account. The account balance is not stored in the phone; rather, it is in a digital account that is tied to the SIM card. If a customer loses their handset they can call their MMO and request that their account be connected to their new SIM. TchoTcho Mobile accounts are accessed using a secret password that the customer has chosen; with T-Cash, passwords were generated by the service provider.

13.4 A vendor wearing a Digicel t-shirt in the Marche en Fer, Port-au-Prince.
© *Erin B. Taylor*

On January 10, 2011, Digicel's TchoTcho Mobile was awarded a US$2.5 million "First to Market" award for having achieved 10,000 cash in/cash out transactions at 100 new outlets in the six months after the award was announced. On October 11, 2010, Voilá's T-Cash received 89 percent of the first scaling award, a total of US$889,000. By the end of 2011, over 800,000 Haitians had signed up for mobile money services; of these, between 6,000 and 9,000 were in development programs at any given time.[4]

---

4. Personal communication from Greta Greathouse, Chief of Party of HIFIVE, February 15, 2012.

After Voilà's acquisition by Digicel in April 2012, T-Cash was disbanded, leaving Digicel's TchoTcho Mobile as the only mobile money service operating in Haiti. In August 2015, Digicel rebranded TchoTcho Mobile as Mon Cash in an attempt to revive interest in, and use of, the service. The major differences between TchoTcho Mobile and Mon Cash is that the agent network is much broader, since any Digicel airtime vendor is now permitted to offer an electronic wallet service if they wish (*Telegeography* 2015). Additionally, the maximum amount of money that a customer can store in their account was raised to 5,000 gourdes (US$80) for a "mini wallet" and 60,000 gourdes (US$980) for a "full wallet."[5] In this chapter, however, we focus on the earlier mobile money service, TchoTcho Mobile, since we are concerned with Digicel's early attempts to teach people to use mobile money.

Within the context of Haiti there are numerous reasons why mobile money could be expected to be a suitable innovation (Baptiste, Horst, and Taylor 2010). First, mobile phone penetration in Haiti was nearly universal at the time, meaning that people were already familiar with basic handset use. Second, people used ordinary phones (not smartphones), and mobile money is specifically designed for text menus and SMS, not Internet access. Finally, sending money around the country was a time-consuming and expensive endeavor. Since only an estimated 10 percent of Haitians had bank accounts, and sending money via formal services was expensive, many Haitians relied upon the much slower method of sending money via public transport (Ibid.). It seemed likely that there would be sufficient motivation for Haitians to learn to use mobile money, a much more convenient and less expensive financial service. In the following section we explore two kinds of materials that mobile money providers produced to teach Haitians how to use mobile money: instructional leaflets and comics.

Designing Financial Literacy

As Smith and Taffler (1996) demonstrate, the design challenges that are part of the broader landscape of financial literacy do not necessarily involve technological "solutions" (see also Parikh, Ghosh, and Chavan 2002; Ghosh, Parikh, and Chavan 2003). During the early roll-out of mobile money in Haiti, service providers needed to account for the fact that, while Haitians are near-universally numerically literate, the textual literacy rate is approximately 53 percent (CIA World Factbook). Digicel's TchoTcho Mobile and Voilà's T-Cash both built literacy considerations into their interface design. Although both services operated via text messaging, they also worked in different ways. Digicel opted for a text interface in which customers navigate through lists of choices. Customers access mobile money services by entering a numerical code. They then receive an SMS in reply asking them to choose an option from a menu, and they use their phone's keypad to select the menu item they desire. Text messages go backwards and forwards between the handset and the

---

5. See Digicel's mobile money FAQs, http://www.digicelhaiti.com/en/help_faqs/products/digicel -moncash-faq

mobile money provider until the transaction is complete. While customers interact with TchoTcho Mobile through their handset's numerical interface, the aesthetics of the service are menu-based and therefore highly textual (see Figure 13.5). Conversely, Voilá's T-Cash used a number-based system that did not require navigating text menus. Instead, T-Cash customers entered a string of numbers to make a transaction, and hit "send." Customers enter strings of numbers that are unique to the kind of transaction they wish to make. This reduces the number of steps necessary to make a transaction, but it requires customers to either remember a greater range of commands or to refer to T-Cash's instructional booklet (see Figure 13.6).

The choice of text messaging versus text menus as the key interface for mobile money services has both aesthetic and functional implications (Taylor and Horst 2014). To be functional, text menus need to be readily navigable and comprehensible, and, to have appeal, thought needs to be put into their design and style. How these needs are balanced depends upon the target market. As Boute's introductory quote highlights, mobile money systems are not necessarily intuitive for people who already know how to use a handset.

13.5 A mobile money transfer using Digicel's TchoTcho Mobile uses French.
© *Erin B. Taylor*

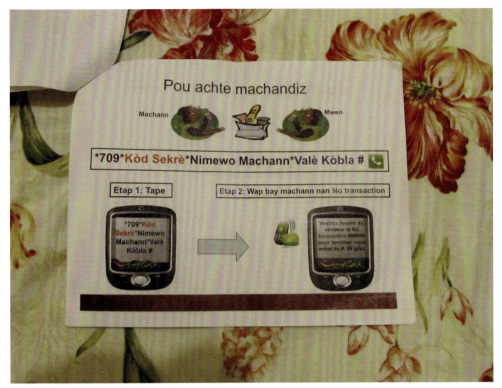

13.6 Mercy Corps developed leaflets in Haitian Creole to explain how mobile money works to recipients of conditional cash grants in Saint Marc, Haiti. © *Erin B. Taylor*

Given the relatively low levels of textual literacy in Haiti, T-Cash's mobile money service should have been easier to use because it only required the entry of numbers. However, textual literacy is necessary to be able to read a T-Cash pamphlet to work out which string of numbers to use. Voilá's use of strings of numbers is not necessarily helpful for people who are not textually literate because figuring out which strings of numbers to use requires them to read a brochure.

Textual literacy issues were also complicated by the fact that Haiti, like many post-colonial countries, has two official languages, Haitian Kreyol and French, and also the increasing encroachment of English in the day-to-day vernacular. Kreyol is spoken by the entire population of roughly twelve million people, and is considered to be the "language of the people," whereas French is the language of administration and formal business and is spoken or partially spoken by about half the population.

TchoTcho Mobile advertises and publishes in Kreyol, but their text menus are all in French. This seems surprising, considering that Kreyol is the dominant language. It suggests that Haiti's poorest sectors were not necessarily Digicel's target market, but rather people who have completed a secondary school education, as French is the primary language in which classes are taught. Indeed, this is in keeping with mobile money deployments elsewhere. Evidence from Kenya, for example, suggests that the middle class was the driving force behind the adoption of mobile money (Kuriyan, Nafus, and Mainwaring 2012). Mobile money became an aspirational product, communicating that the customer was technologically savvy and forward-thinking. Language in this context is deployed not so much for practical purposes as it is for branding a product with a particular symbolic meaning, which may then increase its appeal to poorer social sectors.

These issues relate to different kinds of "literacy" or user knowledge, including language (literacy or fluency), numeric (oft assuming that people are numerically literate), and technological (familiarity with a handset). Additionally, TchoTcho Mobile's television advertisements at the time demonstrated people carrying out mobile money transactions with agents to deposit and withdraw cash, what we might think of as transaction or consumer literacy. Yet the issues around mobile money use cannot be reduced to "literacy." First, this term implies that there are certain skills that consumers should learn. Yet, it is unreasonable to expect Creole speakers to learn French in order to use a mobile phone. Second, as we flagged earlier, "learning" is ongoing, often taking place informally, and occurring in different ways for different demographics. In Haiti, mobile money designers had to take into account not only textual and numerical literacy, but also other kinds of diversity in the target market. One way they addressed social learning was by producing instructional booklets to teach the different ways to use mobile money. These acknowledge that mobile money is not necessarily intuitive and that learning is a process.

Learning through Cartoons

Instructional materials took a pictorial approach to educating Haitians about mobile money. In particular, they drew upon well-established practices of "education-entertainment" in the fields of development (Manyozo 2012). As Waisbord describes in a 2001 report on development communications that builds on a prior definition by Singhal and Rogers,

> Entertainment-education refers to "the process of purposely designing and implementing a media message to both entertain and educate, in order to increase audience knowledge about an educational issue, create favorable attitudes, and change overt behavior." (Singhal and Rogers 1999: xii) (Waisbord 2001: 13)

Waisbord continues,

> Entertainment-education projects are effective in stimulating people predisposed to change behavior to engage in a new behavior (e.g. use contraceptive methods). They provide the push for those already inclined to act to behave differently. (Waisbord 2001: 15)

In this vein, Digicel and Voilá, the two companies that offered mobile money services in Haiti, produced their own entertainment-education materials to teach people to use mobile money (see Figure 13.7). Their brochures, advertisements, and cartoons were distributed through a range of media, including television and radio (advertisements), in the companies' stores (instructional brochures), and through NGO programs using mobile money (cartoons). Mobile money slogans and branding were also painted onto the sides of buildings and walls, especially in Port-au-Prince, to bring visibility and familiarity to the services. However, Maarten Boute's observation about the difficulties of encouraging mobile money use suggests that static promotional materials were not sufficient to convert people into users. The info-tainment materials discussed in this section were introduced by the MNOs as an attempt to overcome this static engagement and train people to use mobile money. In fact, these trials appeared to be successful; the problem was not in the design of the materials, as much as similar efforts were limited to a few small groups.

The cartoons in particular were an attempt to use entertainment to teach product familiarity and overcome textual, numerical, and technological literacy problems. Both Digicel and Voilá produced cartoons depicting people learning to use mobile money. In TchoTcho Mobile's cartoon, one agent explains the service to one woman, who is dressed casually in yellow pants and a white t-shirt. This cartoon creates a story in which she learns how to use the service, solely through

13.7 A T-Cash instructional leaflet and a TchoTcho Mobile cartoon. © *Erin B. Taylor*

interacting with the agent. Conversely, the T-Cash cartoon depicts many Haitians, and always in groups, learning to use mobile money. Though some of the characters are in casual dress and talking with each other, the majority of characters are shown to be working. However, only men are shown to work, and only men talk in the cartoons.

TchoTcho Mobile Cartoon

Opening title: "With TchoTcho Mobile!!!"

A woman goes up to a TchoTcho Mobile tent.

Woman: "Good day! I have come to inscribe in TchoTcho Mobile."

Agent: "Hello madam! Did you know that when you are enrolled in TchoTcho Mobile you can receive your salary on your phone?"

Woman: "How can I receive my money on my phone?"

Agent: "TchoTcho Mobile is a service that Digicel provides to allow you to receive and manage your money in full security on your Digicel phone. It's quick, it's easy and economic!"

Woman: "Perfect!"

Agent: "OK, we will need your identification and your Digicel phone. I will help you complete the form."

A message appears on the mobile phone's screen in French: "Welcome to TchoTcho Mobile, your temporary PIN is 1234."

Woman: "My favorite number is 1980. That year I was born! Let me change the PIN."

The woman receives a message in French: "Your PIN has been successfully changed."

Text: "One week later"

Woman: "Wow! I have received my salary!"

The phone displays a message in French: "You have received an amount of 1,000 Gourdes. Thanks for using TchoTcho Mobile."

The woman goes back to the TchoTcho Mobile tent.

Woman: "Good afternoon! I have come to withdraw 600 gourdes from my TchoTcho Mobile."

Agent: "OK! Give me your ID and your phone."

The woman hands over her phone and ID.

Woman: "This is too cool! I already have my money! TchoTcho Mobile is great!"

The woman shows the reader her phone with a French message: "Your balance is 400 Gourdes. Thanks for using TchoTcho Mobile."

End title: "With TchoTcho Mobile you are your own wallet!"

T-Cash Cartoon

Title: "Presenting T-Cash!"

Parade with a group of people holding signs: "Viva Voilá," "Viva T-Cash," "Thanks Voilá for T-Cash." In the background there are people holding signs that read "Viva Uni-bank" and "Thanks Unibank for T-Cash."

Man in a parade: "Announcement! Announcement! Voilá and Unibank are jointly offe-ring a new service called T-Cash …"

Another man in the parade: "Your wallet is also your bank account and it is in your hands . . . through your Voilá phone."

Worker hanging up a banner that reads "*700# to activate your account": "T-Cash is too cool! You get, set, transfer, buying the same, quick, safe service freely on the phone, Voilá."

A man in casual dress talking to a man in business attire and a man with a machete: "When you have activated your account, you will receive a secret code. To change your secret codes enter *701*PIN*NewPIN. To put money on the account, go to an agent, *707*agentPIN*clientmobilenumber*amount#.

Construction worker laying cinder blocks: "And if I want to send a little money to my father outside [i.e., who is distant]?"

Other construction worker: "Easy, my dear. To make a transfer you enter *707*PIN*mo-bilenumber*amount#. After, to check your balance, enter *702*PIN#."

Man in a group: "How can I verify my transactions? And if my phone is stolen, what do I do?"

Other man: "To check your three last transactions, enter *703*PIN#. If your phone is stolen, to block your T-Cash account borrow any Voilà phone and enter *712*PIN#.

Farmers working in a field: "Things are changing in our lives, since merchants accept T-Cash. To buy, enter *709*PIN*agentnumber*amount# and the vendor will enter *711* PIN*transactionID*amount#.

Other farmer: "The same if you have received your salary or something like that. To take money out of your account, enter *708*PIN*agentnumber*amount# and the agent will enter *711*PIN*transactionID*amount#.

Boy among his family: "You can register easily! Transactions are performed for you secur-ely! That's why we say T-Cash is cash!"

Ends with T-Cash logo and their slogan, "Se lajan kontan" and "For information call client services, *854."

During the first few months after the launch of mobile money, these cartoons were used primarily with people who were part of NGO-run programs using mobile money. These included a Mercy Corps program that was using T-Cash to deliver conditional cash grants to people who were displaced by the earthquake. Mercy Corps gave its participants in Saint-Marc and Mirebalais Voilá phones and SIM cards, helped them register for T-Cash, and trained them to use mobile money through the cartoons and other props. Participants would then receive regular payments on their mobile phones, which they could use to buy food in designated stores. As Boute highlights, mobile money systems need to be straightforward to use. T-Cash is quite complicated, but their cartoon provides advice as to the ways in which everyday practices, such as one-to-one sharing of information, leverages peer learning (and, arguably, also reinforces systems of gatekeeping).

By using the cartoons in a group setting, Voilá and their NGO partners maximized opportunities for social learning. As with many "developing" countries, social learning in Haiti is familiar. Formal schooling rates tend to be low with a primary school completion rate of around 66 percent (World Bank 2013) and so people depend on others to learn skills. Because of the ways that everyday social and economic life is structured, people spend a great deal of time around others, and there are many opportunities to share information. For example, Haitian women traditionally run the country's informal market system and spend a great deal of time in each others' company, traveling together to buy goods and then selling them in markets (Mintz 1961). They learn their trade from one another, often from their mothers (Schwartz 2009). Men also engage in extensive informal labor, much of which occurs outdoors and requires cooperation with others. Moreover, in Haiti there has been a long tradition of creating flexible household structures that span social and economic needs in rural and (more recently) urban Haiti. These are referred to as *lakou* (see LaRose 1975; Stevens 1998; Edmond, Randolph, and Richard 2007; Richman 2009). They emerged during plantation slavery and enabled biological and fictive kin to pool together economic, material, and social resources. Cooperative work teams and everyday household cooperation are enacted through these groups, making for tight-knit networks. Historically, these households were usually distributed within a fairly small geographic area, but today, they may extend between urban and rural environments, and, indeed, transnationally. Mobile phones provide a means for such households to stay connected and informed, thereby facilitating social learning across wide distances.

Other mobile money researchers have noted the use of similar materials elsewhere to teach mobile money use. For example, comic books were used in India to teach people about mobile money (Kc and Tiwari 2015; Tiwari and Kc 2015). As the researchers explain,

Unlike printed matter that is merely disseminated to provide basic information through visual communication, the special comic books in plastic sheaths that the trainers used were designed to actively engage unbanked people. (IMTFI 2015)

These endeavors in Haiti and India both use popular media to educate people in ways that are more visual and textual, thereby confronting problems of financial literacy, language diversity, and aesthetic appeal. However, recent research has noted that mobile money's usability poses further challenges for particular groups of people, such as women and the visually impaired (IMTFI 2013). In some cases, mobile money benefits women as it permits them to gain greater control over money flows (Kusimba, Yang, and Chawla 2015); in others, women's structural position in society may limit their access to mobile phones or other resources (IMTFI 2013). This suggests that, while attempts to teach people to use new products need to take into account that literacy may be an issue, it would be a mistake to reduce the problem to literacy at the expense of other structural issues at play.

Conclusion

While infrastructural and market development matter to the success of mobile money (Baijal 2012), design considerations are central in the planning and implementation of mobile money services. In Haiti, the development and launch of Digicel's mobile money service in 2010 drew upon clear use cases for mobile money in Haiti, and efforts to encourage its uptake were extensive. However, as Boute points out, the hoped-for mass adoption did not occur.

The three cases just described suggest that our conceptualization of the mobile money learning process is partial and limited. People learn in different ways and for different reasons. Sometimes literacy issues (technological, textual, numeric) come into play, but often the learning that needs to take place is not related to a deficit but is simply an ordinary process of learning a new product. In this sense learning in the "developing" world, or the "global south," is no different from anywhere else.

Coupling mobile phones with digital finance products extends access to financial services to populations that have previously had little access to formal financial products. If these products are to achieve their potential to encourage 'financial inclusion' and to 'bank the unbanked,' design and usage context need to be considered. Issues such as literacy (textual, numerical, technical), practice (how users incorporate mobile money into their lives), and context (e.g., integration of digital products into a preexisting financial ecology) are all part of what it takes to stimulate adoption.

From a design perspective, this requires thinking through issues as diverse as the aesthetics and design of the handset and interface, branding, and teaching materials. It also requires considering how these design features form part of a broader landscape of financial and cultural repertoires. As Digicel's and Voilà's experiences with mobile money demonstrate, "teaching" product literacy is as much a social-material activity as it is an issue of training. People often learn from friends and family, relying on "social proof" and informal settings to pick up new skills.

The question of who mobile money is designed *for* is also important. Whereas providers are interested in capturing a market, development programs are often aimed at poor and marginalized members of a population who may have different literacy needs or social demographics. There may be a mismatch in the materials produced by the MMO and the needs of the teaching group, such as was the case when Mercy Corps used Voilà's cartoon depicting men to teach a mixed group about mobile money. Such mismatches can potentially be alienating to certain social groups. Designing for literacy is, therefore, a complex endeavor that must consider the entire "value chain" from production to dissemination in order to produce appropriate technologies and means of learning.

Acknowledgments

This paper was made possible through the support of the Institute for Money, Technology and Financial Inclusion, University of California, Irvine. Research on mobile money in Haiti was also carried out with Dr. Espelencia Baptiste (Kalamazoo College).

References

Baijal, H. (2012), "Promoting Financial Inclusion: Is Mobile Money the Magic Bullet?" *World Bank Blogs*, August 6. Available online: http://blogs.worldbank.org/psd/promoting-financial-inclusion-is-mobile-money-the-magic-bullet.

Baptiste, E., H. A. Horst and E. B. Taylor (2010), "Haitian Monetary Ecologies and Repertoires: A Qualitative Snapshot of Money Transfer and Savings," Institute for Money, Technology & Financial Inclusion, University of California Irvine. Available online: http://www.imtfi.uci.edu/imtfi_haiti_money_transfer_project (accessed on January 25, 2017).

Brown, J. K., T. V. Zelenska and M. A. Mobarak (2013), "Barriers to Adoption of Products and Technologies that Aid Risk Management in Developing Countries," Innovations for Poverty Action. Available online: https://wdronline.worldbank.org/handle/10986/16365 (accessed on January 25, 2017).

CIA World Factbook. Available online: https://www.cia.gov/library/publications/the-world-factbook/geos/ha.html (accessed on January 25, 2017).

Donner, J., R. Gandhi, P. Javid, I. Medhi, A. Ratan, K. Toyama and R. Veeraraghavan (2008), "Stages of Design in Technology for Global Development," *Computer*, 41 (6): 34–41.

Donovan, K. (2012), "Mobile Money for Financial Inclusion," *Information and Communications for Development*, 61–74.

Edmond, Y. M, S. M. Randolph and G. L. Richard (2007), "The Lakou System: A Cultural, Ecological Analysis of Mothering in Rural Haiti," *The Journal of Pan African Studies*, 2 (1): 19–32.

Flores-Roux, E. M. and J. Mariscal (2010), "The Enigma of Mobile Money Systems," *Communications & Strategies* 79 (3): 41–62.

Ghosh, K., T. Parikh and A. Chavan (2003), "Design Considerations for a Financial Management System for Rural, Semi-Literate Users," *ACM Conference on Computer-Human Interaction.*

Goss, S. (2011), "Mobile Money Services Have Arrived in Haiti!" blog (January 18, 2017). Available online: http://www.impatientoptimists.org/Posts/2011/01/Mobile-Money-Services-Have-Arrived-in-Haiti (accessed on January 18, 2017).

GSMA (2015a), Mobile Technical Literacy Toolkit. Available at http://www.gsma.com/mobilefordevelopment /programme/connected-women/mobile-technical-literacy-toolkit-2 (accessed on January 25, 2017).

GSMA (2015b), "Accelerating Digital Literacy: Empowering Women to Use the Mobile Internet." Available online: http://www.gsma.com/mobilefordevelopment/programme/connected-women/accelerating -digital-literacy-empowering-women-to-use-the-mobile-internet-2 (accessed on January 25, 2017).

Ho, M., T. N. Smyth and M. Kam (2009), "Human-Computer Interaction for Development: The Past, Present, and Future," *Information Technologies and International Development*, 5 (4): 1–18.

IMTFI (2013), "Addressing Poverty through Mobile Money Technology." Available online: https://www .youtube.com/watch?v=BMt18nxctEc&feature=youtu.be (accessed on January 25, 2017).

IMTFI (2015), "Financial Literacy through Comic Books in Dharavi & Bihar with Deepti KC," Institute for Money, Technology & Financial Inclusion Blog, October 2013. Available online: http://blog.imtfi.uci .edu/2015/10/revisiting-imtfi-researchers-in-bihar.html.

KC, D. and M. Tiwari (2015), "Financial Literacy for Women Entrepreneurs," Institute for Money, Technology & Financial Inclusion, Available online: http://blog.imtfi.uci.edu/2015/10/revisiting-imtfi -researchers-in-bihar.html (accessed on January 25, 2017).

Kuriyan, R., D. Nafus and S. Mainwaring (2012), "Consumption, Technology, and Development: The 'Poor' as 'Consumer'," *Information Technologies & International Development*, 8 (1): 1–12.

Kusimba, S., Y. Yang and N. V. Chawla (2015), "Family Networks of Mobile Money in Kenya," *Information Technology in International Development*, 11 (3): 1–21.

LaRose, S. (1975), "The Haitian Lacou, Land, Family and Ritual," in A. Marks and R. Romer (eds.), *Family and Kinship in Middle America and the Caribbean*, 482–501, Willemstadt/Curacao: Institute of Higher Studies in Curacao.

Lexander, K. V. (2011), "Texting and African Language Literacy," *New Media & Society*, 13 (3): 427–43.

Ling, R. and H. A. Horst (2011), "Mobile Communication in the Global South," *New Media & Society*, 13 (3): 363–74.

Losh, E. (2015), "Mobile Money, Financial Literacy and Learning Through Digital Media," DML Central, January 5. Available online: http://dmlcentral.net/mobile-money-financial-literacy-and-learning -through-digital-media/.

Manyozo, L. (2012), *Media, Communication and Development: Three Approaches*, London etc.: SAGE Publications.

Mas, I. and O. Morawczynski (2009), "Designing Mobile Money Services: Lessons from M-PESA," *Innovations* (Spring), 77–91.

Mas, I. and D. Radcliffe (2010), "Scaling Mobile Money." Available online: http://www.gsma.com/mobile fordevelopment/programme/mobile-money/scaling-mobile-money (accessed on January 25, 2017).

Mas, I. and O. Morawczynski (2009), "Designing Mobile Money Services: Lessons from M-PESA," *Innovations* (Spring), 77–91.

Maurer, B. (2015), *How Would You Like to Pay? How Technology Is Changing the Future of Money*, Durham, NC: Duke University Press.

Maurer, B., T. C. Nelms and S. C. Rea (2013), "'Bridges to Cash': Channelling Agency in Mobile Money," *Journal of the Royal Anthropological Institute*, 19 (1): 52–74.

Medhi, I., A. Sagar and K. Toyama (2006), "Text-free User Interfaces for Illiterate and Semi-literate Users," *Information and Communication Technologies and Development*, 4 (1): 37-50.

Mintz, S. W. (1961), "Standards of Value and Units of Measure in the Fond-des-Negres Market Place, Haiti," *The Journal of the Royal Anthropological Institute of Great Britain and Ireland,* 91 (1): 23–38.

Osei-Assibey, E. (2015), "What Drives Behavioral Intention of Mobile Money Adoption? The Case of Ancient Susu Saving Operations in Ghana," *International Journal of Social Economics*, 42 (11): 962–79.

Parikh, T., K. Ghosh and A. Chavan (2002), "Design Studies for a Financial Management System for Micro-Credit Groups in Rural India," *ACM Conference on Universal Usability.*

Pertierra, R. (2006), *Transforming Technologies, Altered Selves: Mobile Phone and Internet Use in the Philippines*, Manila: De La Salle University Press.

Pertierra, R. (2007), *The Social Construction and Usage of Communication Technologies: Asian and European Experiences*, Quezon City: The University of the Philippines Press.

Richman, K. (2009), *Migration and Voodou*, Gainsville: University of Florida Press.

Schwartz, T. (2009), *Fewer Men, More Babies: Sex, Family, and Fertility in Haiti*, Lexington, MA: Lexington Books.

Singh, S. (2013), *Globalization and Money: A Global South Perspective*, Lanham: Rowman & Littlefield.

Singhal, A. and Rogers, E. M. (1999), *Entertainment-Education: A Communication Strategy for Social Change*, Mahwah and London: Lawrence Erlbaum.

Slater, D. (2014), *New Media, Development and Globalization: Making Connections in the Global South*, Cambridge: Polity Press.

Smith, M. and R. Taffler (1996), "Improving the Communication of Accounting Information Through Cartoon Graphics," *Accounting, Auditing & Accountability Journal*, 9 (2): 68–85.

Stevens, A. M. (1998), "Haitian Women's Food Networks in Haiti and Old Town, United States of America," PhD diss., Brown University.

Taylor, E. B. (2015), "Mobile Money: Financial Globalization, Alternative, or Both?," in G. Lovink, N. Tkacz and P. de Vries (eds.), *MoneyLab Reader: An Intervention in Digital Economy*, 244–56, Amsterdam: Institute of Network Cultures.

Taylor, E. B. and H. A. Horst (2014), "The Aesthetics of Mobile Money Platforms in Haiti," in G. Goggin and L. Hjorth (eds.), *Routledge Companion to Mobile Media*, 462–71, Oxon and New York: Routledge.

Taylor, E. B., E. Baptiste and H. A. Horst (2011), "Mobile Banking in Haiti: Possibilities and Challenges," IMTFI, University of California Irvine. Available online: http://www.imtfi.uci.edu/files/docs/2012/taylor_baptiste_horst_haiti_mobile_money.pdf (accessed on January 25, 2017).

Telegeography (2015), "Digicel Haiti Revamps Mobile Money as 'Mon Cash,'" August 18. Available online: https://www.telegeography.com/products/commsupdate/articles/2015/08/18/digicel-haiti-revamps-mobile-money-as-mon-cash/.

Tiwari, M. and D. KC (2015), "Stories for Financial Literacy Education of Migrant Workers," IMTFI. Available online: http://ifmrlead.org/wp-content/uploads/2015/05/Migrants_story_book_all.pdf.

Waisbord, S. (2001), "Family Tree of Theories, Methodologies and Strategies in Development Communication," The Rockefeller Foundation. Available online: http://www.communicationforsocialchange.org/pdf/familytree.pdf (accessed on January 25, 2017).

"Why Does Kenya Lead the World in Mobile Money?," *The Economist*, May 27, 2013. Available online: http://www.economist.com/blogs/economist-explains/2013/05/economist-explains-18

World Bank (2013), "Improving Access to Primary School in Haiti." Available online: http://www.worldbank.org/en/results/2013/08/29/primary-school-haiti-education-for-all-project.

World Bank (2015), "Data: Mobile Cellular Subscriptions (per 100 people)." Available online: http://data.worldbank.org/indicator/IT.CEL.SETS.P2.

Yao, H., S. Liu and Y. Yuan (2013), "A Study of User Adoption Factors of Mobile Banking Services Based on the Trust and Distrust Perspective," *International Business and Management*, 6 (2): 9–14.

14 Stirring the Anthropological Imagination: Ontological Design in Spaces of Transition

Arturo Escobar

To nourish design's potentiality for transitions requires a significant reorientation of design from the functionalist and rationalistic traditions from which it emerged, toward a type of rationality and set of practices attuned to the relational dimension of life. This is because life, and all creation, is collective and relational; it involves historically and epistemically situated persons (never 'autonomous individuals').

This chapter introduces key ideas around a post-dualistic relational concept of ontological design that I have brought to bear on my ethnographic research and activism with Latin American communities and the geopolitical power struggles touching all aspects of their lives. In their forceful condemnation of modernism and what we are now slowly recognizing as prophetic criticism of Western capitalist modernity, design visionaries and activists connected to the rising counterculture movement of the 1960s and 1970s foretold a future of intense globalization and warned of the concomitant, interrelated crises affecting climate, food, energy, poverty, and meaning. Owning up to this historiography of design with a sweeping social agenda, a small but growing subgroup among designers today are not only envisioning profound change; they have also already embarked upon bringing about cultural and ecological transitions through design. In taking my main epistemic and political inspiration for this chapter from past and current discourses and practices in design activism (explored in detail elsewhere[1]), I suggest that life-changing transitions—transitions toward entirely new ways of being-in-the-world—are possible however unthinkable they might seem in particular current situations. These transitions are possible based on an ostensibly simple observation: that in designing tools (objects, structures, policies, expert systems, discourses, even narratives) we are creating ways of being. Change, from this ontological perspective, can be understood as residing firmly within the scope of design due to design's capacity to embrace different forms of creation—in short, to contribute to "a world where many worlds fit" or what many increasingly call the pluriverse.[2] In what follows, I provide a brief historiographical outline of design theory and practice geared toward substantial transformation. To this growing range of debates and endeavors that can be regarded as an emerging field of critical design studies (CDS) I then offer a theoretical contribution by imagining, in the best sense of anthropological scholarship and with much needed optimism, how communities suffering from extractive globalization, such as those in Colombia's Cauca River Valley, might thrive if they were able to connect, articulate, and perform their "Life Projects" autonomously, perhaps with the help of design.

The Ontological Turn: From Cartesian Modernism to Designs for the Pluriverse

In 1971, as industrialism and US cultural, military, and economic hegemony were coming to their peak, the Austrian–American émigré designer and writer Victor Papanek opened *Design for the Real World* with the following caustic indictment of the field: "There are professions more harmful than industrial design, but only a very few of them. . . . Today, industrial design has put murder on a mass-production basis"; even more, "designers have become a dangerous breed" (1984: ix). Reflecting on the watered-down governmental agreements at the recent Summit on Environment and Sustainable Development (Rio + 20, June 2012) and the climate change conferences, just to mention two prominent attempts at 'redesigning' global social policy, one might think that not much has changed; but this would be too quick a judgment. To be sure, much of what goes on under the guise of design at present involves intensive resource use and vast material destruction.[3]

---

1. This chapter is part of a book manuscript entitled *Autonomy and Design: The Realization of the Communal*, currently under revision for publication. I thank Martina Grünewald and Alison Clarke for their invitation to contribute to this volume, and for their caring and insightful preparation of the chapter from a much longer text.

2. The concept of ontological design was initially proposed by Terry Winograd and Fernando Flores in the mid-1980s (Winograd and Flores 1986) and, with a few exceptions (Willis 2006; Tonkinwise 2012, 2013, 2015; Fry 2012, 2015) has remained little developed.

3. Indeed, any serious inquiry into contemporary design must equally be a journey into the trials and tribulations of capitalism and modernity, from the birth of industrialism to cutting-edge globalization and technological development, which is beyond the reach of this short chapter.

But, despite the crucial continuities that cast design as a central political technology within the paradigm of Cartesian modernism, today's social and design contexts differ significantly from those of the 1970s.

Papanek's call for taking the social context of design with utmost seriousness is being heeded by many contemporary designers, and statements on the increasingly transformative character of design abound in the literature of the last decade. The intensifying globalization of images and commodities fostered by capitalist modernity has led critical design theorists to advocate new kinds of engagement between design and the world. Claims from the significant to the earth shattering start with everyday life, but move on to infrastructures, cities, the lived environment, medical technologies, food, institutions, landscapes, the virtual, and, in the long run, experience itself. The fact that we all increasingly live within a "Design Cluster" means that design becomes "a category beyond categories" (Lunenfeld 2003: 10), one that opens up a new space for linking theory, practice, and purpose, vision and reality. These supra-categorical relational entanglements engender the endless process of discovering new territories for design through research (Laurel 2003). A key question becomes: "How does one design for a complex world?" Instead of keeping on filling the world with stuff, which design strategies will allow us—humans—to have more meaningful and environmentally responsible lives (Thackara 2005)?[4]

Contemporary Scandinavian design, it seems, has been notably successful at pairing social democratic goals and design, as superbly analyzed by Ehn, Nilsson, and Topgaard (2014) and by Murphy (2015) for the Swedish case. Disalvo's (2012) framework of "adversarial design" makes a cogent case for design approaches that broach explicitly the agonistic connection between design, technology, democracy, policy, and society. These are huge steps. Further inroads into the design–politics relation are being made in the fields of transition design (Kossoff 2011; Tonkinwise 2012, 2014, 2015; Irwin 2015; Irwin et al. 2015) and design for social innovation (Manzini 2015). "Design thinking" has become a key trope in this changing context. This design-led approach to (business) innovation has gained great popularity outside the design professions, as the "editorial" to a recent special issue of *Design Studies* put it, precisely due to the perception of design's real or potential contribution in addressing "wicked" (intractable) problems and of design as an agent of change.[5] It brings about a shift from the functional and semiotic emphasis of design to questions of experience and meaning.

---

4. While the relation between design and politics is frequently found at the forefront of design inquiries, the majority of design treatises still maintain a fundamental orientation that is technocratic and market-centered, and does not come close to questioning its capitalistic nature. Many design professionals navigate the middle ground, alternating between celebration and venturesome ideas and critiques (such as the well-known works by Bruce Mau, 2000, 2003; see also Antonelli et al. 2008).

5. See the special issue on "Interpreting Design Thinking" organized by the Design Thinking Research Group at the University of Technology, Sydney, based on the group's 8th Symposium, *Design Studies* 32 (2011).

As design moves out of the studio, beyond the sphere of the classic design professions, and into all domains of knowledge and applications, the distinction between expert and user/client breaks down. Not only does everyone come to be seen as a designer of sorts, but the argument for a shift to people-centered design becomes more readily acknowledged. Designing people back into situations means displacing the focus from stuff to humans, their experience and contexts. From mindless development to design mindfulness (Thackara 2004), from technological fixes to more design, from object-centered design to human-centered design, and from 'dumb design' to 'just design'—new guiding ideas abound (e.g., Laurel 2003; McCullough 2004; Chapman 2005; Brown 2009; Simmons 2011). These principles summon to the discussion unprecedented methodological and epistemological issues, opening up a welcoming space for disciplines such as anthropology, geography, and ecology (e.g., Clarke 2011; Berglund 2012; Suchman 2012; Julier 2014). New methods highlight front-end research, with the designer as facilitator and mediator more than expert; conceive of design as eminently user-centered, participatory, collaborative, and radically contextual; seek to make the processes and structures that surround us intelligible and knowable so as to induce ecological and systems literacy among users; and so forth. There is an attempt to construct alternative cultural visions as drivers of social transformation through design (Schwittay 2014).

The question of digital technologies, too, is driving crucial design insights. Some, including the architect Malcolm McCullough (2004), theorize 'interaction design practices' as articulations of interface design, interaction design, and experience design. Imbued in phenomenological tenets, design here embodies technologies that, rather than decontextualized and value neutral, are place-based, convivial, and potentially the domain for care (see also Ehn, Nilsson, and Topgaard 2014; Manzini 2015). Grounding digital technologies in human- and place-centered design counteracts modernity's proclivity to speed, efficiency, mobility, and automation. In architecture as well as other domains, this conception means designing systems that are easy to operate—a situated design practice that is bound up with place and community but that through embedded systems nevertheless addresses how people move around through their mobile devices. There is a lot of ethnographic and theoretical work at the interface of the digital and the cultural that contributes to illuminating the meaning of being digital, such as research on postcolonial theory and computing (Irani et al., 2010), the digital divide, digital technologies and the body, social media, virtual environments and communities, and so forth. Some of this work involves ethnographic investigations of the manifold intersections of digital technologies and cultural practices, giving rise to a new field of digital anthropology (Boesltroff 2008, Balsamo 2011, Horst and Miller 2012).

The engagement with ecological issues is one of the most vibrant areas of new design orientations. It took almost three decades after the publication of landscape architect Ian McHarg's anticipatory *Design with Nature* (1969) for a field of ecological design, properly speaking, to take off.[6] Today, approaches range from the conceptual to the technocratic, with the latter predominating a wide range of economic and technological perspectives including proposals that could be said to 'push the envelope' in envisioning a significant transformation of capitalism (as in the well-regarded proposal for 'natural capitalism' by Hawken, Lovins and Lovins 1999), and a plethora of green washing proposals produced by the official UN conferences and mainstream environmental think tanks in the Global North around concepts of climate change, sustainable development, and the 'green economy.'

There have been significant conceptual strides in ecological design, largely through collaborations between architects, planners, and ecologists with on-the-ground design experience. A readily accepted principle is that ecological design involves the successful integration of human and natural systems and processes. Whether this integration is seen as based on learning from several billion years of evolution and from nature's designs, or needs to rely on and hence re-invent technology to meet contemporary situations and needs, the starting point is the realization that the environmental crisis is a design crisis avertible only if humans change their practices radically. The field of fashion and sustainability offers a rather counterintuitive example. Designers embrace the social and ecological challenges of the industry in an attempt to transform it—from reducing the environmental impact of materials and processing to re-use and re-fashion strategies, from place-based production to biomimicry—and turn to collaborative creative practices like 'co-design' in actively crafting, hacking, and tackling difficult issues around alternative knowledges and politics that, ultimately, generate transitions toward other cultural and ecological models for society (see the excellent book by Fletcher and Grose 2011; Shepard 2015).

One of the biggest challenges lies in urbanism. As Tony Fry (2015) puts it harshly, much more than the kind of reactive adaption and retrofitting of buildings that serve the interests of the affluent is needed in facing the universally but differentially experienced condition of unsettlement that has come about as a result of the combined action of climate change, population growth, global unsustainability, and geopolitical instability. The development of new modes of earthly habitation has become an imperative, which means changing the practices that account for contemporary forms of dwelling in ways that enable us to act futurally instead of insisting on strategies of adaptation to defuturing (future-destroying) conditions. Adaptation and resilience will have to be revisited through the creation of grounded, situated, and pervasive design capacities by

---

6. The best treatise on the subject, in my view, remains van der Ryn and Cowan (1996). See also Orr (2002), Edwards (2005), Hester (2006), Ehrenfeld (2008); for more technical treatises, see Yeang (2006); and the large and well-documented tome by Hawken, Lovins, and Lovins (1999). An influential ecological design example is permaculture, for which there is a vast specialized literature. The concepts of biomimicry and cradle-to-cradle are gaining attention in product design. In Latin America, agroecology has become a gathering space for peasant agriculture and ecological design, often in tandem with social movements such as La Via Campesina.

communities themselves who are bound together by culture and a common will to survive when confronted with threatening conditions. In short, the "recreation of urban life should occupy a central position in the structural changes that must occur if 'we' humans are to have a viable future" (Fry 2015: 82). Fry's urban design imagination provides important leads to "the question of finding futural modes of dwelling" (p. 87). Re-imagining the city along these lines will have to be part of any transition vision and design framework.

In conclusion of this brief review, then, I see a field of 'critical design studies' emerging, which, following academic usage, applies a panoply of critical theories (from Marxist and post-Marxist political economy to feminist, queer, and critical race theory, post-structuralism, phenomenology, post-colonial and de-colonial theory, and to the most current post-constructivist of neo-materialists frameworks) to design. Nonetheless, several caveats are in order. First, as it should be clear, the elements and contours of the field are far from being restricted to the academy; many of its main contributions stem from design thinking and activism, even if often in some relation with the academy. Second, beyond this growing range of thought-provoking ideas, there is still a dearth of critical analyses of the relation between design practice and modernity, capitalism, patriarchy, race, and development—even though, the limits of Western social theory in generating the questions, let alone answers, needed to face the unprecedented unraveling of modern and most other forms of human life on the planet at present are becoming patently clear. Third, then, the relation between design, politics, power, and culture still needs to be fleshed out.

Critical design studies must embrace the vital normative questions of the day from "out of the box" perspectives. Design theorists Anthony Dunne and Fiona Raby, for instance, argue for a type of design practice that enables collective discussion about how things could be—what they term "speculative design" (2013). "Design speculations," they write, "can act as a catalyst for collectively redefining your relationship to reality" (p. 2) by encouraging—for instance, through "what if" scenario practices—imaginations about alternative ways of being. Such critical design can go a long way against design that reinforces the status quo. "Critical design is critical thought translated into materiality. It is about thinking through design rather than through words and using the language and structure of design to engage people. . . . All good critical design offers an alternative to how things are" (p. 35). That we are in the age of "speculative everything" is a hopeful thought, assuming it fuels the kinds of "social dreaming" (p. 169) that result in alternative forms of world-making—indeed, "in the multiverse of worlds our world could be" (p. 160). This ontologically open impetus of speculative design is useful in advancing the notion of design for transitions to the pluriverse.

As I argue in detail in the longer manuscript from which this chapter is taken, to nourish design's potentiality for transitions requires a significant reorientation of design from the functionalist and rationalistic traditions from which it emerged, toward a type of rationality and set of practices attuned to the relational dimension of life. This is because life, and all creation, is collective and relational; it involves historically and epistemically situated persons (never "autonomous individuals"), and this ineluctable relationality is acknowledged now by designers in the age of "design, when everybody designs," to quote Ezio Manzini's catchy title (2015). If, indeed, another design imagination, this time more radical and constructive, is emerging among a new breed of designers who come to be thought of as transition activists, then designers have to walk hand in hand with those who are protecting and redefining well-being, life projects, territories, local economies, and communities. They are the harbingers of the transition toward plural and relational ways of making the world, toward the pluriverse.

To contemplate what co-designing for a life-enhancing pluriverse might engender, I now turn to Latin America, where an important part of my empirical research has unfolded. Current debates and struggles around *buen vivir* (well-being), rights of nature, communal logics, and civilizational transitions, particularly as they are taking place in some Latin American countries, give rise to my speculation whether these can be seen as instances of the pluriverse re/emerging (Escobar 2014). A transition exercise for a particular region in Colombia's southwest, in which an ecologically and socially devastating model has been in place for over one hundred years, this region is in fact a prime laboratory for local and regional transition projects, and as such it can provide rich lessons for alternative pluriversal articulations.

In the Global South: Politics of Relationality and the Realization of the Communal

East from Colombia's main Pacific port city of Buenaventura and across the Western Andean cordillera lies the fertile Cauca River Valley, centered on the city of Cali (population 3 million), a region that could well be considered a poster child of development gone awry. Capitalist development based on sugar cane plantations in the plains and extensive cattle ranching in the Andean hillsides started to take hold in the late nineteenth century. It gained force in the early 1950s with the setting up of the Cauca Regional Autonomous Development Corporation (CVC), patterned after the famous Tennessee Valley Authority (TVA), with the support of the World Bank.[7] By now it is not only clear that this model of development based on sugar cane and cattle is exhausted but that it has caused massive ecological devastation of hills, aquifers, rivers, forests, and soils besides profoundly unjust and painful social and territorial dislocation of the region's peasants and Afro-descendant communities. The region can easily be reimagined as a veritable agroecological stronghold of organic fruit, vegetable, grain, and exotic plant production and as a multicultural region of small and medium size farm producers, a decentralized network of functioning towns and medium size cities, and so forth. Other attractive futures can surely be imagined for this region.

---

7. The Tennessee Valley Authority, today an important public power company in the United States, was established in 1933 to control flooding, produce energy, and promote business, forestry, and farming along major stretches of the Tennessee River.

Nevertheless, these futures are at present *unthinkable*, such is the strength of hold of the developmentalist imaginary on most of the region's people and the power of elite control. Though the region is 'ripe' for a radical transition, this proposition is inconceivable to elites and most locals, and certainly to its middle classes whose intense consumerist lifestyle is inextricably tied to the model. Under these conditions, is a transition design exercise even possible? Moreover, could it have some real bearing on policy, mindsets, actions, and practices? I am interested in showing, even if tentatively and as a hypothesis, that even under such antagonistic conditions a transition design imagination can be set in motion. Let us see how.

The Cauca River, Colombia's second most important waterway, runs for 1,360 kilometers, flowing northward from its origin in the Colombian Massif, a group of high Andean mountains in Colombia's southwest. Seventy percent of Colombia's fresh water is said to originate in the Massif. It is there also that the Andean mountain chain splits into three, giving origin to inter-Andean valleys, such as the Cauca Valley. The valley opens up progressively in between the western and central cordilleras (the central cordillera exhibiting several snowed peaks over 5,000 meters). The focus of this exercise is the first part of the Cauca River basin known as the *Alto Cauca*, or upper Cauca. This section of the valley widens progressively, following the river for over 500 kilometers, covering an area of 367,000 hectares; its width ranges between 15 and 32 kilometers. It is an incredibly beautiful valley, flanked by the two cordilleras and traversed by many smaller rivers and streams. The flat plains have an altitude of 1,000 meters, and an average temperature of 25 degrees centigrade. A traveler looking at the valley even in the 1940s with a relational gaze would no doubt conclude that it could easily support a very pleasant and culturally and ecologically rich existence. Locals actually refer to the valley with the name of the most famous colonial hacienda still standing: *El Paraiso* (Paradise). This future, however, was being foreclosed by the 1950s when defuturing forces gained speed and strength.

In terms of administrative divisions, most of the valley falls within the Valle del Cauca department, but an important area lies in the Cauca department to the south. The Alto Cauca starts at the Salvajina Dam, constructed in the mid-1980s by the CVC to regulate the water flow of the river and to generate electricity for the growing agro-industrial complex centered in Cali. The geographic Cauca valley is a bioregion shaped by up to forty smaller river basins, several lagoons, and extensive wetlands. Its soils are very fertile, well-drained, and of relatively low salinity. Superficial and deep aquifers have been a rich source of water of high quality for both agricultural and human consumption. Historically, this ecological complex of mountains, forests, valley, rivers, and wetlands has been home to hundreds of plant and animal species. All of these features have been systematically undermined by the agro-industrial operations.

Even if the majority of the population of the region is mestizo, the Afrodescendant presence is very significant. There are several predominantly black municipalities in the Norte del Cauca, some within the sphere of influence of the Salvajina dam. Up to 50 percent of Cali's population is black, according to some estimates, largely the result of migration and forced displacement from the Pacific over the past thirty years, making Cali's black population the second largest in urban Latin America after Bahia (Brazil). This is an amazingly important social fact for any design project. Most of the black population is poor; at the other end of the spectrum there lies a small white elite, extremely wealthy, who pride themselves on their European ancestry. This elite has traditionally controlled most of the land and owned the largest sugar mill operations. In 2013, 225,000 hectares were planted in cane and 53,000 in pastures for cattle. Although only about 60 holdings are over 500 hectares, the figure is deceiving since the large landholders also lease land or buy the cane produced by a large number of smaller farms exclusively dedicated to cane. The use of water in sugar cane cultivation is intensive, about 10,300 cubic meters per hectare in the region. This sector uses up 64 percent of all surface water and 88 percent of subterranean water. Over 670,000 hectares of hillsides (more than half the total area) have been affected by extensive cattle ranching.[8]

Traveling up and down the valley on the main highway one sees what most locals consider a "beautiful green landscape": hectare after hectare of sugar cane in the plains, almost without interruption, and cattle leisurely roaming in the foothills. But this landscape is the result of over one hundred years of ontological occupation of the valley by a heterogeneous assemblage made up of the white elite, cattle, cane, water, the dam, chemicals (the tons of pesticides and fertilizers used in the cultivation), the State (the political elite, completely wedded to the model), experts (CVC in particular), global markets (demand for white sugar), and of course the black cutters, without whom the entire operation (despite increasing mechanization) would have been impossible. The black cutters, in fact, refer to the sugar cane as the *monstruo verde* (green monster) and associate it with the devil; for them it is far from a beautiful landscape (Taussig 1980). The entire assemblage is 'concreted in' by a large network of roads, trucks (the *trenes cañeros*, or long trailer trucks loaded with cane, are impossible to avoid when traveling by car, as sugar cane is cultivated year-round), and of course the entire industrial, financial, and service infrastructure in Cali and nearby towns.

After more than a century of allegedly smooth functioning, the well-oiled operations of this heterogeneous assemblage—touted as a *milagro del desarrollo* (development miracle) by local elites, and celebrated in folk culture in multiple ways, from soap operas to salsa music—can no longer hide their profoundly defuturing effects. They are visible in the exhaustion, sedimentation, and contamination of rivers and aquifers; in the desiccation of wetlands; the erosion of biodiversity; the deforestation and severe erosion of hills and mountainsides; the respiratory health problems of black workers and nearby populations because of the ashes inhaled during the periodic burning of the cane after cultivation; the repression against attempts by black workers to organize for better conditions; and the persistence of racism and profound inequality, all integral to the 'cane model.' Linked to the inequality and the poverty of 60 percent of the population, as its inevitable result, is the high degree of 'insecurity' and 'delinquency' decried by the middles classes, against which they attempt to find security by living in heavily surveilled apartment complexes and gated

---

8. I am grateful to David Lopez Mata and Douglas Laing for some of the information in this section.

communities, and by restricting a great deal of their social lives to the ubiquitous, well-policed, globalized shopping centers. One wonders how the model goes on, year after year, despite its blatant and obvious failings wherever one looks, failings that some activists and a handful of academics and intellectuals are beginning to identify, despite the apparent unawareness of most of the population and the absence of any critical voice in the dominant media that continues to celebrate the model day in and day out. This is the challenging backdrop (not uncommon for many regions in the Global South) against which any transition design strategy will have to be crafted. Let us discuss a few of the major aspects of this endeavor.

Generating a Transition Design Imagination for the Cauca Valley

Even a purely theoretical transition design exercise for a region such as this one is a daunting task, moreover if the hope exists for some degree of implementation. Yet, considering the huge number of actual 'successful' cases of impactful urban and regional re/development worldwide,[9] the question arises: why not? Conventional regional development builds on the naturalized histories of capitalist development, whereas the type of regional transition envisioned here would take place against the grain of such history and within well-established structuring conditions of unsustainability and defuturing. Many of the design ideas previously discussed may of course be invoked in support of the exercise in question. However, as Colombian design theorist Andrea Botero, from the media lab at Aalto University in Helsinki, argues, "[d]espite these advancements, our understanding of how to go about setting up, carrying on, and more broadly, sustaining collaborative and open-ended design processes in explicit ways is still limited" (2013: 13). As she goes on to say, there is a great need for methods that enable collaborative design over longer periods than usual, that elaborate on the evolving roles of designers under this extended temporality (beyond, say, being initiators or facilitators), and that take at heart the distributed nature of design agency, including, one needs to add, non-humans. The articulation of design-in-use practices in the context of temporally extended collective design activities is particularly important at this point in time.

As ecologists and transition activists and designers, it is relatively easy to propose scenarios to trigger the design imagination. I have just proposed one such scenario. Recall, first, the overwhelming landscape of omnipresent sugar cane and cattle, and their in/visible effects. Then try to reimagine it "as a veritable agroecological stronghold of organic fruit, vegetable, grain, and exotic plant production and as a multicultural region of small and medium size farm producers, a

---

9. Dam-based development projects including the Tennessee Valley Authority in the United States and the Salvajina Dam on the Cauca River as well as many other examples worldwide serve as a case in point for modern development schemes so expressive, and inclusive, of a dominant technocratic mindset they were even likened to sacred spaces worthy of adoration and worship. Let us not forget that the first prime minister of India, Jahawarlal Nehru, called dams and factories "the temples of modern India" on the occasion of the 1963 inauguration of the Bhakra-Nangal multipurpose dam, one of the earliest river valley development schemes in this country.

de-centralized network of functioning towns and medium size cities, and so forth," as I mentioned earlier. Easy to imagine, perhaps, but locally unthinkable, yet. What follows are some elements that might go into a transition design exercise for the Cauca Valley to take place over a number of years (let's call it *Valle del Cauca en Transición*, or VCT).[10]

There are two crucial tasks to be accomplished at the start of the project: gathering together a co-design team and creating a design space with which the collaborative design team would co-evolve. Creating an attractive imaginary for the design space might be useful, but that is just the start. The importance of the design space cannot be underestimated, as rightly underlined by Botero, Kommonen, and Marttila (2013). These design theorists understand the design space "as the space of possibilities for realizing a design, which extends beyond the concept design space into the design-in-use activities of people." (p. 186) The design space involves tools for mapping design activities aimed at locating participants' possibilities in a continuum from consumption to active creation. The design space is always co-constructed and explored by multiple actors through their social interactions involving technologies, tools, materials, and social processes. Through ongoing design activity, it becomes "the space of potentials that the available circumstances afford for the emergence of new designs" (p. 188). The concept thus goes well beyond the focus on objects, workplaces, and design briefs to embrace design-in-use in all of its complexity, including, of course, the multiple users' inputs and designs. This expanded notion of design spaces might be particularly effective in what Botero calls "communal endeavors," those that "stand midway between being the project of a recognized community of practice or teams and being simply the coordinated actions of unidentifiable collectives or ad-hoc groups" (2013: 22).

In this dialogic space, design coalitions would create a new, radical vision for the valley and a vision for large-scale change, well beyond the business-as-usual adjustments. In the first year or two of the project, the coalitions and collaborative organizations involved will be tasked with the construction of an initial framework for the transition(s). One could think of the design space as a kind of lab or set of labs where vision-making and co-design meet, resulting in organized conversations for action (for instance, a Norte del Cauca and southern, central, and northern valley Labs, but also a Cali Lab, given the commanding presence of the city in the valley; or in terms of domains of social and ecological actions).

Given this overall objective (and the highly charged, political, and controversial character that the process will likely take as it evolves), at least in the initial phases of the VCT process, the actors involved in the co-design team will be limited. It will be essential that the main actors share the fundamental goals of the exercise in their broadest sense. That said, the actors should include at least the following sectors: social movement organizations (urban and rural, Afrodescendant, indigenous, peasant, and various urban groups); organizations of women and youth, particularly

---

10. In a recent proposal (Escobar 2014), I envisioned the process to take place over a ten-year period. It should be made clear that Valle del Cauca refers in this section to the Alto Cauca, not to the administrative *departmento*.

from black and other marginalized rural and urban areas; academy and intellectual life; arts and alternative communications and media. It will also be essential that this team be seeded with epistemic, social (in terms of race/ethnicity, gender, generation, class, and territorial basis), and cultural (ontological) diversity from the get go, since this will be the only reasonable guarantee of a genuinely pluriversal design outcome. Activists, intellectuals, NGO people, and academics, including from the natural and physical sciences, are all, in principle, good candidates for the team (it should be said that it is not uncommon in Latin America for individuals to perform several or even all of these roles simultaneously or sequentially; in the Cauca Valley, there is a significant 'natural reservoir' of people already quite adept at carrying out inter-epistemic conversations). It will also be crucial for this team to develop the ability to think 'communally' and relationally, in onto-epistemic terms (although of course not necessarily literally in these theoretical terms).[11]

The actual transition exercise will start to evolve from this initial process, and it will have to include both the continued generation of contexts capable of nourishing the idea of a transition and concrete projects intended to develop particular aspects of the design for social innovation (Manzini 2015).[12] Some of the goals and activities of this phase might include:

- Making visible the structural unsustainability and defuturing practices of the current model (e.g., effects on water; systematic impoverishment of black workers; soil exhaustion; rampant consumerism; destructive forms of extractivism, including gold mining; just to mention a few).
- Creating a sense of a region different from the 'folk' regional narrative that prevails, particularly in Cali, dominated by sugar cane, salsa music, sports, and commerce. This would require articulating a 'pluriversal bioregional notion' for the entire Alto Cauca, beyond the purely geographical or folk concept.
- Getting a sense of the diverse life projects of the communities and collectivities involved, including, of course, those in marginalized urban areas and even those seemingly without place and community.
- Promoting a diversity of actions, such as digital platforms to enable broader participation in the co-design process; thematic clusters and design labs; traveling interactive exhibits to encourage the generation of new imaginaries about and for the region in smaller towns and the countryside; compendia of realistic cases (particularly useful to demonstrate that 'other economies are possible'[13]); competing metastories; the collec-

---

11. Manzini speaks about the importance of the initial "creative community" in collaborative design experiences (2015: 89).

12. Manzini's discussion of design for social innovation (chapter 3) is very useful for thinking about many of these aspects; see especially his discussion of the Slow Food Movement.

13. This was actually the title of a four-day workshop designed and organized by Process of Black Communities, PCN, and held in Buga, north of Cali, in July 2013, with the participation of seventy PCN activists from Norte del Cauca and the southern Pacific, plus a handful of academics, including me.

tive creation of scenarios, whether grounded in existing cases extrapolated to fulfill the vision of a particular community or speculatively imagined to elicit open-ended design reflections.

- Actions should privilege bottom-up, horizontal, and peer-to-peer methodologies and design tools, yet involve top-down elements as needed, although always subordinated to the goals arising from the communal dialogs. There will surely be many methodological hurdles to work through. For instance, how to design spaces where collaborative organizations might create conditions to dignify the manifold memories of the past, acknowledge the multiple overlapping worlds and realities, and consequently provide resonance for the numerous futures that inevitably populate the discursive and emotional space of the broad range of Valle inhabitants.

- A series of "Cali Labs" intended to ascertain the range of answers to the question of "What do you want Cali to be?"—to be followed by scenario building where the various visions can be put on display, along with potential transition and speculative design imaginaries developed by the co-design team—so that more and more people come to entertain the idea of Cali as a truly hospitable space for dwelling, rather than as an unsustainability machine.

- The design of methods and tools to activate the multiple communal design histories (vernacular, diffuse, autonomous), found among so many rural and urban groups and in so many places throughout the valley, and their intersections with expert design.

- The impact of climate change on the various local worlds will have to be an important aspect of imagining the transitions, borrowing from the many transition initiatives in the world that are dealing with this question, and strategically invoking broad transition imaginaries such as *Buen Vivir* and degrowth. This design aspect potentially touches on everything: agriculture—as La Via Campesina (2009) is fond of saying, "small farmers cool down the earth"; energy and transportation (diminishing the exponential growth of private cars toward alternative light, decentralized, transportation systems); city planning; commons; and so forth. The concept of resilience, resituated in the ontological context of autonomous worlds, might be important in this area.

- The creation of art and media for the transitions. Performance art (including about non-humans, for example, about how to 'liberate' soils and bring them back to life), transition music and dance (building on the region's strong musical traditions, including salsa and the black musics from the Pacific and Norte del Cauca), social media, and new mainstream media contents that destabilize the 'folk' discourse about the region and position the new one in the collective imaginary will all be integral to the design task. This aspect will build on strong popular education and communication sectors existing in the region since the 1980s. There is a great potential in the transition imagination to generate an unprecedented wave of cultural activism.

There is a whole range of other issues that could be considered from the transition design frameworks, such as the relation between diffuse and expert design,[14] the creation of knowledges that might travel from one situation to another, the learning process as the project moves on, the role of design research, the use of prototypes and maps, small-local-open-connected (SLOC) scenarios as well as digital and live storytelling, the design of toolkits from and for communal spaces, and questions of scale, among others.

The presentation given in this chapter is of course extremely tentative and general. It is offered more as an indication of the kind of design inquiries that might be at play in transition efforts than as an actual roadmap to be followed. I am perfectly aware of the overly ambitious nature of the proposal. Let us say that it was intended largely as a purely theoretical exercise and, as such, as an anthropologist's contribution to critical design studies. It was also intended to buttress the idea that 'another design is possible,' a design for the pluriverse. At the same time, it might be considered an example of the dissenting design imagination that, as this chapter has indicated, is emerging in various design domains. Perhaps, in the last instance, this effort was my imperfect attempt as a scholar at making a political-ontological statement by relying on those ultra-designed spaces we call the academy, the book, and the thinking process.

References

Antonelli, P. with H. Aldersey-Williams, P. Hall and T. Sargent (2008), *Design and the Elastic Mind*, New York: The Museum of Modern Art.

Balsamo, A. (2011), *Designing Culture: The Technological Imagination at Work*, Durham: Duke University Press.

Berglund, E. (2012), "Design for a Better World, or Conceptualizing Environmentalism and Environmental Management in Helsinki," presented at the 2012 Conference of the European Association of Social Anthropology, EASA.

Boellstorff, T. (2008), *Coming of Age in Second Life*, Princeton: Princeton University Press.

Botero, A. (2013), *Expanding Design Space(s): Design in Communal Endeavors*, Helsinki: Aalto Art Books.

Botero, A., K.-H. Kommonen and S. Marttila (2010), "Expanding Design Space: Design-In-Use Activities and Strategies," in A. Botero (2013), *Expanding Design Space(s): Design in Communal Endeavors*, Helsinki: Aalto Art Books.

Brown, T. (2009), *Change by Design*, New York: Harper.

Chapman, J. (2005), *Emotionally Durable Design: Objects, Experiences & Empathy*, London: Earthscan.

Clarke, A., ed. (2011), *Design Anthropology: Object Culture in the 21st Century*, New York/Vienna: Springer.

---

14. Manzini (2015) differentiates between diffuse design, which is the design capacity possessed by every person regardless of their formal education, and expert design, meaning the knowledge of the design professions.

DiSalvo, C. (2012), *Adversarial Design*, Cambridge: MIT Press.

Dunne, A. and F. Raby (2013), *Speculative Everything: Design, Fiction, and Social Dreaming*, Cambridge: MIT Press.

Edwards, A. (2005), *The Sustainability Revolution*, Gabriola Island, BC: New Society Publishers.

Ehn, P., E. M. Nilsson and R. Topgaard (2014), *Making Futures: Marginal Notes on Innovation, Design, and Democracy*, Cambridge: MIT Press.

Ehrenfeld, J. (2008), *Sustainability by Design*, New Haven: Yale University Press.

Escobar, A. (2014), *Sentipensar con la tierra: Nuevas lecturas sobre sobre desarrollo, territorio y diferencia*, Medellín: UNAULA.

Fletcher, K. and L. Grose (2011), *Fashion and Sustainability: Design for Change*, London: Laurence King Publishing.

Fry, T. (2012), *Becoming Human by Design*, London: Berg.

Fry, T. (2015), *City Futures in the Age of a Changing Climate*, London: Routledge.

Hawken, P., A. Lovins and L. H. Lovins (1999), *Natural Capitalism: Creating the Next Industrial Revolution*, New York: Little, Brown and Company.

Hester, R. (2006), *Design for Ecological Democracy*, Cambridge: MIT Press.

Horst, H. and D. Miller, eds. (2012), *Digital Anthropology*, London: Bloomsbury.

Irani, L., J. Vertesi, P. Dourish, K. Philip and R. E. Grinter (2010), "Postcolonial Computing: A Lens on Design and Development," *CHI'10: Proceedings of the SIGCHI Conference on Human Factors in Computing Systems*, 1311–20, New York, Association of Computing Machinery Publications.

Irwin, T. (2015), "Transition Design: A Proposal for a New Era of Design Practice, Study & Research," unpublished manuscript, School of Design, Carnegie Mellon University.

Irwin, T., G. Kossoff, C. Tonkinwise and P. Scupelli (2015), "Transition Design Bibliography." Available online: https://www.academia.edu/13108611/Transition_Design_Bibliography_2015.

Julier, G. (2014), *The Culture of Design*, 3rd ed., London: Sage.

Kossoff, G. (2011), "Holism and the Reconstitution of Everyday Life: A Framework for Transition to a Sustainable Society," in S. Hardin (ed.), *Grow Small, Think Beautiful: Ideas for a Sustainable World from Schumacher College*, 122–42, Edinburgh: Floris Books.

Laurel, B., ed. (2003), *Design Research: Methods and Perspectives*, Cambridge: MIT Press.

La Via Campesina (2009), "Small Scale Sustainable Farmers Are Cooling Down The Earth," position paper

Lunenfeld, P. (2003), "The Design Cluster," in B. Laurel (ed.), *Design Research: Methods and Perspectives*, 10–15, Cambridge: MIT Press.

Manzini, E. (2015), *Design, When Everybody Designs: An Introduction to Design for Social Innovation*, Cambridge: MIT Press.

Mau, B. (2000), *Life Style*, New York: Phaidon.

Mau, B. and the Institute without Boundaries (2004), *Massive Change*, London: Phaidon Press.

McCullough, M. (2004), *Digital Ground*, Cambridge: MIT Press.

McHarg, I. (1969), *Design with Nature*, New York: American Museum of Natural History.

Murphy, K. M. (2015), *Swedish Design: An Ethnography*, Ithaca: Cornell University Press.

Orr, D. (2002), *The Nature of Design: Ecology, Culture, and Human Intention*, Oxford: Oxford University Press.

Papanek, V. (1984 [1971]), *Design for the Real World*, New York: Pantheon Books.

Schwittay, A. (2014), "Designing Development: Humanitarian Design in the Financial Inclusion Assemblage," *PoLAR*, 37 (1): 29–47.

Shepard, C. (2015), "Exploring the Places, Practices, and Communities of the Subculture of Refashioning Secondhand Clothing through Themes of Bricolage and Sustainability," Undergraduate Honors Thesis, Department of Anthropology, University of North Carolina, Chapel Hill.

Simmons, C. (2011), *Just Design: Socially Conscious Design for Critical Issues*, Cincinnati: HOW Books.

Suchman, L. (2012), "Anthropological Relocations and the Limits of Design," *Annual Review of Anthropology*, 40: 1–18.

Thackara, J. (2005), *In the Bubble: Designing in a Complex World*, Cambridge: MIT Press.

Tonkinwise, C. (2012), "Design Transition Expert Interview." Available online: https://www.academia.edu/5040427/_Design_Transitions_Expert_Interview_-_Full_Unpublished_Version (accessed January 18, 2017).

Tonkinwise, C. (2013), "Design Away: Unmaking Things." Available online: https://www.academia.edu/3794815/Design_Away_Unmaking_Things (accessed July 14, 2015).

Tonkinwise, C. (2014), "Design (Dis)Orders: Transition Design as Postindustrial Design." Available online: https://www.academia.edu/11791137/Design_Dis_Orders_Transition_Design_as_Postindustrial_Design (accessed July 14, 2015).

Tonkinwise, C. (2015), "Design for Transitions—from and to What?" Available online: https://www.academia.edu/11796491/Design_for_Transition_-_from_and_to_what (accessed July 14, 2015).

van der Ryn, S. and S. Cowan (1996), *Ecological Design*, Washington, DC: Island Press.

Willis, A.-M. (2006), "Ontological Designing–Laying the Ground," *Design Philosophy Papers, Collection Three*, 80–98. Available online: https://www.academia.edu/888457/Ontological_designing (accessed December 21, 2015).

Winograd, T. and F. Flores (1986), *Understanding Computers and Cognition*: 163–79, Norwood, NJ: Ablex Publishing Corporation.

Yeang, K. (2006), *Ecodesign. A Manual for Ecological Design*, London: John Wiley and Sons.

Taussig, M. T. (1980), *The Devil and Commodity Fetishism in South America*, Chapel Hill: University of North Carolina Press.

Index